ACRL Publications in Librarianship no. 49

# Restructuring Academic Libraries:

## Organizational Development in the Wake of Technological Change

*edited by*

*Charles A. Schwartz*

Association of College and Research Libraries
A division of the American Library Association
Chicago 1997

The paper used in this publication meets the minimum requirements of American National Standard for Information Sciences–Permanence of Paper for Printed Library Materials, ANSI Z39.48-1992.∞

**Library of Congress Cataloging-in-Publication Data**
Restructuring academic libraries : organizational development in the
    wake of technological change / edited by Charles A. Schwartz.
        p.  cm.  --  (ACRL publications in librarianship ;  no. 49)
    Includes bibliographical refererences  (p.)  and index
    ISBN 0-8389-3478-1
        1. Academic libraries--United States.  I. Schwartz,  Charles A.
    II.  Series.
    Z674.A75  no.  49
    [Z675.U5]
    020 s
    [027.7'0973]--DC21                                    97-40243

Printed in the United States of America.

01 00 99 98 97        5 4 3 2 1

# Contents

## Redeveloping State and Regional Consortia

## Case Studies of the Single-Organization Experience

## Restructuring Library–University Relationships

# Preface

*Restructuring Academic Libraries* is the product of a recent historical discontinuity: Information technology in the 1990s is advancing more rapidly than our profession is prepared to assimilate the changes. Indeed, the acceleration of computer networking has shown no respect for traditional organizations or other institutional arrangements in higher education as a whole. When Stephen E. Wiberley Jr., editor of the monograph series, and I began to talk in summer 1995 about this lag of organizational development, only a handful of articles had recognized the problem. Since then, however, general awareness of it has grown. It was a theme of ACRL's biennial conference of 1997 and the focus of an Association of Research Libraries survey report, which took note of the lack of even internal documents on reorganizations under way.[1] This book is the first major attempt to help fill this gap in the literature.

At no other time have academic libraries been faced with such different, but natural, courses. First, engrossed with the sheer speed and significance of technological change, they might attempt restructuring aggressively and radically. Or, struck by the apparent magnitude of organizational reform, they might put a premium on the avoidance of instability while waiting for some other organization to come up with a "blueprint" or "road map" for the whole profession to adapt. Unfortunately, as plausible as either response might be in these turbulent times, both lead to organizational decay. Ill-planned radical change would prove costly and unwieldy. Prolonged hesitancy—attempting too little, too late—would conserve the library's stability at the expense of its relevance on campus. On a broader plane, if "enough" libraries averted basic organizational changes, our profession would lose its relevance in the scholarly communication system.

The course of action that unites the nineteen chapters of this book is for academic libraries to gradually but surely ("with all deliberate speed," as navigators say) restructure themselves to be more aligned with patterns of computer networking on campus, in consortia, and across the scholarly communication system at large. Organizational development along such lines is called *boundary spanning*. In this perspective, academic libraries would play much more of an integrative role in their institutions' efforts to incorporate new information technology into research and curricular programs.

The scope and organization of this book are outlined in the introductory chapter, which provides a conceptual framework of boundary spanning. This framework—drawn from the other contributing authors as a whole—describes different approaches to the planning process that all focus on ways that problems (once recognized), solutions ("out there"), and decision makers (with competing concerns) sometimes get linked to become restructuring *opportunities*. It then sets out five ranges of restructuring *outcomes*:
- convergence of public and technical services;
- realignment of campus computing partnerships;
- redevelopment of state and regional library consortia;
- redesign of research and curricular programs;
- revisioning the library's and university's joint service mission to society.

In the first section, "Reassessing Traditional and Virtual Ground-Assumptions," David W. Lewis, in an analysis of how public services may be reconceptualized in a networked environment, argues that library management should forego turf battles over control of networked resources and services. Herbert S. White contends, on the contrary, that campuswide networks coupled with decentralized cost centers is a "disastrous strategy" because it lacks both intellectual economy and fiscal control. The second section, "Realigning Campus Computing Partnerships," begins with Richard M. Dougherty and Lisa McClure's overview of the rise and fall of great expectations for easy mergers between academic libraries and computing centers. Meredith A. Butler and Stephen E. DeLong recount a "bottom-up" approach to collaborative realignment at the University at Albany, SUNY, where the library and the computing center have focused on handling an ongoing series of network-to-desktop challenges, rather than restructuring institutional arrangements. In contrast, Nina Davis-Millis and Thomas Owens describe a "top-down" approach at MIT, where joint library–computing center projects were put aside at the start in favor of exploring organizational designs and cultural affinities.

The third section, "Redeveloping State and Regional Consortia," marks a new stage of resource sharing. David F. Kohl examines OhioLINK's radical reinterpretation of library cooperation that became possible only after a virtual infrastructure had been constructed in which the physical location of materials is largely irrelevant. Barbara McFadden Allen and William A. Gosling explain how the Committee on Institutional Cooperation, a midwestern consortium, has repositioned its member libraries not only horizontally (to share resources, particularly expertise, and services) but also vertically—in terms of their campus relationships with faculty, technologists, university presses, and strategic planners. Sue O. Medina and William C. Highfill describe the Network of Alabama Academic Libraries' evolutionary approach to technological and economic collaboration from the perspective of social role theory. Derrie B. Roark recounts a much different experience of the centralized, state-mandated process of restructuring Florida's community college library system.

The next section presents six single-organization case studies. Rebecca R. Martin describes a gradualist, "top-down" approach—"seizing windows of opportunity"—to make a series of reorganizations at the University of Vermont with no blueprint or firm timetable for change. Caroline M. Kent examines how restructuring, rather than flattening, an organization can bolster the administrative arrangements necessary to coordinate a highly decentralized library system, such as Harvard's. Joan Giesecke and Katherine Walter relate a "bottom-up" restructuring process at the University of Nebraska-Lincoln, where technical services librarians, once relatively isolated from public services, took the initiative to create their own choice opportunities. Gloriana St. Clair explains the "best-practice" benchmarking approach, which is much more deliberate than a "windows of opportunity" process, to redesign structures with examples drawn from Penn

State. Peggy Seiden describes seven organizational change strategies prevalent in liberal arts college libraries to provide increasing levels of information-support services given very limited personnel and financial resources. Rita A. Scherrei looks at the human side of restructuring when twenty library administrators in the University of California system had their careers disrupted with significant personal losses.

The last section, "Restructuring Library–University Relationships," concerns the farthest range of boundary spanning. Charles B. Osburn foresees research universities and their libraries at a historic juncture where libraries are instrumental in fulfilling their universities' new social mission to disseminate scholarly information through mass electronic communication systems. Douglas G. Birdsall provides a corollary analysis of the politics of library strategic planning in the "organized anarchy" of the academic enterprise. Finally, the epilogue on "Balancing Restructuring Efforts" puts the transition process in the perspective of four competing organizational orientations. On the external side are *boundary spanning* to meet new environmental challenges and *strategic planning* for productivity and effectiveness. On the internal side are *policy setting* for internal coordination of structural changes and *human development* for morale and commitment to strategic plans. Successful restructuring requires that these orientations be brought into balance periodically by making them roughly equivalent in importance and compatible with one another. Otherwise, boundary spanning runs the risk of generating not organizational development but, instead, decay.

My dominant impression at the close of this project is the prospect for boundary spanning to become an enduring source of organizational innovation. At least, boundary spanning is how innovations elsewhere in the academic institution tend to arise—from interdisciplinary or cross-disciplinary patterns of interaction, which act as a counterweight to the inherent rigidity of disciplinary structures. If that analogy holds, organizational boundary spanning would come to mark the beginnings of yet another historical discontinuity in our profession, given the academic library's relative autonomy on campus not so long ago. Thus, restructuring is a double-barreled proposition, the contemporary lag of organizational development being followed—in perhaps the space of less than a decade—by a more progressive era in which academic libraries take the lead in adapting new information technology to the scholarly system. Dr. Wiberley and I are grateful to the contributing authors for showing us all how these dual transitions can be assessed and managed.

C. A. S.
Boston
August 1997

NOTE

1. *Library Reorganization & Restructuring,* SPEC Kit 215, comp. Joanne D. Eustis and Donald J. Kenney (Washington, D.C.: Association of Research Libraries, 1996), unnumbered attached flyer.

# Restructuring Academic Libraries: Adjusting to Technological Change

*Charles A. Schwartz*

An emerging problem for academic libraries is the lag of organizational development behind technological change. The key factor, which gained momentum in the mid-1990s, has been the rise of sophisticated computer networks that disrupt old organizational arrangements and invade the library's traditional autonomy. Such rapid technological change does not necessarily lead to new structural patterns or new interdependent relationships. But it does create an overriding need for them by broadening the demand for network-to-desktop information resources to support new research and curricular programs. Networked resources require restructured, boundary-spanning library services throughout the academic institution. Forecasts for academic libraries in this transformed environment are mixed. In this book, some of the contributing authors identify, collectively, a broad range of opportunities for expanding the quantity and quality of library services, leading to significant organizational development. Other contributors lean toward an opposing prospect—that, in the absence of such development, academic libraries will face organizational decay, with a consequent deterioration in the library's relevance.

1

Organizational development and restructuring are similar terms. *Organizational development* is a general term for structural–functional adaptation to new environmental challenges. Restructuring is defined more specifically in this book in terms of the changing scholarly communication system: *Restructuring* is the development of boundary-spanning library services—allied with computing center services—to deliver networked information resources campuswide for the broader purpose of supporting new research and curricular programs.

Until now, the literature on technology in libraries has not dealt much with organizational development, restructuring, or organizational decay. Rather, it has focused on a different process which can be called *social adaptation*, occurring primarily at the level of the individual. Social adaptation involves workaday concerns about "keeping current with technology," "using electronic communications effectively," "assisting faculty and students with information resources," and so forth. These were at the top of a 1993 survey by the Association of College and Research Libraries (ACRL) on what its members considered their most pressing challenges at that time.[1]

Although we may never fully adjust on a personal level to the pace of technological change, such adaptation is old hat by now. This book is based on the distinct premise that our profession is now shifting its focus to the more fundamental problem of organizational development. This is a new area for both theory and practice, and has only begun to attract systematic analysis by researchers or sustained attention by administrators. Indeed, before the acceleration of computer networking with the advent of World Wide Web in 1993, there was no *general* movement toward a convergence of public services and technical services, or of public services with either the library automation department or the campus computing center.[2]

Telling in this regard is a 1995 survey by the Association of Research Libraries (ARL) that focused on organizational changes undertaken since the early 1990s.[3] Of the 108 member institutions, seventeen (15%) have undertaken a *librarywide* reorganization, whereas thirty-four (31%) have merged *specific units*, with the main trend involving a reallocation of personnel from technical services to public services. The report concluded that "organizational change in the mid-1990s appears to be incremental rather than dramatic and transformational." The case studies in this book, however, represent much more fundamental, or at least continual, reorganization processes begun rather early in the decade.

### "We Haven't the Courage" versus "Just Do It!"

The newness of restructuring, along with its sweeping implications, has evoked a polarity of assessments on what can be done in the foreseeable future. For example, on one side, Jerry D. Campbell, in a proposal for a new budget model for libraries in transition from the print age to the electronic era, reflected that "technological assault" combines with "organizational rigidity" to produce an "unproductive anxiety" in our profession.[4] To "improve the sense of confidence and control among library staffs," Campbell recommended that planning, training, and team-building programs be run for some years before any restructuring might be attempted. "Given the trauma associated with major changes in libraries," he reasoned, "few librarians, including library administrators, have the necessary courage to risk it."

On the other side of the debate, Carla Stoffle, Robert Renaud, and Jerilyn R. Veldof, against a backdrop of the new realities of the higher education environment, contended that "academic libraries have to undergo radical, revolutionary organizational change quickly":

> The price of failure to act now and to begin building the necessary new structures and paradigms will be the decay and degradation of library services and the narrowing of library roles to the point where it will be impossible to make the shift."[5]

They peppered their clarion call for a restructuring movement with a host of admonitions against slow change: "Be willing to risk errors rather than lose opportunities"; "Be prepared to thrive on chaos"; "Just do it!"

The examples used to illustrate the poles of the spectrum of contrasting viewpoints are more philosophical than real, given Campbell's and Stoffle's similar track records. Campbell is a versatile writer who can argue both sides of the organizational development issue. For example, along the lines of the "lag of organizational development behind technological change posited in this book," Campbell has noted that "technological possibilities always race ahead of the culture's willingness and ability to embrace them." He is perhaps best known as an advocate of restructuring reference service.[6] Stoffle's article on "revolutionary change" should be read with an eye toward her interest in a then-upcoming ACRL conference on organizational change. Her institution—she is dean of the University of Arizona Libraries—has a "Vision Statement" that focuses on becoming a "learning organization"; the statement does not have adjectives such as "revolutionary."[7]

The philosophical difference Campbell and Stoffle have elucidated is nonetheless real in that it reflects a divide in our profession's outlook on prospects for major organizational changes. Campbell sensed that libraries will seek to maintain a predictable world by reducing ambiguity, even at the risk of organizational development; for Stoffle, our energies would be much better spent developing resilient organizations that can absorb and institutionalize rapid change. Against that background of abstract standpoints, the case studies in this book occupy a new middle ground that centers on the planning process for noteworthy programs already under way. This joining of strategic analysis and action, though differing in scope and method from one program to another, demonstrates that the "unproductive anxiety" that Campbell sensed in our profession can be superseded by a certain "creative tension" between converging units. In that regard, these chapters mark far more actual progress than either polar assessment or the ARL survey suggest.

Nonetheless, other chapters on a broader analytical plane than this book's case studies suggest that major organizational change will be a process with recurring bouts of instability. Because even reconsidering library services is usually troublesome, reconceptualizing and restructuring them may prove very difficult. Yet, prolonged failure to move in that direction—by either a library that lacks the capacity to develop, or one that puts a premium on avoidance of instability—will lead to organizational decay. The overarching issue, as David W. Lewis puts it in his chapter titled "Change and Transition in Public Services" becomes, "How is it possible to move a library organization from where it is today to where it needs to be tomorrow and still have a functioning organization when you get there?"

## Approaches and Ranges of the Restructuring Process

The contributing authors' various analyses, taken together, suggest a set of three approaches for "moving from here to there": toward significant restructuring outcomes without undue organizational instability. These approaches to the *planning process* are:

• *coupling independent streams* of problems, solutions, participants, and opportunities;

• *fostering collaborative realignments* between organizations on campus and in a consortium;

• *coordinating academic program goals* related to information resources and services in an integrated campus network.

In addition, the different kinds of restructuring *outcomes*—what is "out there" for a library to move toward—can be categorized in terms of five ranges of a restructured, boundary-spanning organization.

As shown in figure 1, the first range is a reorganization of units within a library; the second range applies to a convergence of the library with the computing center; the third range relates to collaborative programs within a consortium; the fourth range, encompassing the library's parent institution as a whole, involves the redesign of academic programs in an integrated network environment; and the fifth range is more visionary than organizational—it represents a rethinking of the library and the university's societal mission in the age of electronic information.

The abstractions of "ranges" of outcomes are not familiar perspectives in our literature, though they may be intuitively familiar to administrators and researchers. Instead, restructuring efforts are usually couched in terms of the immediate surroundings

| FIGURE 1 | | | | |
|---|---|---|---|---|
| **Ranges of Boundary Spanning** | | | | |
| 1 | 2 | 3 | 4 | 5 |
| Public & Technical Services | Library & Computing Center | State or Regional Consortium | Network & Academic Programs | Library, University & Society |

of a single organization. For example, table 1 shows the outcomes of reorganizations listed in the 1995 ARL survey (with percentiles representing only the third of its members that reported organizational changes).

Except for "partnerships with other academic libraries," those ARL library organizational changes were confined to range 1; indeed, the survey concluded that "there seems to be little involvement by members of the university community outside of the library."[8]

The connection (intervening variable) between the three various approaches of the *planning* process and the five possible ranges of restructuring *outcomes* is boundary spanning. It is the signature activity that makes restructuring a new form of organizational development by virtue of its broadening the scope of restructuring from the relatively bounded areas of library units, work flow processes, personnel, and budgets to campuswide and geographically dispersed fields of opportunity

| TABLE 1 | | |
|---|---|---|
| 1995 ARL Survey "Outcomes" | | |
| Number of ARL Libraries | Percentage of Survey Respondents | Type of Organizational Change |
| 25 | 71% | Reallocation of personnel |
| 11 | 31% | Movement of personnel from technical services to public services |
| 2 | 4% | Movement of personnel from public services to technical services |
| 5 | 14% | Reallocation of monies from materials budget to operating budget |
| 4 | 11% | Reallocation of monies from operating budget to materials budget |
| 9 | 26% | Entered into partnerships with other academic libraries |
| 17 | 49% | Increased allocation of funds for training and development |
| 17 | 49% | Reallocated resources to automation/networking units/activities. |

afforded by networked information resources and services. Boundary spanning is the essential difference between the kinds of organizational changes reported in the 1995 ARL survey and those described or envisioned in this book.

The various planning approaches have certain shared properties. First, they involve a series of incremental, or gradualist, projects that build collectively toward larger, more significant advances in organizational development. Next, the approaches are necessarily quite general. Restructuring academic libraries involves a host of nearly unique variables that no model could take into account: differences in leadership style, technical know-how, and the historical–experiential context which any mature organization draws upon to interpret new information or new challenges. Finally, the approaches are open-ended. The 1995 ARL survey noted that library reorganizations are more often situational than strategic:

> With a variety of forces currently at work, most notably declining resources and the ability of communications technology to deliver information to the desktop, many libraries have been forced to restructure on an ad hoc basis without an opportunity to plan.[9]

The essential point, however, is that there is no Grand Plan that fits our highly decentralized profession. Restructuring challenges and opportunities are necessarily abstract; their results cannot be predicted or even wholly controlled to avoid some disruptions in the process. Efforts to overengineer restructuring actually connote a library unprepared for fundamental change. As some of the contributing authors point out, there are no "blueprints" or "road maps" of this new territory. In that perspective, the three planning frameworks suggest a process along the lines that E. L. Doctorow once used to describe the solving of an ill-structured problem: "It's like driving a car at night. You can never see further than your headlights, but you can make the whole trip that way." The main idea is to start moving in what amounts to an open field, without a detailed plan, and relying on signs along the way to update one's sense of the destinations. Venturing like that requires valuing the *process* of finding one's way from "here to there" and treating obstacles as workshops rather than failures.

## Coupling Independent Streams

Restructuring an academic library entails the design of new institutional arrangements and interdependent relationships, a long-term reallocation of resources, and other more or less formal strategic plans. Such manifestations of orderly development, however, gloss over a certain randomness in the planning process.

The approach termed *independent streams* emphasizes problems, solutions, participants, and choice opportunities being loosely coupled. Problems may be overlooked or avoided. Solutions may be simply "out there," unattached to a given problem. Participants wander in and out of problem arenas. Choice opportunities tend to flow through organizations, and converge and diverge free of human wishes or intents. Although the streams are not always independent of intentional coordination (a choice opportunity may be linked to a recognized problem, a ready solution, and available decision makers), their most prevalent source of order is the variable of *timing*. As a rule, the less organizational control over the streams, the more critical the factor of their simultaneous appearance for a restructuring program to utilize them. This prevalence of temporal order over human design is a departure from the library's classic situation of an autonomous hierarchy in which there are strong mechanisms for arranging the streams into a decision package. For a traditional library, the timing of streams will not usually be critical, and randomness in the planning process will be regarded as a product of poor management. For a contemporary organization being restructured, however, the framework of independent streams recognizes the fortuity of timing and embraces its meaningfulness in the planning process.[10]

In a similar fashion, the ecology of *attention*—who attends to what, and when—is treated as an independent variable. The spread and flow of decision makers' attentions do not depend simply on the choice opportunity at hand but, rather, on a rather complicated mix of problems, solutions, and other choices at any one time. Thus, the attention paid to a restructuring problem can be both unstable over time and remarkably independent of its overall importance. For example, the "false starts" in the title of Meredith A. Butler and Stephen E. DeLong's chapter on the University at Albany's experience refers to missed opportunities for collaborative planning of a new library system when representation from the computing center was only "sporadically available."

Of the six single-organization case studies, five depict academic libraries creating choice opportunities within the independent streams framework, whereas the last study looks at the human side of restructuring when careers get disrupted. Rebecca R. Martin's chapter on the University of Vermont's experience is the most explicit account of administrators taking the initiative to couple problems, solutions, and participants to make choice opportunities happen:

> The primary approach has been one of articulating a mission or redefining a function, focusing on problems and prospects for change, and then seizing opportunities as they arise. There is no specific blueprint nor firm timetable for reorganization. . . . Vacancies at all levels are viewed as opportunities to question the status quo and to redeploy resources. Other changes have been initiated by a particular need to reduce a budget line, by an urgency to offer a particular service, by the changing institutional framework to support a new information technology, by an availability of special funding in an area, or by some other "window of opportunity."

At UVM, long-range planning has a "strategic vision [which] provides a compass but not a road map." Specific strategies and tactics are "continually modified in response to new opportunities and information," and organizational learning becomes an "almost familiar process." Martin calls this approach "evolutionary restructuring."

Caroline M. Kent's chapter on the Harvard College Library's experience shows that, even when problems and solutions arrive together, decision makers may nevertheless be adverse to choice opportunities that fail to mesh with a salient aspect of institutional culture. In this case, some forty divisional and departmental libraries at Harvard—traditionally independent ("every tub stands on its own bottom")—faced restructuring to accommodate the political economy of the campus network:

> A presumption of total organizational and fiscal indepen-
> dence and decentralization can only work at a university when
> there are no development and supportive costs that the com-
> munity must share. . . . Networking and networked resources,
> which require collaborative efforts and payments, made
> Harvard's administrative model vulnerable to failure.
> . . . [Networking, or] "who owns the fiber," emerged as a
> major institutional issue: who installs, who supports, and,
> most important, who pays.

Kent suggests that Harvard's mixed success at aligning organizational development to a highly decentralized culture may be a "microcosm of how academic libraries will face the problem of collaboration on a national scale."

Joan Giesecke and Katherine Walter's chapter on the restructuring of technical services at the University of Nebraska-Lincoln
(UN-L) shows a different, "bottom-up" phenomenon: rank-and-file
librarians taking the main initiative to create their own choice opportunities:

> Outsourcing, purchasing of cataloging tapes, receiving online
> catalog records—all such cost-effective changes bring into
> question the position of the technical services professional.
> Career development becomes a real concern as technical
> services librarians foresee the traditional intellectual as-
> pects of their work dwindling. Although technology does
> not replace the intellectual work that technical services
> librarians do, they must . . . take the initiative in reestab-
> lishing their own futures. These librarians, once relatively
> isolated, have broadened their professional roles to refer-
> ence, collection development, automated services, and bib-
> liographic instruction. Those newly won roles are crucial:
> They create improved access to collections and enrich the
> librarians' careers.

Just a few years ago, migration of technical services to public services appeared to be a rather slight and uncertain phenomenon. In a 1992 survey, for example, Gillian M. McCombs identified some places where catalogers were doing reference work, but she posed the question of whether there was a real restructuring movement under way: "It is not clear whether this is a result of a genuine convergent evolutionary growth, in which librarians themselves are changing, or whether it is the result of enforced redeployment and streamlining due to current budget cuts and staff shortages."[11] In that perspective, Giesecke's and Walter's case study depicts a significant initiative in our profession.

Whereas the Harvard experience concerns an internal factor (institutional culture), Gloriana St. Clair's chapter on Penn State University deals with an external factor: benchmarks—programs of excellence at other places—against which a restructuring program can be designed and evaluated. In the framework of independent streams, benchmarking is less a case of "windows of opportunity" than it is a deliberate process (akin to Giesecke and Walter's experience with technical services at the University of Nebraska-Lincoln) to create choice opportunities. The main variables in Penn State's benchmarking are the availability of appropriate comparators and capable participants:

> A significant investment of time must be made to identify strategic areas for benchmarking, select individuals to participate in the benchmarking process, determine appropriate and meaningful measures, justify the processes selected, discern the best comparators, collect significant data for comparison, make the [investigative] trip, and introduce the changes back into the organization.

Of interest, St. Clair suggests that some restructuring problems (e.g., document delivery) are not amenable to a long-term process of continuous incremental change but, instead, may require a whole new structural–functional model.

Peggy Seiden's chapter, "Restructuring Liberal Arts College Libraries: Seven Organizational Strategies," finds that with the recent proliferation of full-text databases and Web resources the electronic environment has become nearly sufficient for all undergraduate needs. For better or worse—Seiden finds student learning curves going down and demands for support services going up—"the network is the library." In an analysis of new-technology diffusion on campus, comparable to Butler and DeLong's chapter, Seiden looks at prospects for the diffusion of new-technology use in the coming years:

> Up to now, most colleges have done reasonably well supporting the "early adopters," the first 10 to 15 percent of the faculty to use information technology in their teaching. . . . [However], the level and quality of support that was adequate for the first 5 percent of the faculty is probably strained dealing with 15 percent of the potential faculty-user pool and will not scale up for the next 70 percent of the faculty. Thus, an information technology support crisis looms on many campuses—university and college. . . . [Some libraries in the Oberlin Group] have demonstrated considerable determination and inventiveness in redesigning their organizations that better enables them to embrace and exploit new information technologies. The essential approach has been one of creativity, flexibility, and trial and error. These college libraries have demonstrated a willingness to try different solutions and to abandon those that are not successful—a risk taking which, however prudent and necessary, is atypical of much of higher education.

The last case study, Rita A. Scherrei's chapter "Caught in the Crossfire: Organizational Change and Career Displacement in the University of California Libraries," does not relate to the planning process but, rather, looks at the human side of restructuring outcomes. Scherrei focuses on ten variables generally associated with professional self-identity and job satisfaction in a group of thirty librarians whose careers had been disrupted—either positively or negatively. Not surprisingly, the librarians whose careers were negatively changed (twenty of the thirty in the group) had feelings of significant personal loss:

Seven of them had seen their career tracks moving them into associate university librarian or large unit-head management jobs. At the time of the interviews, these librarians were almost all unclear as to what they would be doing in the future. They felt derailed; most expressed great disillusionment and reduced loyalty to the library and the university. Some talked about going through a process similar to grieving, not only for their career loss but also for the loss of the relationship with the institution. . . . Some had decided to drop outside activities for the foreseeable future as they struggled to find new niches—usually in subject areas for which they had very little background and, in some cases, limited interest.

What is surprising, however, is that most of them had been left by library management almost completely unprepared for the rather drastic change in their lives. They felt "genuine anger at the absence of complete information and an opportunity for dialogue and input with decision makers." In Scherrei's assessment, "It is possible . . . to mitigate much of this negativity if the job restructuring process is open, consultative, and placed in an overall strategic context."

## Fostering Collaborative Realignments

Collaborative realignments go beyond the boundary of a single organization to encompass a functional convergence of the library with the computing center (range 2) and with other libraries in a consortium (range 3). At first glance, such cross-organizational development would seem to entail a higher order of complexity, or difficulty, than that for range 1 boundary spanning between the relatively limited area of public and technical services. However, the degree of complexity depends more on the character of a particular problem than on the scale of boundary spanning (the number or diversity of organizations involved). Moreover, although the character of a given restructuring problem can be categorized as, say, technical, political, cultural, cognitive, or economic, there is no practical method of comparing degrees of complexity for such different types of restructuring problems.

Consider the various problems of realigning campus computing relationships. Richard M. Dougherty and Lisa McClure take up *political* matters underlying alternative organizational models; Butler and DeLong identify *technical and cognitive* barriers to network user support; and Davis-Millis and Owens focus on *cultural* differences in library–computing center alliances.

None of these cross-organizational boundary-spanning problems is inherently more complex than the long-standing single-organization issue of restructuring the library reference desk, which has sparked bitter debates resembling paradigm conflicts between traditional, print-medium knowledge structures and electronic, network-based skills.[12] The essential point is that attempts to measure the degree of complexity of various restructuring programs, whether at different organizational levels or even for different problems at the same level, will not likely produce useful generalizations.

Range 2 organizational development dates back to Patricia Battin's 1984 proposal for a new "scholarly information center," which would combine functions of the library and of academic computing to create a campus telecommunications infrastructure:

> According to the traditional cliche, the Library is the heart of the University. I think it is time for a new metaphor— and that metaphor is more appropriately DNA. The new process will be a helix—we can provide a basic set of services and technical capacities, users interact and experiment with the new technical dimensions and develop new requirements which then influence the evolution of a new shape for the infrastructure. As the genetic code of the University, the character and quality of the Scholarly Information Center will determine the character and quality of the institution.[13]

Dougherty and McClure's lead chapter to this section of the book, "Repositioning Campus Information Units for the Era of Digital Libraries," provides a survey of that "field of dreams" over the past decade, where great expectations of what once seemed logical or plausible, or even inevitable, have largely disappeared:

What happened to the merger debate? For all the theoretical debates, the promise of quick and easy mergers proved to be illusory. Consequently, the goals of reorganization have generally become more modest.

Against that background, Dougherty and McClure coined the term *collaborative realignment*. Their analysis of this "more modest" framework becomes a practical guide for academic library and computing center directors facing the prospect of working together. On a broader plane, the authors' conclusions bear on the chief dilemma of development versus decay: "Although at first glance some costs may eclipse the benefits, the consequences of doing little or nothing will be severe. Networked resources are powerful, and any institution that does not adapt to exploit them will find itself in a technological backwater."

Butler and DeLong's chapter on the University at Albany's experience presents what is basically a "bottom-up" approach to collaborative realignment. A new building was constructed for an electronic library together with computing services, but no integrated planning process involving library and computing directors was established for some years. Instead, collaboration between the two units was confined largely to pilot projects: Buy a server, bring up a system, expand network connectivity, design a gateway, and so forth. Now, even with a more integrated administration, collaboration retains its initial focus on resolving salient challenges, such as user support, rather than restructuring institutional arrangements:

> But user support and training have continued to be problematic, and they can only get worse because as we upgrade our infrastructure, the number of users will jump from 2,000 to 20,000. Furthermore, although the current users tend to be "early adopters" and much more likely to be comfortable with technology, *each of the next 18,000 will probably need substantially more training and help*! This realization prompted us to put 'user support' under a magnifying glass as a distinctly new boundary-spanning, value-added service function.

The chapter by Davis-Millis and Owens on MIT's experience presents a "top-down" approach to collaborative realignment of the library and the computer center. That university emphasized not only new institutional structures but also staff development groups whose main agenda was to explore their units' cultural differences rather than to initiate pilot projects:

> Ironically, each unit saw the other as being at an advantage politically. The libraries were concerned that they would be absorbed and controlled by IS [Information Services] which, in turn, feared that the libraries had deeper service contacts across campus and could build powerful alliances demanding unsustainable services. Picking up on the 'marriage' metaphor, [the directors] . . . saw the possibility that the partnership would be a 'deadly embrace' as each tried to leverage resources from the other while retaining complete control—ending with both parties squandering staff and financial capital on fruitless projects. To avoid that, . . . the initial focus was actually on defining the scope of the partnership, awareness of each other's organizational structure, and then the respective professional cultures. . . . [The directors] . . . avoided discussions about specific projects but, instead, focused on sharing organizational goals and values. . . .

The long-term differential effect of bottom-up versus top-down realignment may be a significant question for future research. On the one hand, it is possible that neither approach would generally leave much of an imprint—that the differences between them are exaggerated on paper because any convergence of an academic library and the computing center involves, over time, a series of shifts between strategic plans (from "above") and specific projects (from "below"). On the other hand, the case studies presented here do suggest a certain long-term differential effect. At Albany, the bottom-up approach has a universitywide corollary: Responsibility for selecting and funding PCS, and even for funding increased network support, now resides in the individual schools. (Thus, a dean might have to decide whether to fund a computing need or a faculty position.) At MIT, by contrast, the top-down approach has fostered more expansive interunit convergence: The libraries collaborate in the creation of software development methods and in the reengineering of computer services, whereas the computing center runs all the major library servers and audits security of library-operated systems.

## Redeveloping State and Regional Consortia

The section of the book on state and regional consortia focuses on range 3 organizational development, which has a longer history than any other area of boundary spanning for academic libraries. Whereas range 1 development (public and technical services) is just a few years in the making, and range 2 development (libraries and computing centers) began only last decade, range 3 development dates back a half-century. A brief sketch of its historical discontinuities puts prospects for academic library consortia in better perspective.[14]

In the 1940s, Robert B. Downs made a precursory case for coordinated collection development in consortia on the ground that it was impossible for even the largest libraries to hold more than a fraction of the world's literature.[15] Yet, this proposition took thirty years to become a professionwide norm. Until the mid-1970s, organizational autonomy—reflecting the "bigger is better" philosophy of collection management—overshadowed the idea of library interdependency.

Strikingly different was the latter half of the 1970s, when coordinated collection development became an institutionalized concept about "the way things ought to be done." Whereas only a handful of consortia had been previously established, fifty-three new consortia, each comprising at least one member of the ARL, were set up between 1975 and 1982.[16] The early 1980s, however, marked the beginning of a third period of discontinuity as the immense difficulty of moving collection development interdependency from theory to practice became evident. In 1983, the Resources and Technical Services division of ALA published a model of "combined self-interest," based on the ideal assumption that academic libraries' strengths and weaknesses could be rationally combined into regional schemes of coordinated collection development:

If enough libraries would combine with major research libraries—and if each library could state specific needs for its own core collection based on the library's strengths, weaknesses, and special local conditions—a rational, coordinated collection development scheme could be created to satisfy all participants' self-interest.[17]

Yet, according to a survey conducted that same year by Joe A. Hewitt and John S. Shipman, nearly all consortia became stymied in the attempt to move beyond the beginning stage of fostering cross-institutional relationships to the point of determining specific goals and responsibilities.[18]

Once consortia participants became aware of the sheer diversity of institutional interests and collection management structures, they found themselves unable to specify even the general aims of their respective programs.

From the mid-1980s to the mid-1990s, discussions in the literature about the fruits of cooperative collection development nearly disappeared as the gap between theory and practice became increasingly evident. Groups and agreements were announced, but without follow-up reports on the complexity or outcome of particular ventures.[19] (Dougherty and McClure, in their chapter on theory versus practice of library–computing center relationships, note the same phenomenon: a sharp decline of reports since the mid-1980s.)

This book's section on collaborative realignment of consortia marks a new stage in the historical development of this problem and its literature. The focus is now on practical problems and prospects, particularly in a networked environment, rather than on plausible assumptions about a "rational" or ideal system reflective of the print age. David F. Kohl's lead chapter, "Farewell to All That . . . Transforming Collection Development to Fit the Virtual Library Context: The OhioLINK Experience," describes this stage in terms of "two complementary frameworks—based on a new model of technological unity, the other on a radical reinterpretation of library cooperation." The technological vision is on the use of common hardware and software at all of OhioLINK's many members (as opposed to a "diverse, historical crazy quilt of individual-institution automation choices"). That infrastructure, notable for enabling patrons to receive interlibrary loan materials within a few days, makes OhioLINK one of the first truly feasible opportunities for reassessing old assumptions about cooperative collection development:

> In retrospect, it seems fairly obvious that [statewide coordination of] collection development must follow, not precede, the construction of a virtual library and delivery system. Until librarians and patrons are convinced by personal experience that the physical location of materials is largely irrelevant for their purposes, it is difficult to make the case for a genuine division of statewide (or regional) collection responsibilities. Once that Rubicon is crossed, however, significant opportunities for cost-effective resource-sharing open up.

Kohl's analysis of OhioLINK's experience covers an array of practical concerns: institutional versus consortium collection responsibilities (the "tragedy of the commons" problem), economies of scale in statewide acquisition of electronic resources, a consortium's political leverage in licensing issues, and the transforming role of local subject bibliographers.

Barbara McFadden Allen and William A. Gosling's chapter, "Facing Change and Challenge through Collaborative Action: The CIC Libraries' Experience," describes the Center for Library Initiatives of the midwestern Committee on Institutional Cooperation (CIC), in which collaborative realignments are vertical (intra-institutional)—involving nearly all academic and administrative units—as well as horizontal (cross-institutional):

> Because the CIC is organized as a consortium of *institutions* (as opposed to a consortium of *libraries*), there are ample opportunities for academic libraries to work with other key academic groups, such as the directors of campus computing centers, the university press directors, and other faculty and administrative units. . . . Together, such boundary-spanning activities provide a range of opportunities for wide-scale experimentation.

Experiments now under way include electronic scholarly publishing by a CIC university press and university library planning group; a Learning Technologies Initiative on the part of faculty, librarians, and technologists; the virtual electronic library of digital information; an electronic journal database; a collection of electronic texts in the humantites; and a task force on the preservation of digital as well as print media.

The concluding section of Allen and Gosling's chapter points up some lessons learned, such as the need for "constantly evaluating goals and programs with particular regard for a decision-making infrastructure." Although the lack of an established culture of electronic resources facilitates cooperation, subject bibliographers tend to have difficulty in thinking "globally rather than locally" about more traditional areas of coordinated collection development.

Sue O. Medina and William C. Highfill's chapter, "Shaping Consensus: Structural Cooperation in the Network of Alabama Academic Libraries," describes that consortium's evolution from the perspective of certain overlapping constructs of organizational theory and social role theory:

> Most definitions of [social] role assume the existence of consensus regarding expectations. Divergence in expectations for individuals, however, may result in conflict because of the pressure created by incongruent or countervailing forces. Organizational theory, unlike role theory, lacks well-defined concepts of role. Research on role has been concerned primarily with *intra*organizational issues, the role of the individual within the organization. There is little empirical research on how an organization's role is defined. . . . As in the case of roles of individuals, conflict can result from incongruent expectations placed on the organization. . . . Acceptance [of NAAL] presupposed a change in the status quo. Responsibility for library quality had always been the exclusive domain of the individual institutions. How would the institutional representatives to NAAL define the consortium's role relative to those of the parent institutions?

There was a period of several years for discussion and planning for NAAL before funding became available to establish actual policies and programs. That early period was lent not only to philosophical discussions about the nature of Alabama's libraries but also to research projects on social role theory. Medina and Highfill's application of social science to NAAL is thus not post ad hoc (hindsight) but, rather, explains a conscious effort by NAAL's leaders from the start to prepare for certain issues of collaborative realignment among academic institutions whose rivalries extend from football games to state resources.

Derrie B. Roark's chapter, "Directed Technological Change in the Florida Community College System," describes a fundamentally different approach to collaborative realignment in terms of a "centralized, top-down process of technological restructuring":

> District oversight and campus autonomy make strange bedfellows. However, as HCC [Hillsborough Community College] has participated in the development of a district-level instructional technology plan, its LR [learning resources] program . . . is viewed as a model of centralized training and purchasing. [Such centralization of learning resources services] has benefited both the LR program and its academic institution. Change, which sometimes must be imposed from above, is easier to accept from below if done across the board. At the same time, HCC's general experience suggests not only that strong coordination is necessary to ensure that technological development is done expediently but also that staff input and two-way communication on problems and processes are needed to make the whole process socially acceptable.

Staff who participated in state library automation projects during the 1980s naturally became technology leaders within their respective institutions in the 1990s. "By generalizing what has worked well within libraries to assist educators and students, librarians have much to offer the broader institution in its attempts to foster social adaptation to new technology in the workplace and in the curriculum."

## Coordinating Network-Based Academic Program Goals

The third and final framework of organizational development in the wake of technological change involves the role of the library in setting the academic institution's goals for the campus network. In the highly decentralized academic system, this framework is one of "harnessing organized anarchies." It encompasses the broadest and most ambiguous areas of boundary spanning:

• range 4—redesigning Internet-based academic programs in a networked environment;

• range 5—revisioning the library and the university's societal mission in the electronic communication system.

As the scope of boundary spanning expands, the concept of "organization" changes as well. At range 1 (public and technical services), the organization is a *rational order* of relatively specific goals and formal structures. At both range 2 (libraries and computing centers) and range 3 (consortia), the organization is an *alliance*, less formally structured, with more problematic and collective pursuits. At ranges 4 and 5 (concerning the networked university's societal mission in the electronic scholarly communication system), the organization is an *open system* of coalitions of shifting interest groups that develop goals by negotiation; the structure of a particular coalition, its activities, and their outcomes are all strongly influenced by environmental factors.

The concept of "organizational development" also changes at different organizational levels of boundary spanning. At ranges 1 and 2, such development centers on *institutional structures and technologies*. At range 3, it mainly involves *technological processes and economics* (Allen and Gosling's chapter providing the fullest account of the "significant and intractable economic pressures that require completely new service models and budget strategies" through consortia). At ranges 4 and 5, organizational development is primarily about *environments and politics*. The very openness of the "organized anarchy" of the university makes distinctions between what is "out there" and what is "in here"—and whether something is an "opportunity" or a "threat"—more matters of perception or sense making than discovery or analysis.[20]

Both the first and last sections of this book—"Reassessing Traditional and Virtual Ground-Assumptions" and "Restructuring Library–

University Relationships"—relate to range 4 organizational development involving a redesign of research and curricular programs in the networked environment. The authors of the chapters in those sections provide remarkably diverse assessments of the basic situation academic libraries face in the latter half of the 1990s. Pervading (implicitly if not expressly) practically all scenarios of restructuring is the metaphor of the academic library as a "bottomless pit" of escalating costs, which do not have even theoretical limits.[21]

In Herbert S. White's chapter "Dangerous Misconceptions about Organizational Development of Virtual Libraries," the combination of integrated network-to-desktop information services and decentralized university cost-center budgetary arrangements for such services is a "disastrous strategy" because it lacks intellectual economy for both the user (in terms of information overload) and the university (in terms of fiscal management):

> [The] rate of growth might at least be alleviated if [electronic access] costs were centralized under the control of librarians, rather than decentralized and scattered among faculty cost centers (ultimately still funded from the same university budget). If university administrators are concerned about costs, they should consider a different approach—improving the productivity of faculty in the spheres of teaching and research. The purpose of information, after all, is to enable the recipient to do something better. Information is not an end in itself, it is a means to an end.

However, White is not optimistic about academic librarians' willingness to take up their former "institutional turf" as the intermediaries in the scholarly communication system (i.e., as buffers and brokers in the network-to-desktop information flow now afforded by campus networks) because the option of standing aside seems to be a "way out" of the "bottomless pit":

> . . . [L]ibrarians seem all too willing to cede the process of information intermediation—to abdicate their expertise in analyzing the content and the value of information to the

desks and terminals of the faculty through the virtual library—because in such an organization, though costs may indeed be much higher, they will no longer be our responsibility. In that framework, the virtual library may be understandable, but it remains unworkable.

White's message is straightforward: "One cannot fritter away money into the budgets of countless and traditionally irresponsible user groups! . . . [If the library manages and controls] these funds, the result will be a great deal more palatable for the institution."

David W. Lewis makes the opposing argument that library management should "forego turf battles and take a broad institutional view of information, even when that risks a loss of exclusive control of some resources":

> Historically, most [library] efforts to network information began with dial-up access to OPACs and networked CD-ROMs, applications that were generally developed and controlled by the library. It might be tempting for the library to try to maintain control, but that would not be a good strategy. Unless networked information is closely tied to institutional and departmental programs and delivered in a way that matches ever-changing local needs, it will not be used effectively. At any rate, the enormous economic costs involved would prohibit total library control.

In Lewis's approach to resolving the "bottomless pit," cost-benefit analyses are necessary to move forward in political debates on how campus resources are allocated. Thus far, however, little is known in any systematic way about that kind of analysis. As Charles R. McClure and Cynthia L. Lopata found in a 1996 survey, universities have had a very difficult time attempting to determine an operational definition of the campus network because each of its manifold components—infrastructure, resource content, user services, user support, and management (governance, planning, and fiscal aspects of the network)—involves a different kind of cost-benefit analysis.[22]

Charles B. Osburn's chapter, "One Purpose: The Research University and Its Library," is a more optimistic assessment of the "bottomless pit" problem, based on his view that the university has reached a historical turning point in the "need for serious institutional strategic planning and the establishment of operational academic priorities":

> . . . [F]aculty can no longer avoid the truth that for so long had been overlooked or ignored: There really are trade-offs to be made and priorities to be applied. Library issues need to be addressed as they have not been for decades. That means that the library will be given closer scrutiny, no longer taken for granted. There will even be occasional debates on campus about the future role of the library in the electronic environment. There will also be opportunities to involve both faculty and administration in library planning in significant ways, thereby creating an overture for the reintegration of the library into the academic enterprise.

Of potentially greater import is the university's and library's prospective relationship to society (range 5 organizational development). Osburn foresees a shift in higher education's institutional response to mass electronic communication systems—away from "ad hoc projects and programs undertaken evidently out of desperation"—toward a recognition that the university "will function in the best interests of society" by disseminating scholarly information through those mass systems. He argues:

> We have now arrived at a crucial moment, perhaps a historical juncture. For the first time, both the emergent medium of scholarly communication and the communication medium in demand by all segments and strata of society at large (not just an elite) are the same, the common feature being the seductive convenience of electronic information technology. This concurrent emergence of the so-called information society and the electronic scholarly communication system opens an era of unprecedented opportunity for the university to serve society through a new kind of relationship.

In that perspective, the mission of the university and that of its library have the potential to become perhaps not identical, but highly congruent.

The final chapter, Douglas G. Birdsall's "Strategic Planning in Academic Libraries: A Political Perspective" deals with practical considerations of range 5 organization development. His analysis of the university as an "organized anarchy" having a variety of decision processes, power bases, and influence strategies brings us full circle to the earlier frameworks of "coupling independent streams and "fostering collaborative realignments":

> There are three main political strategies for maximizing planning outcomes. These are to build upon the diversity of stakeholder interests, to form alliances and coalitions for the advancement of the library's own interests, and to market a persuasive planning document.

Specific strategic plans used by Harvard University, the Massachusetts Institute of Technology, the University at Albany, Michigan State University, and Wayne State University are discussed by Birdsall.

Unlike White's emphasis on "turf" issues, Lewis's emphasis on cost analyses, and Osburn's emphasis on historical turning points, Birdsall emphasizes that academic governance of the virtual library will continue to be highly pluralistic and evolutionary in character—the "accretion of hundreds of largely autonomous actions taken for different reasons, at different times, under different conditions, by different people." Hence, a strong and growing importance is attached to the formation of alliances and coalitions that benefit the library's stakeholders, as well as its own institutional interests.

Finally, the epilogue on "Balancing Restructuring Efforts" describes the difference between organizational development and decay in terms of four competing orientations that must be periodically weighed against one another: boundary spanning and strategic planning (on the external side) versus policy setting and human development (on the internal side). What makes restructuring such an interesting, sometimes emotional, undertaking is that these organizational needs represent contradictory moral positions about what makes a good manager and a good organization.

## Concluding Remarks

The nineteen chapters of this book are variations on a distinct theme for academic libraries in the latter half of the 1990s: The lag of organizational development behind technological change. The key factor that will spell the difference between development and decay is *boundary spanning*. Within a library organization, boundary spanning centers on a convergence of public services and technical services. In the broader environment, it ranges from a realignment of campus computing structures, to a redevelopment of consortium relationships, to a readjustment of the library and university's dual mission to serve society through the electronic scholarly communication system.

The overall problem of "getting from here to there"—moving toward significant restructuring outcomes without undue organizational instability—thus involves several goals and destinations. To conceptualize the various transition processes, three overlapping approaches may be helpful: (1) coupling independent streams of problems, solutions, participants, and choice opportunities; (2) fostering collaborative realignments; and (3) coordinating academic program goals related to the campus network. The approach that appears to have the broadest prospects of change for the library staff as a whole is the third one, in terms of integrating networked information resources into research and curricular programs. That will be a process characterized by open-ended goals, problematic choices, "paradigm conflicts" among academic departments over electronic versus print-age library resources, and drifting participation of different groups in the decision arena over time. The library's role will be to help foster and maintain collaborative strategies among the different stakeholder groups: the scholars in the sciences, in the social sciences, and in arts and humanities; the librarians themselves; the computing center staff; and the university administrators, with each group having its own worldview and spheres of influence in the decentralized academic environment. The end result would not be just organizational development for the academic institution as a whole but a significantly higher level of organizational relevance for the library.

For now, the "unproductive anxiety" that Jerry Campbell identified as the product of "technological assault" and "organizational rigidity" is real enough to reiterate the first step for "moving from here to there": Start in a general direction and make greater sense of the various destinations along the way. When faced with an ambiguous environment, restructuring might seem to require a good map or, what amounts to the same thing, a detailed strategic plan. But we should remember that organizations are judged by what they *do*, not by what they plan.

## NOTES

1. Althea H. Jenkins, "Members Shape ACRL's Future," *College & Research Libraries News* 55 (June 1994): 368–72.

2. For reports at the turn of the 1990s on the very slow involvement of either technical services or the library automation department in public services, see: Barbara J. Moran, "The Unintended Revolution in Academic Libraries: 1939 to 1989 and Beyond," *College & Research Libraries* 50 (Jan. 1989): 31; Gillian M. McCombs, "Technical Services in the 1990s: A Process of Convergent Evolution," *Library Resources and Technical Services* 36 (Apr. 1992): 135–48; Mike Ridley and Charles W. Bailey Jr., eds., "Symposium on Staffing Issues and Public-Access Computer Systems," *Public-Access Computer Systems Review* 1, no. 2 (1990): 15–49, access at http://info.lib.uh.edu/pacsrev/html; Patricia M. Larsen, "The Climate of Change: Library Organizational Structures, 1985–1990," *Reference Librarian* 34 (1991): 79–93.

3. *Library Reorganization & Restructuring*, SPEC Kit #215, comp. Joanne D. Eustis and Donald J. Kenney (Washington, D.C.: ARL Office of Management Services, 1996).

4. Jerry D. Campbell, "Getting Comfortable with Change: A New Budget Model for Libraries in Transition," *Library Trends* 42 (winter 1994): 451.

5. Carla J. Stoffle, Robert Renaud, and Jerilyn R. Veldof, "Choosing Our Futures," *College & Research Libraries* 57 (May 1996): 219; see also "Commentaries on 'Choosing Our Futures,'" *College & Research Libraries* 57 (May 1996): 226–33.

6. Jerry D. Campbell, "Choosing to Have a Future," *American Libraries* 24 (June 1993): 560–66; and "Shaking the Conceptual Foun-

dations of Reference: A Perspective," *Reference Services Review* 20 (winter 1992): 29–35.

7. *Library Reorganization & Restructuring,* 11–13.

8. Ibid., unnumbered attached flyer.

9. Ibid.

10. For discussions of planning in the framework of "independent streams," see James G. March, *A Primer on Decision Making: How Decisions Happen* (New York: Free Pr., 1994); Nitin Nohria and James D. Berkley, "The Virtual Organization: Bureaucracy, Technology, and the Implosion of Control," in *The Post-Bureaucratic Organization: New Perspectives on Organizational Change,* ed. Charles Heckscher and Anne Donnellon (Thousand Oaks, Calif.: Sage, 1994), 108–28.

11. Gillian M. McCombs, "Technical Services in the 1990s," 136.

12. For such debate, see: Campbell, "Shaking the Conceptual Foundations of Reference;" Larry R. Oberg, "Rethinking Reference: Smashing Icons at Berkeley," *College & Research Library News* 54 (May 1993): 265–66; Daniel F. Ring, "Searching for Darlings: The Quest for Professional Status," *College & Research Library News* 54 (Dec. 1993): 641–43.

13. Patricia Battin, "The Electronic Library: A Vision for the Future," *EDUCOM Bulletin* 19 (summer 1984): 14.

14. Charles A. Schwartz, "Social Science Perspectives on Cooperative Collection Development," in *Impact of Technology on Resource Sharing: Experimentation and Maturity,* ed. Thomas C. Wilson (New York: Haworth Pr., 1992), 47–60.

15. Robert B. Downs, "American Library Cooperation in Review," *College & Research Libraries* 6 (Sept. 1945, part II): 411.

16. Joe A. Hewitt and John S. Shipman, "Cooperative Collection Development among Research Libraries in the Age of Networking: Report of a Survey of ARL Libraries," *Advances in Library Automation and Networking* 1 (1987), 202.

17. Paul H. Mosher and Marcia Pankake, "A Guide to Coordinated and Cooperative Collection Development," *Library Resources and Technical Services* 27 (Oct. 1983): 417–31; as summarized in Richard M. Dougherty, "A Conceptual Framework for Organized Resource Sharing and Shared Collection Development Programs," *Journal of Academic Librarianship* 14 (Nov. 1988): 289.

18. Hewitt and Shipman, "Cooperative Collection Development among Research Libraries in the Age of Networking"; see also Joseph J. Branin, "Cooperative Collection Development," in *Collection Development: A New Treatise*, ed. Charles B. Osburn and Ross Atkinson (Greenwich, Conn.: JAI Pr., 1991), 81–110; Richard Hacken, "The RLG Conoco Study and Its Aftermath: Is Resource Sharing in Limbo?" *Journal of Academic Librarianship* 18 (Mar. 1992): 17–23.

19. A significant exception to the lack of informative reports on cooperative collection outcomes is John Rutledge and Luke Swindler, "Evaluating Membership in a Resource-Sharing Program: The Center for Research Libraries," *College & Research Libraries* 49 (Sept. 1988): 409-24.

20. Karl E. Weick, *Sensemaking in Organizations* (Thousand Oaks, Calif.: Sage, 1995), 70.

21. Analyses of the "bottomless pit" phenomenon include Dennis P. Carrigan, "The Political Economy of the Academic Library," *College & Research Libraries* 49 (July 1988): 325–31; Larry Hardesty, "The Bottomless Pit Revisited," *College & Research Libraries* 52 (May 1991): 219–29; Richard M. Dougherty and Carol Hughes, *Preferred Futures: A Summary of Six Workshops with University Provosts and Library Directors* (Mountain View, Calif.: Research Libraries Group, 1991); and Carol A. Hughes, "A Comparison of Perceptions of Campus Priorities: The 'Logical' Library in an Organized Anarchy," *Journal of Academic Librarianship* 18 (Mar. 1992): 140–45.

22. Charles R. McClure and Cynthia L. Lopata, *Assessing the Academic Networked Environment: Strategies and Options* (Washington, D.C.: Coalition for Networked Information, 1996); see also Vartan Gregorian, Brian L. Hawkins, and Merrily Taylor, "Integrating Information Technologies: A Research University Perspective," *CAUSE/EFFECT* 15 (winter 1992): 5–12.

# Change and Transition in Public Services

*David W. Lewis*

Academic libraries and, more important, all of higher education have been in the midst of a fundamental transformation over the past decade. Changes in information technology, requirements for increased accountability from stakeholder groups, and pressures to accomplish more with fewer resources have combined to produce a period of organizational restructurings that will require librarians to reshape their professional identities and roles.[1]

This combination of rapid technological advances, rising demands for improved services, and long-term economic constraints may have profound effects on the societal role of the university:

> Instead of prospering with the new tools, many of the traditional functions of universities will be superseded, their financial base eroded, their technology replaced, and their role in intellectual inquiry reduced. . . . Accomplishing each of these functions is based on a set of technologies and economics. Together with history and politics, they give rise to a set of institutions. Change the technology and economics, and the institutions must change, eventually.[2]

Eli M. Noam, author of that dictum on organizational development as a function of technological and economic change, argues that a historic reversal of information flow has taken place. In the past, people went to information by attending universities and visiting libraries. Now and increasingly in the future, information goes to the people via computer networks. In the emerging electronic communications environment, organizations outside higher education may be better positioned than universities to provide information services to society at large.

Underlying the restructuring of the organizational and technological bases of information is the accelerating growth of the World Wide Web, which enables multimedia, hypertext information to flow without mediation to individuals who, with trial-and-error experience, can find a wealth of resources that were not easily available just a few years ago. No one with online access must visit a library, or be affiliated with higher education, to explore the networked electronic scholarly communication system. Although the Internet and its Web are still "under construction," with a broad range of technical, informational, and economic problems to be resolved, the reversal of information flow posited by Noam has clearly begun.

Academic librarians generally acknowledge that their profession is undergoing fundamental change. Still, there is remarkably little consensus on specific future directions. Michael Buckland provides important insights for our coming to a consensus in *Redesigning Library Service: A Manifesto*, which sets forth three historical stages of library development: the paper library of old; then, the automated library, where bibliographic access became electronic but primary resources remained largely in paper format; and now, the electronic library, where both bibliographic structures and primary resources are increasingly digital.[3] That is a useful taxonomy because it distinguishes among ways of providing library services with different sets of technologies. By looking at distinct stages of development, we are encouraged to go beyond the usual incrementalist mode of assessing the future and consider the prospect that ongoing change may accrue, over some years, into a fundamental transformation of the academic library enterprise.[4]

In recognizing the electronic stage of development, we need to reconsider academic library professional identities and roles. Such a reconsideration is hardly new for reference librarians. For example, in an article published nearly twenty years ago, Brian Nielsen caused quite a stir with his argument that online searching would soon be done by *all* library users, thereby causing a "deprofessionalization of librarianship."[5] Although difficult to imagine now, that was considered an alarming prospect; online searching had then given reference librarians the powerful role of gatekeeper to the world of electronic information, so the idea of giving up such power was not generally welcomed. Beyond that, Nielsen made several points that bear on the contemporary scene:

• Reference librarians have a certain ambivalence about technology: Although it brings them increased professional status, it also promises to make a traditional role for them obsolete.

• An important distinction exists between librarians' enthusiasm for new technology and their enthusiasm for the new roles that are imposed on them.

• As unmediated technology develops, librarians are likely to be ambivalent to the extent that unmediated services scramble old and new workloads, identities, and statuses in ways that may not be to the advantage of individual librarians.

We are now in the midst of the transition from the automated to the electronic library. The earlier transition from the paper to the automated library was not really difficult because it did not seriously challenge the role of the librarian or the library. Even with the influx of online databases in the mid-1980s (and the subsequent alarm over a "deprofessionalization of librarianship"), things remained fundamentally unchanged. Computers had come into technical services earlier, but the buildings looked and operated much as they did in the 1970s. Terminals and then computers replaced index tables and card catalogs, but the basic role of the library and the librarian—what we did and how we did it—was much as it had been decades earlier. We should not, however, take comfort in the fact that we have managed this first transition. The transition we now face—to the electronic library—will not be so simple or easy. It is more problematic, for at this juncture technology allows the information flow to begin its reverse course: to be wherever people are connected to a network.

It is hard to say with any confidence what public services in academic libraries will be like in ten years—but such services and our professional identities will certainly be different. Fundamental change will stamp all parts of the library, altering or obliterating the traditional boundaries between public and technical services. Although this chapter takes a public services perspective, one of the most likely results of the coming transition will be the vanishing of that boundary which has for so long defined the way library organizations and functions are viewed.

## Fundamental Changes

Although there are many ways to frame prospects for the future, three particular frames seem to capture the predominant trends. The first two are driven by changes in technological capabilities, and the third is the resulting organizational adaptation to technological change. The combination of the three will surely have profound effects on academic libraries and their staffs.

In the first frame, information tools have, for most of recorded history, been place-bound, mainly in library buildings. Now, however, information tools can be not only electronic but network based, and thus freed from their traditional spatial limitations. The library as a space on campus will remain, but no longer as the only information place. As Noam suggests, information will flow to, and be available in, all places it is needed. Equally important, information resources are being combined with productivity tools—word processors, spreadsheets, and animation and video-editing packages—which are increasingly demanded by students and expected by faculty.

In the second frame, the nature and methods of instruction in higher education will be transformed by new information technologies. The one-hour lecture presented by a single faculty member using a chalkboard as the primary tool is as doomed as the paper-format card catalog. Librarians should play a significant role in integrating information resources into the networked instructional environment, but this role is not ensured because the political issues surrounding the whole area of instruction may prove difficult to resolve.[6]

In the third frame, such technological advances require a restructuring of organizational models. Libraries must become adept at boundary spanning. Traditional library organizations generally lack the flexibility and adaptability to respond to rapid environmental change, especially when players from outside libraries become central to what we do. Team-based structures will be required if we are to maintain effective collaborations with computing organizations and other campus units. And in working with faculty, librarians must carve out a new professional role in the development and delivery of networked curricular resources.

All three kinds of changes are sweeping, and their combination will transform academic libraries and librarianship in some ways that are foreseeable and in other ways that are not yet known. Each of the three changes—in information tools, in instructional approaches, and in organizational structures—is reviewed in turn.

## Information Tools

Networked information resources and services have come to dominate prospects for the academic library in recent years. OPACs and networked CD-ROMs set the stage a decade ago, but these are mainly bibliographic tools more representative of the automated library than the emerging electronic one. Lexis/Nexis made the first large-scale set of primary resources available in academic libraries in the early 1990s. Other sets of full-text general and business journals became available, first on CD-ROM and then over the Internet; but the real explosion has been World Wide Web, which in its first year (1993) proliferated at an astonishing 341,634 percent annual growth rate (based on service traffic).[7]

Although libraries generally provide access to the Web, in many cases (because of limited hardware or because of philosophical concerns about the appropriateness of "Net surfing" in libraries) this information is more easily available in computer labs, dorms, offices, or homes. Although much of the information available through the Web has been rightly ignored by academic libraries, there are many scholarly sites that offer more current or comprehensive materials than typically found in local collections. Another important development is the use by commercial sites, such as Britannica Online, MUSE, Engineering Village, and MathSciNet, of IP (Internet protocol) address filtering as a mechanism for controlling access. That allows campuswide access to a given resource without having to maintain complex hardware or software, manage passwords, or be limited by simultaneous-use constraints.

In the near term, we can expect to confront a variety of changes in service patterns. Although such changes may be evolutionary in libraries that confront the issues forthrightly, the overwhelming need to restructure organizations could lead to crises in those libraries that do not accept change easily, raising the prospect of organizational decay.

*Crisis #1: Redesigning services for a distributed and integrated computing environment.* The influx of terminals, and then workstations, that accompanied the deployment of OPACs and CD-ROM networks in the 1980s required academic libraries to develop on-site support for computer hardware. As networked information becomes more important in the latter half of the 1990s, and as libraries respond by deploying large numbers of workstations, user-support issues will become increasingly demanding. Library sites that combine word processing and other productivity software will need to provide the kind of assistance offered in computer labs. At the same time, as library resources are networked across campus, reference questions about them (e.g., their content, source, reliability, timeliness) will need librarian expertise. Collaboration with computing organizations in both cases is the only sensible approach. Because it is not possible to spread librarians across all potential service points, questions of where and how reference staff should be deployed, and when other levels of staffing would be an adequate substitute, will arise. This reconceptualization of reference work as being spatially distributed and involving technical troubleshooting may lead to the conclusion that current assumptions about the combination of expertises required to provide all-around service are unrealistic and that alternative strategies using less-credentialed staff with either technical skills or just an ability to answer directional questions will be more effective and less costly.[8] In short, reference librarians may not be able, if only because of time constraints, to manage the constantly changing technical basics of the networked environment as well as the newly created reference questions.

*Crisis #2: Integrating computer and information support services.* As information resources spread over campus networks, and remote users require both technological and research assistance, there will be an inevitable blending of the reference and the computing help desks. Current service arrangements, based on assisting users in person on-site, will give way to strategies that support remote users at any location. Over the long run, tiered strategies that focus differently on giving immediate answers, on teaching research techniques, or on arranging consultations for large projects or complex questions will prove more effective. At the same time, when networked information comes to users through personal workstations, users might take responsibility for mastering important sources, just as they now do for books in their personal collections. Given such personal initiatives, there may be a "light at the end of the tunnel" in the sense of a gradual reduction of incessant technical and/or reference queries directed at library–computing units. Still, significant short-term problems abound: Triage will be required, and some users will go unserved until support services are restructured.

*Crisis #3: Reconceptualizing reference service to apply worldwide expertise locally.* Another way to view the remote-support issue leads to a more challenging reorganizational prospect. Traditional reference service has been based on maximizing the effective use of local collections by developing local expertise. In a networked environment, this arrangement will give way to new strategies that provide access to worldwide resources and worldwide expertise.[9] Although outsourcing has traditionally been a technical services option, it is not difficult to envision the outsourcing of certain reference services to remote-subject specialists or to commercial firms that have the resources to develop sophisticated support structures and economies of scale which are simply beyond the capabilities of individual libraries. There will be legitimate local concerns about the quality or relevance of reference services "out there," but (as with similar concerns about outsourcing cataloging) they can be addressed in terms of staff efficiency and organizational effectiveness. An important part of considering this issue is to have a clear understanding of both the quality and the cost of current services, for the cost might be higher and the quality lower than generally assumed.

*Crisis #4: Reassessing local cataloging costs.* The local catalog, traditionally the core resource for reference service, has always commanded considerable resources for its maintenance. The proliferation of Internet resources now drives libraries to either create parallel organizational tools or attempt an integration of networked resources into the catalog. Neither strategy, however, makes much sense in the long term because each one is extremely labor-intensive and therefore expensive. Commercial firms may come to provide products that organize the Web better, and at a lower cost, than individual libraries are able to do.[10] Paying a few thousand dollars a year for dedicated access to an academic version of, say, *Yahoo!* or AltaVista could turn out to be a better deal than doing this ever-growing job in-house. When the library's more important resources are on the network and good indexes with links exist, the local catalog's value may decline. At some point, important questions about continuing the expense of maintaining the Internet part of the local catalog seem inevitable.

*Crisis #5: Rethinking bibliographic instruction.* The training of library users requires new approaches, for the traditional approach no longer works.[11] The fifty-five-minute, one-shot session as part of a term paper preparation can rarely cover even the basic skills required to manipulate complex information tools. Moreover, the "shelf life" of some skills is so short that teaching them as part of a freshman composition course—and then hoping for relevance over the student's college career—may also be doomed to failure. In the long run, information literacy will have to be integrated into, and taught across, the curriculum. For now, a variety of strategies will need to be tried and retried to cover, as best we can, the skills needed to use increasingly sophisticated information tools effectively.

Each of these changes in service strategies entails difficult choices. On the one hand, service patterns in most academic libraries target users who come into the building and provide roughly equal, though generally limited, help. On the other hand, specialized reference assistance may require a rerouting of basic or directional queries to less-credentialed staff. Empathy—an ability to handhold the inexperienced—will be increasingly important as reference services become more technical. As contemporary patterns do not suffice, it will be necessary to conduct a series of careful, objective reevaluations of user needs. Attempts to restructure without such formal planning will inevitably run into entrenched staff habits and assumptions that are not likely to be compatible with restructuring public services. Overall, fundamental change in reference services is likely to be more important in the long run than the transition of cataloging operations in the mid-1970s, when the availability of national cataloging databases transformed those operations. The keys to success will be similar: a hard-nosed, cost-conscious approach to management, a shift of some responsibilities to less-credentialed staff, and a commitment to continuous retraining.

## Instructional Approaches

On a broader level, there is much debate and marked controversy about the effectiveness of information technology in higher education. Stephen C. Ehrmann, manager of the Educational Strategies Program at the Annenberg/CPB Project, argues that confusion abounds because higher education has only a vague notion of what methods of instruction work and even what instructional goals should be. "Unfortunately, this means one can't ask, 'How well is this technology-based approach working against the norm?' since there isn't any norm."[12] As he points out, there is little way to state in rational economic terms what it ought to cost to educate a student properly because colleges simply spend all the money they manage to raise. Moreover, there are no salient relationships among patterns of spending, even for similar institutions. Kenneth C. Green and Steven W. Gilbert concluded from an extensive review of the literature that, although information technology has the potential to change the way instruction is delivered in the academy, there is much to be learned and that information technology will not likely increase instructional productivity:

> Content, curriculum, and communications—rather than productivity—are the appropriate focus of—and rationale for—campus investments in information technology. But even if this argument is compelling, we must still be careful not to foster inappropriate expectations. . . . The academic enterprise can do great things with—and will experience significant benefits from—information technology. But it won't be cheap, and it will not save money soon.[13]

When many knowledgeable commentators agree that the academy cannot reliably ascertain whether investments in technology (or, for that matter, in other teaching resources) make a real difference, there should be cause for concern. Clearly, students and parents (who pay higher and higher tuition bills) and funding agencies (especially state legislatures) no longer show much tolerance for this situation.

A way out of this untenable situation is, at least in theory, not terribly difficult to ascertain, though it will be hard to implement. Robert B. Barr and John Tagg distinguish between two approaches to the mission of the university: instruction versus learning.[14] The *instructional* approach generally involves only rudimentary, stimulus-response interactions limited in meaning to a particular course. The method and the product are the same—a class taught or a lecture given. The assumption is that to get more learning you must do more teaching. In contrast, the *learning* approach embraces "education for understanding—a sufficient grasp of concepts, principles, or skills so that one can bring them to bear on new problems and situations." Barr and Tagg go on to argue:

> Under the Instruction Paradigm, colleges suffer from a serious design flaw—they are structured in such a way that they cannot increase their productivity without diminishing the quality of their product. . . . Under the Learning Paradigm, productivity is redefined as the cost per unit of learning per student. . . . Under this new definition, however, it *is* possible to increase outcomes without increasing costs. An abundance of research shows that alternatives to the traditional semester-length, classroom-based lecture method produce more learning. Some of these alternatives are less expensive; many produce more learning for the same cost. Under the Learning Paradigm, producing more with less becomes possible because the more that is being produced is learning and not hours of instruction.[15]

Alan E. Guskin reaches the same basic conclusion regarding productivity in higher education—that faculty roles must be restructured to enhance and facilitate student learning and, although this will help control the costs of higher education, it will be a "monumental undertaking" for faculty to acquire such new skills.[16] In that vein, William Massy and Robert Zemsky focus on productivity enhancements arising from the substitution of new information technology for faculty and other labor; and Donald Langenberg cites a 1993 Pew Higher Education Research Program study which calls for cost savings by a reduction of full-time faculty *employment* by 25 percent.[17–18] Lanenberg suggests, however, that a better way to resolve the problem is by increasing faculty *productivity* by 25 percent. Whatever happens, it is clear that faculty work needs to be restructured to become more effective.

If changes in instructional strategies are not based on this need to improve productivity, universities will not be competitive in the coming education marketplace.[19] Langenberg suggests the analogy of industrial deregulation in describing the competitive environment that higher education has entered:

> It is not written anywhere that the apex of American higher education will always be associated with brand names that once were the surnames of New England gentlemen or western railroad barons. It is not even written that the apex will continue to be occupied by colleges and universities.[20]

William Plater suggests that we "Imagine what Steve Spielberg's new company could produce for the education market within the decade or what Bell Atlantic might do if it actually could purchase the Public Broadcasting System."[21] He argues that it is only because universities and colleges have a monopoly on credentials and certifications that more rapid development of media-based, private-sector competition in higher education has not been forthcoming.

The combination of rising costs and other competitive pressures will likely require most academic institutions to move from an instructional paradigm to a learning paradigm. As part of this shift, they will apply new information technology widely as a substitute for faculty or staff labor. Moreover, as universities and colleges migrate to the learning model, opportunities will be created for libraries and librarians to play new and potentially exciting roles. A broad area of new opportunity is in the design and implementation of computer-based teaching and learning environments. Such environments will rely on instructional teams comprising faculty, librarians, technologists, and experts in pedagogy. Another principal area of new opportunity will arise in the creation of both physical and electronic spaces where the learning paradigm will take place.

## Instructional Teams

Restructuring the curriculum and creating alternative learning structures and environments will require that faculty members learn new skills and, in some cases, give up their exclusive role as proprietor of individual courses. An effective approach will be to create instructional teams that redesign and deliver new courses or, more generally, create the learning environment that will replace the course.[22] Faculty, as the content experts, will generally provide leadership for the team, which will include members with different skill sets—representing, in the main, technology, pedagogy, and the research library. Most teams will function intensely during the design and construction stages but may have differing memberships or activities later in the delivery and evaluation stages.

Integration of information resources into courses and the development of information competencies across the curriculum are the librarian's role on instructional teams. Such integration may be the only means of solving the library's current bibliographic instruction dilemma. Librarians have for some time been using the term *information literacy* as a way of adapting bibliographic or library instruction to the environment of the automated and now electronic library. That effort has been largely ineffectual because librarians have neither the means to influence curricula nor the resources to teach large numbers of students more than a cursory overview. With new instructional teams, however, a fundamental integration of all aspects of information literacy—from the mechanics of information tools to the societal impacts of networked technologies—may be possible.[23]

## New Learning Spaces

As instructional approaches change, the spaces in which these activities take place will also need restructuring. Universities and colleges have large inventories of classrooms designed for lecture presentations, and academic libraries are designed to store books and to encourage individual study. In the classroom, technology is not universally deployed; in the library, it is not effectively utilized. Where technology is in place on most campuses—in computer clusters and labs—it is generally structured for individual, not group, work. The instructional approaches we can anticipate will require large-scale access to technology, through either the installation of many workstations or the creation of new space with network access for student laptops. In either case, an emphasis on facilitating group work will be required on a broad scale as group projects and peer or faculty coaching become common instructional strategies.

The library, as the central space for scholarly activity on campus and as the facility that has traditionally offered the longest hours of operation, should be the primary locus of these new spaces. Early examples of this kind of restructuring are the Leavey Library at the University of Southern California, and the Information Commons at the Estrella Mountain and Mesa Centers in the Maracopa Community College system.[24] Such pioneering spaces, however, are in conflict with certain traditional values of libraries. They are noisy places designed to encourage interaction, not quiet contemplative spaces. They also require heavy investments in technology and support. Designing and staffing of these spaces will involve librarians, computing center personnel, and student-tutoring or study-skills assistants. All this will require collaborations across existing administrative boundaries, which may prove especially difficult because physical space and pedagogical turf are at stake. Other spaces on campus will be designed to accommodate activities with a library component but will not be library based. In those cases, the library will always need to be involved, sometimes as a consultant and sometimes as a full partner. Interesting examples of this can be found in the new undergraduate library at George Mason University, which shares a building with the student center, and in the Media Union at the University of Michigan, located with computer classrooms and laboratories.

In addition to physical spaces, electronic spaces to support the new styles of teaching and learning will be built. This will take place on dual—infrastructure and course—levels. On the infrastructure level, librarians will need to be involved as part of the campus team that plans and operates the networked scholarly environment. Historically, most efforts to network information began with dial-up access to OPACs and networked CD-ROMs, applications that were usually developed and controlled by the library. It might be tempting for the library to try to maintain control, but that would not be a good strategy. Unless networked information is closely tied to institutional and departmental programs and delivered in a way that matches ever-changing local needs, it will not be used effectively. At any rate, the enormous economic costs involved would prohibit total library control. Libraries will need to restructure public services in a campuswide collaboration that will require shared controls of information resources with departments and computing centers. On the course level, the required collaboration among faculty, librarians, and technologists will likely be accomplished with the aforementioned instructional teams which jointly develop ways to use information resources effectively.

## Organizational Structures

In 1986, I proposed an organizational paradigm for academic libraries.[25] It was based on a professional bureaucratic model to provide individual librarians the authority and support structures necessary to operate independently within a certain organizational philosophy. That model became the basis for a 1994 article on the reorganization of reference services.[26] Both articles focused on library operations primarily from an internal perspective. However, what I have come to appreciate in recent years is the significant extent to which the library needs to be integrated with other university organizations. It is now clear that libraries will be restructured outwardly in new and radical ways and that *boundary spanning* will be central to all library activities. Two organizational changes can be expected: The first is the use of teams, the second is a truer user orientation.

## *Teams*

As noted above, librarians will be involved in team-based collaborations with computing and telecommunications organizations to provide support for clusters of workstations both within the library and across campus. Additionally, collaborations with computing organizations will grow to design and construct the campus-networked information system. Neither kind of collaboration can be based on a division of traditional institutional turf. Rather, a mutual commitment to ongoing programs and a willingness to share both resources and responsibilities will be necessary. Beyond the computing organization, collaborations with other information-support units can be expected. For example, it is likely that libraries, bookstores, and graphic-reproduction operations will collaborate on the production and sale of supplementary course materials. The library collaboration having the greatest potential will be with the faculty (or departments or entire schools) in instructional teams to redesign the curriculum.

Teams will be used not only as a boundary spanning mechanism across campus but also to create more flexible library organizations internally, with all levels of staff more fully involved in decision making.[27] Teams will be increasingly required because existing hierarchical structures are not adequate to the tasks we now face—to be productive and more focused, to do more with less.

Adapting to team structures will require librarians to rethink their professional identities and roles. Librarians on most campuses have a status that is between faculty and other professional support staff. The importance, or even the appropriateness, of faculty status for librarians has been challenged, and this challenge will undoubtedly continue.[28] If academic librarians use faculty status to insulate themselves from accountability for organizational success or failure, or when it distracts them from core organizational functions, it will be counterproductive. As Plater points out, the use of all faculty time is likely to be subject to more institutional control.[29] Librarians should anticipate a similar reconsideration of their activities. It seems clear that an inflexible adherence to faculty status will not be useful in a team-based organization. Teams that involve staff from a variety of job classifications and categories, as most library teams inevitably will, have a potential to cause stress because of differences in philosophies about public services, as well as differences in salary and benefits. The potential for this type of conflict increases when the teams include staff from units outside the library where different organizational cultures prevail.

Teams can, ideally, channel individual energies and creativity toward organizational goals. This ideal is more likely to be approached or achieved when teams have both clear, tangible objectives and outcomes by which their success can be gauged. The development of activity-based cost models for team activities (and other forms of strategic planning) will assist in the evaluation process. Administrative clarity on institutional goals is needed, along with a strong commitment to team building and, concomitantly, to decentralization of authority.

Richard M. Johnson argues that a political model of decision making will predominate in higher education. In that model, two keys to assessing the prospective role of the library are whether it is identified as an academic unit, rather than a support unit; and the extent to which librarians, particularly library leaders, are identified as campus academic leaders, rather than managers of academic support enterprises:

> The library must be recognized as a core element of the academic enterprise rather than peripheral to it, a focal point for the development of an advanced information-based university for the next century. Seeing the library solely as an academic support makes it easy to give its function a secondary status, thus making it vulnerable to the budgetary knife.[30]

Having a salient role in restructuring the information core of the academic enterprise, as members of either instructional teams or other boundary spanning units, will position librarians to be, and to be perceived as being, central to the academic mission of the university. Actually, one could go further than Johnson and say that librarians will be either part of the team that restructures the academic enterprise or simply not relevant to that process of institutional development.

## User Orientation

The other major element of restructuring academic libraries is a truer user focus which, despite a lot of rhetoric, is often low in our services. Industry initiatives in total quality management have much to teach libraries about focusing on product improvement and meeting the real needs of users.[31] Michael H. Harris and Stan A. Hannah even argue that a service-based strategy is critical to the survival of libraries:

> It is now apparent that the linkage between access and ownership has been severed, and users now can 'access' information in a myriad of information markets. It also appears that most of the new entrepreneurial competition for traditional library service is intensely user-centered. And unless libraries are radically reengineered, they will be quickly supplanted by more sophisticated and accessible client-centered information services.[32]

Explicit user-oriented approaches will require new research on the design of focus groups and survey instruments.[33] Even more important to meeting library user needs will be a commitment to flexibility—to adjusting services and redirecting resources in response to changing times and needs. A corollary is the ongoing need to re-evaluate low-demand, high-cost-per-use services. As always, it will be difficult to agree on which users "count" and for "how much." Traditionally, academic libraries have responded to faculty needs because of their political clout, even though the bulk of demand for library services comes from students. In the future, responsive information services may become a known point of competition between academic institutions. If so, student needs will be accorded greater weight.

The technology underlying a truly electronic library significantly improves access to information. Networked access to full-text periodical collections with printing from workstations across campus appears to be much more efficient for the user—and less costly for the organization broadly defined—than a print collection of periodicals, which must be individually retrieved and photocopied in the library (though a definitive cost-benefit study in this area has yet to be published). Networked electronic *reserves* may well provide for better and more economical service than a print *reserve* collection, which also requires a student to go to the library, stand in line, and then photocopy items (though here again cost-benefit analysis is needed, given the accrual of copyright fees every semester). However, it is alarmingly easy to design these services in ways that recreate the bureaucracy and staff frustrations of our current service models. As noted above, the keys to building a user-oriented library depend on valuing the users' time and delivering what they ask for—not what librarians assume are compelling time or cost factors. Collaborations with other campus units to provide a holistic response to student needs may turn out to be more effective than the most well-constructed response solely from the library's point of view. Libraries that are able to provide truer user-oriented services will create a competitive advantage for their institutions which should, in turn, lead to success in the competition for students.

## Managing the Transition

The overarching issue is, How is it possible to move a library organization from where it is today to where it needs to be tomorrow, and still have a functioning organization when you get there? In his book on managing transitions, William Bridges draws an important distinction between changes and transitions:

> It isn't the changes that do you in, it's the transitions. Change is not the same as transition. *Change* is situational: the new site, the new boss, the new team roles, the new policy. *Transition* is the psychological process people go through to come to terms with the new situation. Change is external, transition is internal.[34]

Public service librarians will need to manage a number of significant personal transitions in response to a broad range of changes—in information technology, in the nature of instruction, and in the nature of organizations. They will need to get out of the library and more about campus to manage the networked information system and assist in the restructuring of the curriculum. To do this, they will deemphasize traditional routines and activities, including some reference services. Academic librarians will be collaborating with a variety of groups from different backgrounds who will be making contributions in areas that were once thought to require a master's degree in librarianship. When successful in such collaborations, librarians themselves will acquire new skills to be campus players and to make the library a valued institutional resource. Otherwise, they face the real possibility of being displaced by computing specialists, paraprofessionals, or even some futuristic, smart technology.

To transform the library as an organization, library management will need to create and project a realistic vision of the future and to be frank about dangers as well as opportunities. Managers must figure out the actual costs of services in order to make good judgments about alternative uses of resources. Cost-benefit analysis of services will be necessary, on a broader level, to move forward in political debates on strategic plans for the academic institution. A primary strategy for all campus players will be carving out resources, including personnel, to undertake new initiatives that will be important, in turn, as professional development opportunities for staff. A commitment to retraining programs for existing staff will be necessary, as will a willingness to go outside traditional pools to bring new talent into the library. A trust of teams and their local authority will be critical to decentralizing the organization in favor of boundary spanning. Finally, library management must forego turf battles and take a broad institutional view of information, even when that risks a loss of exclusive control of some resources.

When librarians make such personal transformations and library leadership has the required strategic perspectives and skills, there will be a successful transition to the electronic library. Restructuring will center on effective provision of networked information services and on boundary spanning teamwork. However, if librarians and library leadership fail, the library organization will become a drain on the institution's resources and its ability to compete in the higher education system.

## NOTES
1. A good review of the changes confronting higher education can be found in Donald N. Langenberg, "The University and Information Tech-

nology: Interpreting the Omens," in *Information Technology and the Re-making of the University Library*, New Directions in Higher Education, no. 90, ed. Beverly P. Lynch (San Francisco: Jossey-Bass, 1995), 5–17; see also William M. Plater, "Future Work: Faculty Time in the 21st Century," *Change* 27 (May/June 1995): 22–33.

2. Eli M. Noam, "Electronics and the Dim Future of the University," *Science* 270 (Oct. 1995 ): 247.

3. Michael Buckland, *Redesigning Library Service: A Manifesto* (Chicago: ALA, 1992).

4. This position is exemplified by Walt Crawford and Michael Gorman, *Future Libraries: Dreams, Madness and Reality* (Chicago: ALA, 1995).

5. Brian Nielsen, "Online Bibliographic Searching and the De-professionalization of Librarianship," *Online Review* 4 (Sept. 1980): 215–24.

6. For examples of how fundamental academic battles will be, see Plater, "Future Work: Faculty Time in the 21st Century"; and William F. Massy and Robert Zemsky, "Information Technology and Academic Productivity," *Educom Review* 31 (Jan./Feb. 1996): 12–14.

7. Robert H'obbes' Zakon. *Hobbes' Internet Timeline v3.0*, available at http://info.isoc.org/guest/zakon/Internet/History/HIT.html [8 July 1997].

8. Critiques of undifferentiated reference services include: Virginia Massey-Burzio et al., "Reference Encounters of a Different Kind: A Symposium," *Journal of Academic Librarianship* 18 (Nov. 1992): 276–86; William L. Whitson, "Differentiated Service: A New Reference Model," *Journal of Academic Librarianship* 21 (Mar. 1995): 103–10; *Rethinking Reference in Academic Libraries: The Proceedings and Process of Library Solutions Institute No. 2*, ed. Anne Grodzins Lipow (Berkley, Calif.: Library Solutions Pr., 1993).

9. The Internet Public Library is a prototype of what is possible: http://www.ipl.org/ [July 8, 1997].

10. An example of an attempt to create a local organizational structure for the Internet is described by Ann Koopman and Sharon Hay, "Large-Scale Application of a Web Browser," *College & Research Libraries News* 57 (Jan. 1996): 12–15. Issues of cataloging Internet resources are addressed in Martin Dillon and Erik Jul, "Assessing Information on the Internet: Toward Providing Library Services for Computer-Mediated Communication," *OCLC Systems and Services* 10 (summer/fall 1994): 86–92.

11. A good review of the current state of library instruction is provided by Virginia M. Tiefel, "Library User Education: Examining Its Past, Projecting Its Future," *Library Trends* 44 (fall 1995): 318–38. As an example of the limits of current practice, a study by Trudi E. Jacobson and Janice G. Newkirk found little or no relationship between training, in either classes or one-on-one, and skill level in using CD-ROMs. Trudi E. Jacobson and Janice G. Newkirk, "The Effect of CD-ROM Instruction on Search Operator Use," *College & Research Libraries* 57 (Jan. 1996): 68–76.

12. Stephen C. Ehrmann, "Asking the Right Questions: What Does Research Tell Us about Technology and Higher Learning?" *Change* 27 (Mar./Apr. 1995): 22.

13. Kenneth C. Green and Steven W. Gilbert, "Great Expectations: Content, Communication, Productivity, and the Role of Information Technology in Higher Education," *Change* 27 (Mar./Apr. 1995): 18.

14. Robert B. Barr and John Tagg, "From Teaching to Learning—A New Paradigm for Undergraduate Education," *Change* 27 (Nov./Dec. 1995).

15. Ibid., 23.

16. Alan E. Guskin, "Reducing Student Costs and Enhancing Student Learning: Part II, Restructuring the Role of Faculty," *Change* 26 (Sept./Oct. 1994): 25.

17. Massy and Zemsky, "Information Technology and Academic Productivity," 13.

18. Langenberg, "The University and Information Technology," 13–14.

19. Noam, "Electronics and the Dim Future of the University," 248.

20. Langenberg, "The University and Information Technology," 17.

21. Plater, "Future Work," 25.

22. Two invitational workshops sponsored by the Coalition for Networked Information, the first at the Estrella Mountain Community College Center in July 1994 and the second at Indiana University-Purdue University Indianapolis in November 1995, focused on instructional teams. Each workshop brought existing instructional teams together to discuss issues and to share experiences. See also Joan Lippincott, "New Initiatives in Teaching and Learning Strategies," *College and Research Libraries News* 57 (Apr. 1996): 216–17.

23. See Jeremy J. Shapiro and Shelley K. Hughes, "Information Technology as a Liberal Art: Enlightenment Proposals for a New Curriculum," *Educom Review* 31 (Mar./Apr. 1996): 31–35; Taylor E. Hubbard, "Bibliographic Instruction and Postmodern Pedagogy," *Library Trends* 44 (fall 1995): 439–52.

24. The philosophical basis for the design of these facilities can be found in Philip Tompkins, "New Structures for Teaching Libraries," *Library Administration and Management* 4 (spring 1990): 77–81.

25. David W. Lewis, "An Organizational Paradigm for Effective Academic Libraries," *College & Research Libraries* 47 (July 1986): 337–53.

26. David W. Lewis, "Making Academic Reference Services Work," *College & Research Libraries* 55 (Sept. 1994): 445–56.

27. An early example of this is at the University of Arizona; see Joan R. Giesecke, "Reorganizations: An Interview with Staff from the University of Arizona Libraries," *Library Administration & Management* 8 (fall 1994): 196–99.

28. See, for example, Beth J. Shapiro, "The Myths Surrounding Faculty Status for Librarians," *College & Research Libraries News* 54 (Nov. 1993): 562–63; Bruce R. Kingma and Gillian M. McCombs, "The Opportunity Costs of Faculty Status for Academic Librarians," *College & Research Libraries* 56 ( May 1995): 258–64.

29. Plater, "Future Work."

30. Richard M. Johnson, "New Technologies, Old Politics: Political Dimensions in the Management of Academic Support Services," in *Information Technology and the Remaking of the University Library*, 28.

31. See the winter 1996 issue of *Library Trends*, particularly Thomas Seay, Sheila Seaman, and David J. Cohen, "Measuring and Improving the Quality of Public Services: A Hybrid Approach," *Library Trends* 44 (winter 1996): 464–90; Philip Tompkins, "Quality in Community College Libraries," *Library Trends* 44 (Winter 1996): 506–25; Sarah M. Pritchard, "Determining Quality in Academic Libraries," *Library Trends* 44 (winter 1996): 572–94. See also Christopher Millson-Martula and Vanaja Menon, "Customer Expectations: Concept and Reality for Academic Library Services," *College & Research Libraries* 56 (Jan. 1995): 33–47.

32. Michael H. Harris and Stan A. Hannah, "'The Treason of the Librarians: Core Communication Technologies and Opportunity Costs in the Information Era," *Journal of Academic Librarianship* 22 (Jan. 1996): 8.

33. On a consumer approach to total quality management, see Karl Albrecht and Ron Zemke, *Service America!: Doing Business in the New Economy* (Homewood, Ill.: Dow-Jones-Irwin, 1985).

34. William Bridges, *Managing Transitions: Making the Most of Change* (Reading, Mass.: Addison-Wesley Publishing Co., 1991), 3.

# Dangerous Misconceptions about Organizational Development of Virtual Libraries

*Herbert S. White*

Academic library leaders have generally taken the term *virtual library* to mean a concept in which as much information as possible is transferred directly to the offices of faculty members, usually through their computer terminals. Some of this information may come through the library, some may bypass the library entirely, but, in any case, it is suggested that this will reduce the need for faculty members to depend on the library for specific answers or general help. The conventional wisdom is that this new concept is considered attractive by faculty members, that it is favored by university administrators because they perceive it as a reduction in cost, and that it will also benefit academic librarians by increasing our status to the role of information advisors or consultants—but, in any case, by transferring costs from the library to the budget of the faculty member's department. This chapter suggests that all of these assumptions—of the virtual library's benefits for faculty members, benefits for university administrators, and benefits for academic librarians—are totally erroneous.

The phrase *virtual library* is sufficiently vague to allow anyone to apply his or her own definition, much as we can make almost anything we like of the "information superhighway," including a growing repertoire of bad jokes about traffic jams, speed traps, potholes, road repairs, and traffic police. The dictionary definition of *virtual* leads us to an approximation of the almost ideal library. However, what is that library, and what makes us think we are approaching it? Furthermore, whose ideal are we talking about? Ours, those of academic administrators, or those of our users? Finally, which users—undergraduate students; graduate students; teaching faculty, who care very little about research; research faculty, who care very little about teaching; tenured faculty who may care very little about either teaching or research; or university administrators, who no longer resemble faculty at all (even though they came from the academic disciples) but whose information needs are now a cross between those of public officials and corporate executives? Or, do we think that all of these communities have the same information needs, something we can subsume under the term *reference*, which, if it is designed to serve anyone, is designed to serve the directional information needs of undergraduates (or at least anything else that can be answered in two minutes or less)? Perhaps we believe, even hope, that the virtual library will absolve us of the responsibility—and the cost—of providing reference service at all, as an expensive nuisance.

If there is anything we certainly do understand, it is that technology has made significant changes in the way information can be announced bibliographically and in the way it can be delivered physically. We also seem to understand that technology has broadened the definition of what we mean by "information," at least in the setting of the library. We used to define information in the context of what we, and perhaps others, considered worthy of indexing and announcing. In general, libraries limited such indexing and announcing to books and were usually willing to make the end user wait until we were ready to state that an item was completed. Journal articles were included in the worthy category if some group, usually a professional society, took the trouble to analyze them. But if this did happen, it was done in separate retrieval systems with various indexing systems that allowed for both gaps (the things nobody wanted to analyze) and duplications (the things everyone analyzed but differently). Other nonbook materials, defined not by value but by format (simplistically what could not stand up on the shelf unaided), were largely ignored.

Technology, which looks at information far more impersonally than we do, has some of the same faulty biases of announcement validity but, with its great speed of sorting and the storage capacity of machines, announces far more things than we were ever willing or able to consider. Moreover, the databases that sprang up more prolifically than weeds (because for weeds there are weed killers to get rid of the noxious ones and here there are none) "announced" things to end users whether libraries had analyzed them or not. This has created certain problems for us, insofar as requests for service can be described as problems. People now want more and more documents from us, and these are more likely to be materials we are not prepared for them to request (at least unprepared in that we have not yet rung the symbolic bell to indicate that people could come and get it).

There is, at the same time, an "out" for us. The organizations that are happy to announce documents directly to end users are also often willing to supply them directly, and more rapidly, than the workings of our own creaking interlibrary loan systems (which are based on the tenuous premise that the owner is just dying to drop everything to supply a copy to the nonowner). Document delivery services and interlibrary loan systems both cost a good deal of money, but cost is irrelevant to the provision of a service or a product that is considered essential. We should understand this (though we frequently do not) because management writers such as Peter Drucker have told us often enough that there is no safety in appearing to be inexpensive. There is only safety in being essential.

What, then, do we know about the options of new technology, the so-called virtual library? We know that there is more information and that it can be delivered directly to the terminals of our end users, particularly faculty members. Is this a good idea? The organizations responsible for developing databases, for selling hardware and software, and for pushing end-user searching obviously think so; certainly it is a good business for them. Is it, therefore, a good idea for everybody else? We also know that even as this process of increased information access might be crucial for survival in a competitive world (and academia is a fiercely competitive world) and that it might be cost-effective (with more return on investment), it will be more expensive. Strangely, though we certainly know all this, to a large extent university administrators do not—some even think that the virtual library will save money for the overall university budget. Much as they might wish this to happen, we certainly know that it will not save money in aggregate terms.

Why, then, have we not told them the truth, and what is our professional responsibility for telling them even what they might prefer not to hear? I know of library administrators who will acknowledge privately that the virtual library will cost a great deal of money but that the cost will "fortunately" be charged to the budgets of the academic departments, not to the budgets of the library, and that, therefore, this transfer of costs—even if it involves an overall increase over the alternatives—is a "good thing" for us. How does that rank as a political strategy and, quite separately, as an ethical strategy?

It is time to assess the implications of the virtual library as they apply to (1) professional librarians, (2) university management, and (3) our end users, who range from uncaring freshmen to know-it-all professors, with administrators also figured in there somewhere. The order I have used is intentional, because the first and most important question is how all of this affects us. Librarians (but probably only librarians) might be shocked at such selfishness, but we need not worry. It is always possible, and indeed essential, to be able to rationalize that what is best for us also happens to be best for everyone else. This is a process that engineers call *retrofitting*—making facts fit conclusions—and, of course, our own researchers working under the time line of grants and dissertation schedules do this all the time. Elected political officials and university presidents do it instinctively or they do not survive. It is what Charles Wilson, president of General Motors, meant when he stated that, "What was good for General Motors was also what was good for the country." His statement shocked some, but on what other basis can anyone be president of General Motors? Therefore, if academic librarians are not willing to postulate that what is best for them is also what is best for the university and its faculty and students, they might as well cover themselves with ashes and live in a cave. However, reassuringly and comfortingly, the statement is true.

## The Impact of the Virtual Library on Us

In the most direct and simplistic scenario, all information moves either directly from the data creator or, through us, to the terminal of the end user, who now functions quite comfortably without ever setting foot in the library or even contacting it. Where does that leave us? Obviously, without a role in information intermediation but perhaps still with a role in document supply for those items that the database providers are unable to supply. However, document supply, whether done well or poorly, is a clerical function, as is the operation of any stockroom or warehouse. What this role, then, presumably does is "rid" us of contacts with faculty members entirely. It frees our budgets of reference costs so that we can devote them more directly to meeting ever-increasing periodical costs. It frees the public areas for students who, at least in my observation, tend to use them for social contacts, except perhaps for the forty-eight hours just before a final exam. When I teach management, I stress that in the area of unionization the only ultimate power of workers is the threat, real or implied, that they will withhold their services. If the virtual library is on "automatic pilot," will anyone even notice that we are not there?

Some individuals, particularly in special libraries but also in academic libraries, suggest a new and higher-level role for librarians— that of virtual-information advisor or consultant or guru. It is an attractive concept but one that cannot succeed because of two major fallacies. First, one's acceptance of some individuals as being information experts or consultants is based on a confidence that those individuals really are experts who know what they are talking about. For example, I accept on faith that the service manager in an automotive repair shop used to be a master mechanic. If we are going to get individuals to allow us to teach them how to do their own information work, our credibility must be based on their confidence that we are truly experts who can do such searching better than they could. The fallacy in that argument from the typical view of the typical faculty member should be immediately apparent. Apart from one or two exceptional librarians on a given campus (who are usually explained away by the faculty as aberrations from the librarian norm), librarians have established no real credibility as being experts, more knowledgeable in the handling of their literature than the faculty. I am not saying that we could not do this, or even that there are not librarians who would like to do it. I only note that we have trivialized reference service to common-denominator "quickies" of directional services aimed primarily at undergraduates who want to know how the journals are shelved, when the library will close, or where the rest rooms are. Is it any wonder that our best reference librarians, capable of doing more than this, hate the time they must spend at the reference desk? For proof that all of this makes sense we need look only at the prestige and success of the occasional bibliographic specialist, who is embraced as a colleague by faculty in such diverse fields as history, French literature, and music. Their prestige stems not from their being librarians but, rather, from being seen as acting differently from the way librarians are somehow expected to act. I have on occasion been paid the dubious compliment of being told that I do not act like a "typical" librarian, and I still do not know how to deal with that. Such extensive reference service is probably worth our time and consideration, but do we foresee it in the virtual library—and would our budgets allow it? (I can anticipate the observation that the levels of information service I have suggested are undemocratic, in that they are geared to the importance of the client. That is obviously true, but who ever suggested that a university was a democratic institution?)

The greater reason that a strategy based on librarians as virtual-information consultants cannot work is the contemporary environment of downsizing—the elimination of jobs considered to be unrelated to the main mission of the parent institution. Corporations have few techniques for downsizing. They occasionally lay off perfectly satisfactory people (usually librarians) and they eliminate middle management slots, but generally they wait for attrition or early retirement and sometimes they force early retirement. They certainly do not add master's-level individuals to the payroll with job titles such as information consultant or advisor. Although they might contract such skills for a short time, they will not add them to the head count.

Academia, trapped in the tenure system that makes any new action difficult, is even more likely to count on attrition and retirement to trim the payroll (though it will take years to realize any savings from such techniques). It is easiest to eliminate the adjunct and part-time teachers, regardless of the impact on the classroom, and to leave vacated positions unfilled. I know of one university in which half the deanships are now vacant and no search committees have been appointed. A system such as this (in an environment ranging as far as we can see) is not going to invest in virtual-information counselors.

Still, it might invest in librarians who, as information *doers*, could make other employees, particularly faculty, more productive as teachers or researchers. That kind of reliance on librarians might make it possible to save money, probably the only justification in which academic administrators are now really interested. However, how are we even going to introduce this subject if we are not willing to tell them that: (1) Adapting to new information technology is a growing requirement for higher education; (2) it will entail a great deal of additional money from the university; and (3) if they agree to put the entire process under the control of librarians, the increased cost outlay could be lessened or at least controlled.

## The Impact of the Virtual Library on University Administrators and Budgets

I did not realize until after I had joined academia in an administrative role how well my twenty-five years in corporate and government management had prepared me for what happens in universities, for I came to understand that the management process is substantially the same. However, academic administrators have far less flexibility in decision options than their counterparts in the corporate environment. Part of that difficulty is related to the tenure system, part of it comes from the faculty's stubborn refusal to concern themselves with whether something can be afforded (if they need it, they can make it an issue of academic freedom), and part of it reflects the faculty's similar refusal of a hierarchical relationship to administrators. In other words, faculty have a great antipathy toward authority and very little financial responsibility. Academic librarians understand the budget process quite well (because they, like administrators, have a good deal of responsibility with relatively little authority). Students, we understand, occasionally make noise but have virtually no power in academia simply because they are considered transients who will, in a few years, take their pleasantness off campus. Librarians have no power either, in large part because their authority is recognized by neither administrators nor faculty (but, unlike students, we do not even make noise).

Long before I joined academia in 1975, I was given valuable information by my own boss, an IBM official who had spent several decades as a faculty member and administrator of an Ivy League university. When I complained about the negative impact of corporate politics, he told me that corporate politics was nothing when compared to academic politics. I have learned since that Robert Maynard Hutchins, former president of the University of Chicago, understood this even better when he noted that political battles in academia are waged so ferociously precisely because the stakes are so small! The issue in academia is one of intellectual turf—controlling a unique area of expertise that nobody else dares challenge. Professors with exalted titles or obscure specializations earn control over their turf automatically and, as I saw on many academic committees, everyone readily yields to the expertise of others that they do not understand.

Academic librarians control no turf as such. Our job is seen as purchasing material for the collection, the "heart of the university," but faculty retain a right to say what should be acquired. The job of librarians is to find the money with which to do it. It should be obvious that the faculty, by and large, are in no position to make decisions about priorities for the library because, at best, their knowledge is a balkanized one about a discipline or subdiscipline. Who but librarians can make a decision about the relative merits of spending additional money on the collection in English literature versus organic chemistry? Certainly not the professors in either discipline, and the faculty members in other disciplines are simply not interested.

At any rate, the "turf" that represents library collection development decisions has been abdicated to faculty, whereas budget responsibility remains with librarians. This tends to annoy administrators because pressures to spend more money on library materials follow relentlessly in the wake of both publication proliferation and price inflation—two growth patterns bolstered by publishers' realization long ago that librarians are often merely purchasing agents for the faculty. The strategy of library administrators in the face of this dilemma remains as predictable as it has proved disastrous. We beg for more money with which to meet rising prices, from both the administration and potential donors. We place all of our other priorities—including resource sharing, technology, adequate reference service, proper salaries, continuing education, and library operational research—on the back burner because the faculty do not see these as their own priority and because the administration is too preoccupied to consider planning much more than faculty pacification.

It is little wonder, then, that in such an environment librarians seem all too willing to cede the process of information intermediation—to abdicate their expertise in analyzing the content and the value of information to the desks and terminals of the faculty through the virtual library—because in such an organization, though costs may indeed be much higher, they will no longer be our responsibility. In that framework, the virtual library may be understandable, but it remains unworkable. Academic libraries will simply underlie what Robert Munn called "bottomless pits" and continue to be a constant source of annoyance to university administrators because there is always pressure to spend more money on research materials without any tangible credit accruing to administrators for authorizing such "necessary" expenditures. Actually, although academic administrators grouse that they are spending a great deal of money—perhaps too much money—on the library, the reality is quite different. They are spending an ever-declining percentage of the university budget on the library, and they are spending it precisely on the materials budget because they and the faculty have been unwilling to control price inflation by presenting a united front to threaten boycott—not as customers but as authors, a far more credible threat.

Librarians have not only transferred funds from all other budgets to the materials budget (at a time when they know that ownership is not nearly as important now as access), but they have abdicated what remained of their turf by allowing administrators and faculty to decide that the funding priority for the library is (in the view of these individuals, not librarians) the purchase of materials. Foisting off electronic materials costs on the end user in the virtual library is the next step in this pattern of planned invisibility.

It is a disastrous strategy for librarians but, perhaps more important, it is a disastrous strategy for university administrators. The growth of electronic access will most certainly increase university costs and, painful as this prospect is, university administrators must face it. However, that rate of growth might at least be alleviated if costs were centralized under the control of librarians, rather than decentralized and scattered among faculty cost centers (ultimately still funded from the same university budget). If university administrators are concerned about costs, they should consider a different approach—improving the productivity of faculty in the spheres of teaching and research. The purpose of information, after all, is to enable the recipient to do something better. Information is not an end in itself, it is a means to an end. Academic librarians should make a case that less money would be spent if librarians, suitably empowered, were given control over the university's information-access budget. To reiterate, successful management in any environment does not call for planned invisibility or appearing inexpensive or even frugal. Rather, successful management is to control the process and resources. (Perhaps I understood this instinctively when, as a twenty-five-year-old corporate librarian, I argued that if there was not enough money to allow my library to buy a certain periodical, I wanted assurance that nobody else would be able to buy the same journal with corporate funds.) We should not assume that faculty will object to our becoming the managers of the information-access channels. As the following section will demonstrate, many might even be pleased or relieved, provided that they have confidence in our ability to manage the process in a way that would enable them to know what they need to know in order to accomplish their own research and curricular objectives, for which information is a means and not an end.

## The Impact of the Virtual Library on Our Faculty Colleagues

The manner in which faculty members' work has long been romanticized is understandably their doing, not ours. When the general public thinks of what researchers do, film versions of Marie Curie and Louis Pasteur, Schliemann's digs at Troy, and the decoding of the

Dead Sea Scrolls immediately come to mind. Undoubtedly, there are such people now, and some may even reside in the faculty of research universities. However, they are a small minority; and in institutions oriented toward teaching they may not exist at all. As Herbert Brinberg noted at an International Federation of Documentation conference, whereas basic researchers seek facts, applied researchers, technologists, and practitioners want specific answers to specific questions (rather than tools that "might" contain an answer), and managers need to know the range of their options. All three types exist among the clientele of a university library but, as notable a humanist and librarian scholar as Charles Osburn has observed, we treat all faculty as though they were researchers, even though basic research disappears rapidly under the siege of funded grants and contracts that demand not just an answer but the promised answer within a promised time frame.

As senior vice president for operations for the Institute for Scientific Information during the 1970s, I presided over the preparation of *Who Is Publishing in Science*, an annual author–address directory drawn from that year's *Science Citation Index* and various editions of *Current Contents*. I once worried about overlap and redundancy in the annual indexes until it was demonstrated to me that half of the authors appear in this collection of scientific and scholarly articles only once, never again. That single article, which may have sprung from their dissertation, is their life's contribution. And yet we presume in our treatment of faculty that all are basic scholars who must have access to scholarly raw materials.

Producers of databases and online services extend the same presumption to end users as a whole, who are supposed to be fascinated with access to more and more information tools. I can certainly understand why it is to the producers' advantage to do so. End users search more sloppily and, thus, more expensively than do librarians, and that means greater profits. But does that benefit the university? Is it helpful to the librarians? Is it even to the advantage of the mythical end user?

For many faculty members, the presumed fascination for information self-service in the virtual library does not hold. University libraries that offered end-user training to their faculty have found that the level of interest is small, perhaps as small as five percent. Moreover, many of the faculty who do sign up send surrogates, such as graduate assistants and even secretaries. The business press informs us of the development of a new industry, rather delightfully dubbed the "meatware" profession, because the meatware people are the ones who use the hardware and software on behalf of the reluctant end user. I can only conclude that the market niche for the meatware industry was created by the failure of librarians to fill the gap because of either a reluctance to do so or a failure to persuade a management besieged by budget pressures to allocate the money which will now be spent in even greater quantities. Of course, there are end users who want to do their own searches all of the time, and perhaps more who want to do them some of the time. However, there are many who would be happy to delegate and even abdicate this process, *if* they could find someone willing to do it—and *if* he or she were someone they could trust.

## Summary and Conclusions

The future leads to the possibility of some disasters, as well as some glorious opportunities. In what is bound to be an environment of increasing options, confusions, and costs, there may be several plausible reasons for academic librarians to decline from the process of acquiring and analyzing information, but all of them lead to disaster. One reason might be despair of getting adequate funds with which to do our jobs, particularly with ever-darkening clouds of publisher invoices hanging over our heads. Another reason might be our belief that end users *ought* to do such access and analysis themselves (just as we entertain that sort of morality play in our insistence that students learn how to do their own searching). It may be that we really think that end users are better able to fend for themselves than we are. However, there is something fundamentally wrong with any academic library budget that puts a higher premium on buying things than on investing in staff.

We have a problematic future in the current conception of the virtual library because there will not be money to engage us as consultants and advisors, and because many faculty have seen no evidence of our willingness or capability to do the work that we now want to teach them to do. Our future, nevertheless, remains in the process of information intermediation. Furthermore, it is the only alternative that makes economic sense for the institution. Certainly, the waves of information that will be dumped on the terminals of people who are really being paid to do something else creates an economic disaster for the university. If administrators have been slow to figure this out, it is because the software and hardware people are not equipped to tell them and we have not been willing to say so. Our message is very simple: One cannot fritter away money into the budgets of countless and traditionally irresponsible user groups! You need to give us the funding. Unfortunately, the virtual library will entail a great deal of additional money. But if you let us manage and control these funds, the result will be a great deal more palatable for the institution.

# Repositioning Campus Information Units for the Era of Digital Libraries

*Richard M. Dougherty and Lisa McClure*

T oday's chief academic officer (CAO) faces an array of daunting challenges, not the least of which is to ensure that the
campus information system effectively supports the needs of
the academic community in the twenty-first century. With technology rapidly transforming the academic workplace, cognizant administrators are seeking ways to restructure library–computing center relationships with a balance of technological and financial effectiveness. They assume the payoffs will be worth the cost. There seems to
be a growing consensus that colleges and universities which are the
most successful at incorporating technology to create a new campus
information infrastructure will be well positioned to compete in the
higher education market. Numerous academic administrators are now
considering, if not pursuing, this challenge, albeit with differing levels of commitment and creativity.

Reorganization of the library with the computing center involves
a complex set of challenges. First, these units do not fit easily into
standard academic organizational models. Second, although both units
offer support services, each possesses a distinctly different organizational culture. Third, there is a broad range of possible institutional
arrangements for libraries and computing centers to work together

more effectively, from simple shared-administrative structures to complete mergers with integrated staffs, convergent operations, and blended cultures.

With all the rhetoric surrounding new information technology and the so-called digital library, it may be difficult for a CAO to separate fact from fiction, reality from fantasy. This paper addresses organizational issues of campus computing relationships from a variety of perspectives. Its intended audience includes library and computing center directors facing the prospect of working together, and CAOs considering a partial or complete merger of units that provide either information services or support for the creation of new information products (e.g., multimedia classroom software).

## Field of Dreams

Computer magazines and the popular press tend to suggest that capitalizing on the latest technology to create completely new information delivery systems is a relatively straightforward process. For example, a 1995 "Focus on Technology" report in *Newsweek* cited the then-planned California State University-Monterey campus as a prime example of a vision of technological change.[1] Barry Munitz, chancellor of the twenty-two-campus system, asserted, "You simply don't have to build a traditional library these days." The report interpreted Munitz's attitude to be, Why bother wasting all that money on bricks and mortar and expensive tomes when it could be better spent on technology for getting information via computer?

The message is simple: As technology advances, we simply create new systems and move on to new technological visions. The *Newsweek* article implied that the new campus in Monterey would not bother having a traditional library. However, when the Monterey campus opened its gates, a recognizable library was there with printed journals and monographs—as well as plenty of technology for networked access to information. Chancellor Munitz should be commended for his willingness to pursue a visionary future, but such visionary rhetoric alone is plainly unrealistic for the foreseeable future and could, if left unchallenged, create the impression in the minds of academic administrators that libraries are passé. On the contrary, a campus without a balanced library of print and electronic resources short-changes its faculty and students as they seek research and information sources.

The new Leavey Library at the University of Southern California shows how traditional library services, new information technologies, and campus computing units can be merged effectively into one building. The recently remodeled undergraduate library at Stanford University is another prime example of print-age strengths allied with electronic-era capabilities. (Both cases are drawn, not from press reports but, rather, from site visits which found certain functional and spatial synergies.)

## Creating the Future

Most information professionals would agree that technological advances generate even greater opportunities for further innovation. Yet, in practically any exciting vision, reality inevitably intrudes. Technology has enabled many rudimentary changes, but it has not yet transformed library and information organizational structures. For example, although the array of scholarly resources available through the Internet is vast and growing at remarkable rates, such resources are often poorly organized and difficult to locate. Moreover, most core journals and monographs will not be easily available online until copyright issues are resolved. Many campuses cannot yet afford to invest in or update new systems as quickly as they appear. One group of experts, the Task Force on a National Strategy for Managing Scientific and Technological Information, recently concluded that electronic formats will not soon dominate science and technology publishing, even though the traditional, paper-based model is becoming both unaffordable and unresponsive to new scientific communication. [2]

Chief academic officers, faced with increasingly tight budgets, are naturally on the lookout for opportunities to eliminate redundant operations and develop more cost-effective services. Although libraries and computing centers are logical candidates for reorganization and possible merger, these units have very different organizational structures and professional cultures, with staffs who may intensely resist convergence despite outward similarities. The central position of the CAO in the restructuring process is another consideration.

Given the inexorable demand for the new resources throughout the academic institution, CAOs tend to spend more time explaining to colleagues how resource constraints limit what can be done than they do serving as catalysts for innovation. (Perhaps this becoming the proverbial *no!* person is part of the reason for the high turnover rate among CAOs. ) Centrality of position makes it particularly important that a CAO make choices carefully. Because most CAOs are neither librarians nor technologists, they rely on being well advised when it comes to planning new campus information infrastructures.

## Background

In the mid-1980s, several librarians and computing professionals noted that, in many respects, the functions of libraries and computing centers were becoming more and more alike. Both units provide access to information resources and services; store, organize, and distribute information; and rely heavily on networking technologies. A few scholars even then came to the view that, as campuses move toward the era of the electronic library, merging these units would make sense. Administrators, for their part, hoped that mergers would generate organizational and budgetary, as well as intellectual, benefits. Raymond K. Neff was the first to describe several technological trends that were leading to a joint library–computing center mission.[3] Pat Molholt described the converging paths of the computing center and library, foreseeing a fast, personalized information system based on existing similarities between the two units.[4] Many others described visions of a new cooperative future. Expected benefits of this future included:
- elimination of redundant operations;
- reduction of costs for shared facilities and equipment;
- shared expertise on information discovery, access, and processing;
- innovation of services.

In light of these and similar predictions, it is little wonder that some academic administrators began to envision a grand restructuring of library–computing relationships.

In the late 1980s, a few research institutions, including Columbia University and Carnegie Mellon University, reorganized their computing centers and libraries to fall under the direction of a single vice president. In both cases, however, later organizational reforms reestablished much of the former units' independence. Detailed assessments as to the eventual success of those cases have not been published. Although case studies on restructuring campus information systems are rare, anecdotal evidence supports the view that such changes are more likely to be successful in smaller academic organizations than in larger, more complex research universities. In 1994, for example, Eugene A. Engeldinger and Edward Meachen reported successful mergers at the University of Wisconsin-Parkside and at Carthage College. They cited a common vision, mutual goal setting, and cordial communications as essential ingredients.[5]

Although many campuses have considered restructuring over the past decade, actual mergers are not yet common. As early as 1989, Pat Molholt raised the question, "What happened to the merger debate?"[6] For all the theoretical debates, the promise of quick and easy mergers proved to be illusory. Consequently, the goals of reorganization have generally become more modest. Even a simple streamlining of information units under one person has not always produced financial savings because the creation of new administration often adds yet another layer to the hierarchy.

## Why Reorganization Is So Difficult

Too many restructuring projects are undertaken without considering fully the significant differences that exist between libraries and computing centers. Each unit has its own organizational culture encompassing distinct gender ratios, professional values, and personality makeups. Jobs have different academic requirements, statuses, and salaries. For example, technologists tend to command higher salaries than librarians but possess lesser academic credentials. Unfortunately, a lack of mutual respect between these professions is not uncommon. Each one has a unique—to the other, unintelligible—jargon. Academic administrators, for their part, tend to hold stereotypes about each unit: librarians being adverse to risk taking but willing to collaborate; computing professionals being risk takers and innovators more comfortably when working independently.

Although parallels between mergers in the corporate world and those on campus should not be drawn too closely, analysts who study why corporate mergers fail often point to dissimilar organizational cultures. Certainly, an edict that the library and computing center will be brought together under a chief information officer as a prelude to an eventual merger is bound to set off loud alarm bells in both units. An imposed merger will likely trigger efforts to preserve respective organizational turfs through increased jockeying for power. Both units will then compete for scarce resources in an effort to become the dominant provider of information services. Each unit will fear a loss of prestige, as well as power, as traditional services and structures are being reexamined. All these conflicts can only impede a merger.

A new CAO may not be aware of the frictions brewing as professionals from each unit begin to maneuver for their side of the campus operation. Librarians are symbolic of traditional scholarship and enjoy the support of faculty who do not want to see the library transformed. It may well be helpful for the CAO to acknowledge up front the existence of library–computer center organizational distinctions and cultural dissimilarities, while at the same time working to cultivate common ground for interunit collaboration.

## Options for Reorganization

A CAO considering a reorganization has a variety of options that largely depend on the initial level of commitment among administrative staff, the realism of the planning framework, and the monetary resources available. The literature focuses primarily on cross-organizational mergers, but a reorganization may take at least three general forms:

- administrative realignment of reporting and budgetary lines;
- collaborative realignment to provide greater working-level linkages;
- blending realignment of the two units into a single, cohesive information services division.

### *Administrative Realignment*

An administrative realignment of reporting and budgetary lines is intended to simplify the hierarchical structure and to save money in the process. The prevailing method is reorganization of the library and the computing center under a single officer, frequently designated the chief information officer, or CIO. The CIO's control may be over those two units only, or include administrative computing, or extend to units in charge of campus telecommunications and multimedia courseware development. Although designation of a CIO may reduce the number of people reporting to the chief academic officer, this kind of realignment usually adds a new middle layer to the hierarchy as the office of the CIO develops. Not surprisingly, the library director, academic computing head, and other computing administrators—all of whom no longer enjoy direct access to the campus chief academic officer—tend to view the new reporting line as a bureaucratic obstacle. Other patterns of administrative realignment include placing department heads of units over their counterparts in other units, or relegating an entire unit (e.g., the library or the computing center) under another. Although this type of reorganization often begins as a relatively superficial change aimed at more effective staff and budget control, it can be the first step toward future restructurings more extensive in scope and function.

### Collaborative Realignment

Collaborative realignment also places academic computing and the library under a CIO. But it goes significantly beyond combined reporting and budgetary lines to make provisions for formal collaboration between the two units. The library and the computing center remain structurally independent but form collaborative links on working levels. Each unit's professional distinctiveness tends to remain intact. In order to facilitate interunit work, a coordinating mechanism is established to identify areas of overlap and to initiate collaborative efforts. For example, at Rice University the computing center and the library established a combined information services unit which brings together reference librarians and computing center staff to provide user services jointly.[7] This kind of middle-range realignment offers distinct advantages for trying new ideas and structural reforms without investing in wholesale reorganization.

### Blending Realignment

The most ambitious restructuring involves a complete merger of the library and the computing center into a new organizational and even cultural body. The elements of each unit are evaluated for the purpose of converging their functions, activities, and cultures on a higher level of organizational development. This approach has at once the most dramatic and the riskiest outcomes. It is a great opportunity for innovation but may lead to confusion and anxiety as well. In such ventures, the CAO should move carefully and be particularly sensitive to prospects for interunit cultural clash. Above all, the CAO should avoid any perception that the units are being pushed together willy-nilly.

## Choices for the CAO

The basic objectives of the reorganization are the keys to determining which of the three general restructuring options to pursue. Although administrators may be inclined to pursue a total merger, initially trying a more limited reorganization might prove to be more productive in the long run. Either a relatively simple realignment of reporting and budgetary lines, or a reorganization that promotes formal collaboration on working levels, can be quite beneficial in the short term, whereas a full integration requires an extraordinary amount of planning and resources, as well as risks. At the very least, a CAO ought to consider the motives of any plan for an immediate, comprehensive restructuring. If the intent is to reduce expenditures while maintaining control, an administrative realignment under the leadership of a CIO might be all that is necessary. Or, if the goal is to improve specific services, a broader reorganization that includes formal collaboration short of a structural merger might be sufficient. Of course, if necessity or opportunity dictates a wholly different campus information infrastructure with a new culture, then nothing short of full integration of the library and the computing center will do.

Before any reorganization option is undertaken, however, the CAO should assess the institutional climate. First, how much time are administrators willing to invest in studying and planning to restructure? If time is short, the goals of the project ought to reflect that reality. Second, collaborative and blending realignments require particularly strong commitments from the staffs directly involved. Are they willing and able to take on additional responsibilities despite the burden of existing duties? Third, although most administrators hope that restructuring will increase production and cut expenditures, any reorganization is likely to be time-consuming at first and require seed money.

A strategy often used as an incentive for organizational change from below is "priming the pump" with seed money. However, such a tactic, which essentially entails a zero-sum game by which funds are drawn from existing unit budgets, runs the risk of creating a series of win-lose situations. Under such conditions, organizational change is made more difficult as units compete to ensure that they are the winners, not the losers, of the sums involved. A generally preferred option is to cut the budget of each unit and recycle the released funds to interunit innovative ventures.

### Suggestions and Tasks for Achieving Successful Reorganizations

A CAO is more likely to orchestrate a successful reorganization if the administrators and staffs of the affected units are willing to negotiate working relations among themselves and to devote the time necessary to create, eventually, a shared vision of the future. Prospects improve when the personal chemistry between the librarians and the computing professionals is synergistic, and when their supervisors exercise a certain firmness balanced with tolerance and patience. If a CAO is able to construct a win-win budgetary scenario (by avoiding a zero-sum game) for the merged units, there is a much greater likelihood that long-term incentives for collaborative efforts will fall into place. The shared vision must be one that not only excites the staff but goes far beyond the usual rhetoric to provide a framework for implementation. A visioning/planning process that involves, and accounts for, staff at all levels will have far greater chances for success than just declarations of a merger emanating from the office of the CAO.

Overall, the shared vision should include broad statements of an ideal information future, and it should provide realistic parameters for short-term cooperation and collaboration. The vision should thus be a basis for interunit negotiation and team building. It should allow a good deal of leeway for planners and participants. If a vision does not provide for the evolution of realistic implementation plans from below, there is a strong possibility that the reorganization effort is attempting too much, too quickly, from above.

Once the decision to initiate a reorganization is made, administrators can more accurately gauge its scope and potential for success by carrying out various tasks of discovery. Such tasks include:

- researching similar efforts at comparable institutions;
- appointing an advisory team composed of affected individuals;
- hiring an outside consultant;
- assessing staff readiness;
- determining the amount of time and money available;
- remaining patient.

### Researching Similar Efforts

A survey of comparable institutions to learn what restructuring steps they have taken and to distinguish significant from not-so-significant outcomes can be invaluable because so much that has occurred has not been reported in the literature. In that regard, articles announcing restructuring plans should not be taken literally unless the facts are verified. For example, in 1990, it was reported that UCLA's Business School Library was being merged with the computing center in a new building to provide better access and resources. Bob Bellanti, the library's director, described the projects's philosophy:

> In years to come, libraries are going to be so electronically based that it's going to be difficult to tell where the library stops and the computing services start. . . . In the new building, the library and computing services will not only occupy the same facility, but will be intermingled so that they become a true information resource center for students and faculty. [8]

By the latter half of the 1990s, however, neither the facility nor the merger had been completed. This story is not told to criticize those involved but simply to illustrate the value of talking with those who have announced restructurings.

## Appointing an Advisory Team

The appointment of an overarching advisory team might seem obvious, but it is a crucial step that is often either overlooked or given short shrift. A CAO should make certain that all stakeholder groups are represented and that advisory team members support the institution's strategic plan. The team should advise but not impede interunit negotiation and team building from below (as often happens in restructurings of academic units).

## Hiring an Outside Consultant

There are two types of consultants who provide different types of guidance. First is the *expert consultant* who strives to provide *technical* solutions to systems issues. The second is a *process consultant* who seeks to develop *teamwork* among participants. Each type of consultant plays a distinctive role. Whether both types are necessary for every restructuring is impossible to say in the abstract.

The *expert consultant* will assess technical system issues by gathering data and making recommendations—and then will leave the scene. The recommendations may create a framework for future actions and/or help clarify technical directions, but such reports rarely serve as a blueprint for action. Why? The staff who will be directly involved in the reorganization had little or no opportunity at that point to participate in the evaluation, so they would not be inclined to accept the expert's recommendations wholeheartedly. Because successful reorganizations require staff support and commitment, the change strategy needs to include, as one objective, the gaining and maintaining of support—thus, the importance of the process consultant.

The *process consultant* can help staff create a shared and realistic vision of the relationship between technical development and organizational development, and help the units develop necessary teamwork skills. It cannot be assumed that teamwork comes naturally to either technologists or librarians, though both are certainly capable of interunit collaboration. Overall, restructuring would benefit from the services of both types of consultants. One is not better that the other, each serves a different purpose.

*Assessing Staff Readiness*
A CAO should inventory staff skills and qualifications. Is the necessary chemistry for interunit collaboration present? Do the staffs possess necessary technical and group dynamic skills? Is there a critical mass who are willing to work for change? Are staff generally excited by the prospects? Or, are they more inclined to hunker down and resist? Because the strategy a CAO adopts to bring about change ultimately depends on the staffs involved, overlooking such staff-readiness issues in the planning process would simply court long-term frustrations.

*Determining the Amount of Time and Money Available*
Because many reorganizations will require reallocations of workloads and budgets already stretched, each unit will need to identify activities that can be streamlined or cut. In particular, reorganization will require a considerable investment of staff time above and beyond expected traditional services. With most staff already stressed, launching a reorganization without a clear assessment of time constraints, monetary resources, and workloads may lead to continual negotiations on the workday level of activities.

*Remaining Patient*
Patience is important. Although administrators and committed staff tend to like instant results and frequently do not exhibit much tolerance for setbacks, temporary and even longer delays in restructuring a campus information infrastructure are normal. Time must be allowed for staff to work through problems. Quick fixes might simply result in superficial changes that end up costing more and producing less.

## Conclusions
The vision of a networked campus information environment will no doubt be achieved in some academic institutions. But there are no guarantees, road maps, or quick fixes. On the one hand, libraries and computing centers are complex organizations with rather distinct infrastructures, philosophies, and cultures. On the other hand, librarians and computing professionals now realize that they are interdependent. Librarians, for their part, have the

ability to interpret information needs and conceptualize methods of access; technologists have the expertise to design and construct systems for that access. Sharing knowledge in a consolidated organizational framework should improve operations and services, particularly with regard to networked resources. Nonetheless, fundamental change involving such complex and highly valued campus units is a formidable task.

Administrators should not be put off by pitfalls of restructuring the campus information infrastructure. Although at first glance some costs may eclipse the benefits, the consequences of doing little or nothing will be severe. Networked resources are powerful, and any institution that does not adapt to exploit them will find itself in a technological backwater. Can a college or university realistically compete for faculty and students if its campus has plainly limited information technology capabilities and services?

Overall, a CAO can expect a payoff roughly commensurate with the level of institutional commitment. If the staff is convinced that restructuring is not simply a guise for cost cutting and that the institution is genuinely interested in reconceptualizing campus information systems, no reorganization need unduly disrupt essential services, incite a turf battle, or foster cultural conflict. With adequate preparation of the staff and their participation, any of the three levels of reorganization—administrative, collaborative, or blending—can lead to organizational development.

## NOTES

1. Katie Hafner, "Wiring the Ivory Tower," *Newsweek* (Jan. 30, 1995), 62.

2. Association of American Universities, *Report of the Task Force on a National Strategy for Managing Scientific & Technological Information of the Research Libraries Project* (Washington, D.C.: Association of American Universities, submitted to the Steering Committee on April 4, 1994), 62–63.

3. Raymond K. Neff, "Merging Libraries and Computing Centers: Manifest Destiny or Manifestly Deranged," *EDUCOM Bulletin* 20 (winter 1985): 8–12, 16.

4. Pat Molholt, "On Converging Paths: The Computing Center and the Library," *Journal of Academic Librarianship* 11 (Nov. 1985): 284–88.

5. Eugene A. Engeldinger and Edward Meachen, "Merging Libraries and Computing Centers at Smaller Academic Institutions," *Library Issues* 16 (July 1994): 1–4.

6. Pat Molholt, "What Happened to the Merger Debate?" *Libraries and Computing Centers*, special issue of *Journal of Academic Librarianship* 15 (May 1989): 96a–b.

7. Kevin Brook Long and Beth J. Shapiro, "On Paths That Have Converged: Libraries and Computing Centers," *Library Issues* 14 (July 1994): 1–4.

8. Natalie Hall, "Are Libraries and Computer Centers Converging? A Match Made Online: Two Service Providers at UCLA Plan to Wed Form and Function in the 1990s," *American Libraries* 21 (Jan. 1990): 70.

# Planning Information Systems at the University at Albany: False Starts, Promising Collaborations, Evolving Opportunities

*Meredith A. Butler and Stephen E. DeLong*

I f, according to Flannery O'Conner, all that rises must converge, do we necessarily diverge as we descend? Administrators of research libraries and academic computer centers are struggling to find answers to this question as they, and the research universities they serve, respond to the fundamental and transformative changes in today's higher educational environment. The factors that are driving these changes are well known: economic decline; erosion of enrollments; an economy that produces many fewer employment opportunities; the public's disenchantment with higher education; the rising costs but stagnant productivity of human resources; and new technological developments affecting nearly every aspect of the processes of teaching, scholarship, research, and publication. What is not well known, however, is how libraries and computing centers are changing their organizational structures, functions, work processes, services, and staffing as they plan for and cope with the networked distributed world in which they now operate. This case study attempts to provide some insight on these topics.

Although there is no doubt that information and communication networks have had a profound impact on higher education and are transforming the culture of academic libraries and computing centers, this change has been accompanied by overheated claims of even greater technological advances. Such claims have generated a lot of "rise" (some would say hot air) on our campuses and in our information organizations. We have seen our profiles and workloads, if not our paychecks or budgets, rise as our expertise and facility in managing electronic information are acknowledged by faculty and students. We have also seen our users' expectations rise in response to new technologies and services that have made information access easier and faster. And, of course, we have seen our costs increase as we have added electronic and networked resources and services to our traditional, labor-intensive organizations. Although the claims of the transformative power of technology may be overheated, there is no doubt that the convergence of computing and telecommunications technologies has caused us to rethink our information organizations—their mission, structure, roles, services, and staff responsibilities. We are looking at these issues from the point of view of the wants and needs of our users, not only those who come into our organizations for information and assistance but also those users distributed throughout the academic systems and networks in which we operate.

In this decade of austerity for higher education, we have witnessed a significant decline of our research libraries and our campus computing centers—declines caused in part by the drop in purchasing power of the dollar, the rapidly rising costs of information products and services, and the need for reinvestment in expensive and sometimes transient technology. In response, we have built local campus and regional networks, integrated them with national and global networks, and facilitated the distribution of computing devices and networked information resources to the desktop. Yet, an overriding question remains: Are these transformative trends making our information organizations more cohesive, or are they fragmenting our organizations at the very time that we need to be more entrepreneurial and productive, more collaborative and cost-efficient? Given the need for strong leadership to integrate new technologies into research and curricular programs, are we focusing on new ways to integrate our experience and expertise on campus and within the profession at large? In short, are we restructuring our libraries and computing centers as cohesive units, or are we continuing to foster traditionally parallel structures that may cooperate on projects without having developed a collective and comprehensive understanding of their interdependent roles and shared responsibilities in the networked environment?

## National Trends in Library–Computing Center Relations

Following a period of distant and strained relationships between libraries and computing centers in the 1960s and 1970s, there emerged in the early 1980s a recognition that economic and technical changes required universities to look at their information organizations as having shared goals and interests. During the 1980s, discussion centered on libraries and computing centers converging or even merging. Merged library–computing organizations were actually created on some campuses. Such consolidated organizations had varying models of leadership: Some were administered by the library director (the Columbia model), others by the director of computing (the Carnegie Mellon model), and still others by shared leadership (the Stanford model).[1] The early literature (particularly by Patricia Battin, Richard Dougherty, David Weber, Anne Woodsworth, and James Williams) made large claims for the value of integrating library and computing operations into a single unit. The assumption was that administrative control would either remain with the library director or be shared by a triumvirate of the chief information officer, library director, and computing director.[2] Brave pioneers in this first wave of restructuring included: Columbia, Vanderbilt, Rutgers, and, to a degree, Stanford, among large research universities; Oregon State, Virginia Commonwealth, Rice, and Carnegie Mellon, among medium-size universities; and some colleges and community colleges.[3] Although those early efforts met with varying degrees of success and may have served as models for other universities planning organizational redesigns, at least some of them seem to have been based more on expediency than on any careful organizational analysis or planning. Certainly, the common focus on issues of administrative control and hierarchy left broader issues of organizational development and cultural integration largely unaddressed.

A central issue that emerged from these early experiments with mergers was the need to redirect attention from organizational structures to organizational cultures and particularly to explore reasons for "clashing cultures" and "barriers to cooperation" between librarians and computing professionals.[4] The more recent literature has emphasized broad differences in professional training, role, and status (including remuneration); technological expertise; and service values and orientations.[5] One institution that created a collaborative model to address such cultural differences is Indiana University. The work of its Inforum group has served as a catalyst for other universities seeking to create collaborative structures and cultures on campus. Building strong collaborative organizational cultures has also been a focus of the Coalition for Networked Information (CNI) and its Working Group on Management and Professional Development. Inspired by Indiana University's Inforum, as well as by workshops sponsored by the Committee on Institutional Cooperation (CIC) of the Big Ten university consortium, CNI invited teams of senior library and computing center administrators to participate in a 1994 workshop on building collaborative partnerships. This workshop reflected a key goal of CNI: "to integrate efforts to support the overall information resources and services mission for the entire academic institution [by providing administrative teams an] opportunity to work together in a common enterprise directed toward a shared future." [6] It was judged quite successful by participants and has served as a model for continuing work by a number of groups.

Sheila D. Creth and others strongly support this shift from talk about consolidated or merged organizations with clashing cultures and competing values to a concerted focus on collaboration to create a virtual information environment with value-added services for users.[7] Of course, as Michael Schrage points out, collaboration must go beyond simply working together to accomplish specific projects to become an "act of shared creation and/or shared discovery."[8] Schrage sees this synergism as occurring between equals who engage in a process of creating value. Such collaborations are marked by "people who realize that they can't do it all by themselves. They need insights, comments, questions, and ideas from others. They accept and respect the fact that other perspectives can add value to their own."[9] For such people, there are no one-person organizational problems anymore.

The literature on library and computing center partnerships, however insightful over the years, offers insufficient guidance on many issues of library–computing center relations in the latter half of the 1990s. Such issues center on the need to help our academic institutions facilitate a restructuring of the teaching and learning process; the need to plan for a distributed information environment in which the principles of affordable, equitable, and open access to information resources are preserved for our users; and the need for cost-effectiveness in all these endeavors. As we grapple with such issues, it is worthwhile to look back on our recent past—at our successes and failures fostering collaborative relationships—to determine what lessons we can learn, what mistakes should not be repeated, and what strengths we can build upon. What follows is a case study of organizational developments at the University at Albany, SUNY, over the past decade. It describes some near successes, real achievements, and remaining challenges for the year 2000. Although library and computing operations at Albany are too small to be on the cutting edge of technological change, they have been steadily moving forward and may be representative of the great middle range in higher education—those moderately sized, fairly progressive academic institutions faced with economic austerity, and unprecedented challenge and opportunity.

## Libraries and Computing at Albany as Parallel Organizations, 1980–1990

The University at Albany initiated an organizational framework to enable centralized planning of information technology in the early 1980s with the creation of the position of associate vice president for academic affairs (AVP), to whom the directors of libraries, of computing, and of education communications (audiovisual and other media services) reported. The AVP reported, in turn, to the vice president for academic affairs, as did the director of libraries, who retained a dual reporting relationship (unlike the director of computing, who reported only to the AVP).

Before 1990, there was little reason for the university library and the computing center to plan for a common future. The library had been operating its automated services (integrated circulation, reserve, online catalog, fund accounting, serials control) successfully on a turn-key, in-house minicomputer since 1984 with its own systems staff of three professionals. An early pioneer in computerized search services, the library offered a full array of databases, as well as some datafiles through the Inter-university Consortium for Political and Social Research (ICPSR). Library systems staff consulted computing center staff as needed, but there were few collaborative projects.

In those years, Albany's computing center had a traditional mainframe orientation, whereas its modest staff in user services provided assistance in an increasingly PC-based environment. In spite of frequent changes in leadership and the burden of running several different mainframe systems, computing center management and staff began to plan actively for the expansion of the campus network and prepared the way for the integration of networking technologies into the mainframe environment. No attempt was made, however, to reassess organizational and managerial structures.

## Early Collaboration, 1990–1994

During the latter half of the 1980s, the University at Albany developed a comprehensive planning process that tied together program development, budget preparation, and resource allocation. With the appointment of a new dean and director of libraries in 1989, the library's planning process became more integrated with that of the university. Every dean or director on campus was involved in library planning, as were faculty and students. Although the strategic plan completed in 1990 focused on the libraries, it was also shaped by the goals and plans of the computing center and it addressed the role of the library as a "gateway" to networked resources. At that point, there was no comprehensive planning process for computing or for information technology in general. Two projects, however, eventually led to library–computing center collaboration: installing a new library automation system, and planning for a new library building.

The need for a new library automation system at the turn of the 1990s induced a convergence of library and computing interests. Early on, however, this project had some missed opportunities for collaborative planning and it also experienced frustrating financial delays. For example, when systems evaluations and functional specifications were being determined (a difficult process in the best of circumstances), representation from the computing center (due to the press of other demands) was only sporadically available. Later, we all realized that more extensive collaborative planning in the beginning would have made the subsequent stages of system procurement, system migration, and system implementation much easier.

Space shortage on the campus had become increasingly acute during the 1980s and nowhere was it felt more acutely than in the library. Campus planning for additional library space was initiated at about the time that the more comprehensive 1990 strategic plan was being drafted. At first, a third library facility—of rather traditional style and function—was envisioned to house the science collections, special collections, and archives. Even before the ink was dry on the architect's drawings, however, a fiscal crisis in the state froze all capital construction. That delay proved quite fortuitous because it allowed those who had a growing awareness and understanding of telecommunications and networking developments to rethink the original building and to redefine it as an "electronic library"— one in which library and computing functions would be integrated.

The revised plan for a merger of the library and the computing center called for a new kind of information resource that would expand and enrich the traditional role of the library:

> By bringing all our information specialists together in a single building, and fully integrating library, computing, and telecommunications expertise, we have an opportunity to create the national model for a network-oriented, regional information tool. [Such a] merger will create models for generation, capture, and delivery of information with the aim of making this precious resource accessible to schools, government, business, and every citizen. Our challenge is to forge these disparate elements [library, computing, telecommunications] into a unified tool, one which defines how they can

best be used, and harnesses their explosively changing capabilities.[10]

This plan defined the environment of the new facility as a "research laboratory where faculty and students explore ways to teach,
to learn, to discover." With its vision of a convergence of libraries and
computing centers, the plan assumed a single, merged facility, rather
than questioning that assumption at a time when the trend was toward distributed access in the networked university. As the year pro-
gressed, however, it became clear that the library and the computing
center were coping with a flux of both confluent and diverging developments that would make their operations too complex for any quick
merger.

In 1992, a large steering committee of administrators and faculty began to develop plans for the new building in which library and
computing services would reside in some yet-unspecified relationship. Nonetheless, the vision had shifted away from a singular emphasis on a new facility as a physical object, to a concern for how the
facility would serve the changing information needs of its users. The
mission statement for the revamped project saw the electronic library
as a "comprehensive information resource that draws on the expertise
of all the institution's information specialists, including those from
the library, computing, and communications." Goals for the electronic library included its becoming a regional resource for research
and development projects, such as distance learning; promoting information literacy and information management skills; fostering collaboration among librarians, computing professionals, and teaching
faculty; promoting interactive teaching and learning; and serving as
a catalyst for information research and electronic publishing. With
this foundation of mission and goals, a collaborative and integrated
planning process was launched to develop a whole new facility that
would reshape the information environment of the university. (Eventually, renewed state funding reinstated the construction program.)

During the planning process just described, we experienced difficulties not uncommon to complex academic organizations. Notably, we had not set up an integrated planning process to engage library and computing directors, other administrators, staff, faculty,

and students in the articulation of a comprehensive scheme for information systems and services for the networked university. Certain difficulties we encountered could be attributed to insufficient resources of staff, time, and money. Other difficulties reflected the newness of such technological development then. And, of course, problems always arise from inertia, from an unwillingness of some staff (at all levels) to change work habits. Despite such difficulties, however, the trends and pressures of technological change drew library and computing administrators and staff together in shared decision making to manage increasingly convergent operations (e.g., user assistance and instruction in new technology) and to solve common problems (e.g., expanding Internet resources, increasing user demands, decreasing staff resources). Such collaboration, in turn, enabled librarians and computing professionals to seize new opportunities to serve their users.

## Fundamental Reorganization since 1994

With the implementation of the new library system in 1994, the cornerstone of the "electronic library" was laid. The library and computing center evolved from having been parallel organizations engaged in complementary processes, to converging units in those areas of information systems and services where they shared common interests and expertise. The process of collaboration gained momentum during the planning of the campuswide information system and was strengthened in the design of the new library building to include computing laboratories and user facilities and several university research centers. The success of early collaborative projects was, in part, due to certain planning necessities: clear institutional priorities and concomitant budget allocations. But we believe that they succeeded for a subtler reason as well. For all their individual complexity, each of these projects focused on a discrete problem: Buy a server and bring up a system; plan a building; design and craft a collection of Web gateways. Those are problems that may have appeared new to some of the staff, but they could be handled by thinking through the needs of users and clients in largely known ways.

Recent years, however, have witnessed mounting frustrations on campus over unmet needs for more equipment, network connectivity, and user support. We have succeeded in renewing equipment and upgrading the network. But user support and training have continued to be problematic, and they can only get worse because as we upgrade our infrastructure, the number of users will jump from 2,000 to 20,000. Furthermore, although the current users tend to be "early adopter," and much more likely to be comfortable with technology, *each of the next 18,000 will probably need substantially more training and help!*

This realization prompted us to put "user support" under a magnifying glass as a distinctly new boundary spanning, value-added service function. In that framework, user support is not a discrete or familiar problem amenable to traditional bureaucratic structures or norms. It can only be met by bringing together many more support providers than one would ordinarily expect; and, as an organizational responsibility, the "help desk" (for want of a better phrase) must be fluid with layers of functions akin to a group of hyperlinked resources. Of course, if we are able to do user support well, our clients will not even realize any of these difficulties; they will simply get information and solutions.

In the past, information resources and services—print materials, telephone, television, fax, and computing—were each provided and supported separately. They were disjointed from each other, fundamentally unidirectional, and straightforward for user help. The contrast with the integrated networked information environment since the 1990s is remarkable. Library collections, much "print material," fax and television transmission, and computing cycles are all available from the desktop PC. More important, information has become bidirectional: Consider Web home pages being put up by offices, departments, faculty, and students; each individual can become a publisher, with everyone who is connected able to browse.

The implication of all this multifunctionality is that user support is now very complex because the services are so interrelated, sometimes in ways that make it difficult for the support staff itself to clarify. Certainly, many users would prefer a return to the old intellectual and bureaucratic structures for figuring out where to go for help online. But those no longer apply as this example shows: Imagine yourself as a user trying to connect from Albany to an OPAC in

California, but when you hit "Enter," you do not get the expected result. Whom do you call for help (at least in Albany)? Library staff? Computing staff? You have heard rumors about a new router, so what about Data Communications? Or maybe you have a modem, so what about Telephone Systems? Maybe your hard disk is making funny noises, should you call the staff who do PC maintenance? Or you are on a LAN, and the LAN coordinator is usually very helpful, if hopelessly overworked, so what about calling her or him? Whomever you call, that person must be ready to span the technological boundaries that link your PC to the OPAC in California.

As multifunctional technology has converged to the desktop over the past decade, choices have decentralized. Choice of applications software was the first. For example, although most units (and therefore users) at Albany are using one of two word-processing packages, that is not a formal restriction. (We have allowed a similar choice of operating systems, both desktop and now LAN servers. Most PC users still have Windows 3.1, but there are others with Windows 95 or NT, and a few with OS/2; and of course there are Mac devotees, plus those with various flavors of UNIX. On the server side, we run a mixed shop of Novell and NT.)

Two recent university policies have decentralized technology choices even more. First, rather than buy equipment in bulk and distribute a fixed package to users, we have transferred funds and the responsibility of choice for new or upgraded PCs to the schools and colleges. Although that gave up some economies of scale, it has provided greater satisfaction to the users. Second, all resources for increased staff support must now come from internal reallocations, so that when a dean recognizes the need for more network support of a school or college, the balancing question must be, Which faculty position will we *not* fill? The two policies, in part, aim to foster a climate in which users will look first for support nearest to "home"— whether a faculty office, a computing center, a library, or a residence. Therefore, we are establishing a structure in which the first line of assistance is the "local" technology coordinators in schools and colleges, administrative units, and residence halls. The chief central role is to provide the second line of assistance (the backup-to-the-backup role) for local coordinators who cannot readily solve geographically distributed problems. But the essential point is that the user should not need to know that all this organizational boundary spanning is going on; he or she simply makes one call to a "local number" and someone with responsibility—and connections—answers.

Although relatively simple on paper, it is a protracted restructuring problem. The biggest obstacles are insufficient local staff resources (or insufficient central ones to reallocate), the natural resistance of users to forgo old reliances on previous intellectual or organizational boundaries, and the need for training different groups of local users to call the help number geared for them (and not the one that a colleague or friend suggested as being particularly helpful). We are optimistic, however, because experiences on other campuses suggest that such a local-and-backup approach works well.[11]

## Evolving Opportunities

If we had written this paper at mid-decade, we probably would have talked about the difference between content and computing, and perhaps about the need for librarians to become steadily more technically sophisticated but to concentrate on their traditional "information" role, however that content may be delivered. That view now seems naive. The explosive growth of the World Wide Web has put enormous amounts of content at everyone's fingertips. We would not conclude that all systems programmers should now learn the most elegant search-engine protocols that librarians have to offer. Nor would we suggest that all bibliographers should be learning Java so that they can write their own application scripts. But we are reasonably confident that very soon the proportion of staff in each of the two units that can still get along barely acknowledging that the other group exists will have to shrink severely. This will arise largely because of expectations of users, who will use ever-changing technology to access vast numbers of information sites. Those helping them will have to be intimately familiar with the technology, the information, and the ways in which they are now inextricably linked (or hyperlinked), whereas the professional title or organizational home of those offering the help will matter far less than their appreciation for the blending of the information and the technology.

We recently redefined the mission of campus computing services, restructured the organization to distribute user support to the university's schools and colleges, and refocused the workload of computing professionals involved in technical support. The library has not experienced a redefinition of mission, but it has undergone continuous evolutionary change over the past decade. We now speak of the library systems and network environment, rather than of the OPAC, database services, or online systems. Although the library's organizational chart is a classic hierarchy, figure 1 is a more accurate picture of its functional design.

## University Library Network/Systems Environment

The issues on which we will be working for some time include redefining reference and user assistance services to move them away from

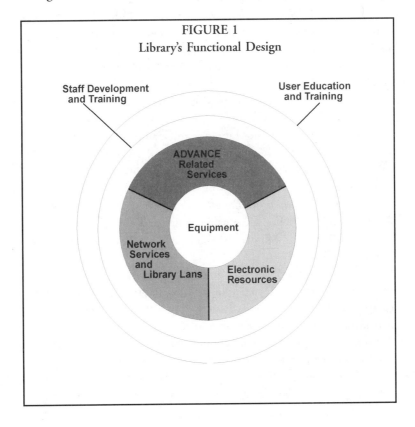

**FIGURE 1**
Library's Functional Design

Staff Development
and Training

User Education
and Training

ADVANCE
Related
Services

Equipment

Network
Services
and
Library Lans

Electronic
Resources

the user-at-the-desk paradigm. We also need to reset the balance of user services responsibilities in the library to provide more time to educate users in the effective use of information technology. If we are successful, we will have more knowledgeable, self-sufficient users and thus will reduce the grinding demand for individual ad hoc reference services. Over time, we will reallocate professional lines from traditional reference and collection development services to user education support and network services. None of the changes we have discussed and are engaged in implementing will be successful without a vigorous and sustained commitment to staff training and development. Library and computing staff are our most precious resource, the foundation on which we can restructure our organizations.

## NOTES

1. Donald J. Waters, "We Have a Computer: Administrative Issues in the Relations between Libraries and Campus Computing Organizations," *Journal of Library Administration* 13, no. 1/2 (1990): 121.

2. Patricia Battin, "The Electronic Library—A Vision for the Future," *EDUCOM Bulletin* 19 (summer 1984): 12–17, 34; Richard M. Dougherty, "Libraries and Computing Centers: A Blueprint for Collaboration," *College and Research Libraries* 48 (July 1987): 289–96; David C. Weber, "University Libraries and Campus Information Technology Organizations: Who Is in Charge Here?" *Journal of Library Administration* 9, no. 4 (1988): 5–19; Anne Woodsworth and James F. Williams II, "Computing Centers and Libraries: In Passage toward Partnerships," *Library Administration and Management* 2 (Mar. 1988): 85–90; Raymond K. Neff, "Merging Libraries and Computing Centers: Manifest Destiny or Manifestly Deranged?" *EDUCOM Bulletin* 20 (winter 1985): 8–12, 16.

3. Patricia Battin, "Stanford Names VP for New 'Info Resources' Structure," *Library Journal* 112, no. 13 (July 1987): 20; Brian L. Hawkins, "Managing a Revolution—Turning a Paradox into a Paradigm," in *Organizing and Managing Information Resources on Campus*, ed. Brian L. Hawkins (McKinney, Tex.: Academic Computing Publications, 1989), 4; Kay Flowers et al., "Collection Development and Acquisitions in a Changing University Environment," *Library Acquisitions: Practice & Theory* 19, no. 4 (1995): 463–69; Denise Troll, "Information Technologies at Carnegie

Mellon," *Library Administration and Management* 6, no. 2 (spring 1992): 91–99; Waters, "We Have a Computer."

4. Anne Woodsworth, *Patterns and Options for Managing Information Technology on Campus* (Chicago: ALA, 1991), 74–75.

5. Woodsworth and Williams, "Computing Centers and Libraries." See also Paula T. Kaufman, "Professional Diversity in Libraries," *Library Trends* 41 (fall 1992): 214–30; Jack Widner and Andrew Lawlor, "Library Computing Center Relations: A Comprehensive State University View," *Cause/Effect* 17 (Sept. 1994): 45–46.

6. Quoted from a memo from Paul Evan Peters, Executive Director of the Coalition for Networked Information, to task force representatives, July 27, 1994.

7. Sheila D. Creth, "Creating a Virtual Information Organization: Collaborative Relationships between Libraries and Computing Centers," in *Libraries as User-Centered Organizations: Imperatives for Organizational Change*, ed. Meredith A. Butler (New York: Haworth Pr., 1993), 111–32.

8. Michael Schrage, *Shared Minds: The New Technologies of Collaboration* (New York: Random House, 1990), 6.

9. Ibid., 39.

10. "The Digital Library," unpublished report, University at Albany, SUNY, Dec. 1991.

11. Brad Stone, "Organizing Support in a Distributed Computing Environment," CAUSE presentation, Nov. 15, 1992; see also: http://www.byu.edu/csr/www/solutions/compsup/compsup.html.

# Two Cultures: A Social History of the Distributed Library Initiative at MIT

*Nina Davis-Millis and Thomas Owens*

B efore the 1990s, libraries and campus computing centers had a long history of working together, but the typical relationship could hardly be called a partnership. Libraries prevailed on the computing centers to provide expertise and services but generally operated their own stand-alone minicomputers. Housed in library buildings and operated by library staff, those systems delivered information solely to library locations. Dial-up access represented the furthest reach of the library computing environment.

Several trends during the latter half of the 1980s, however, led to a nationwide reexamination of this precursory relationship. On the computing side, the microcomputer revolution changed the nature and scope of the services required by traditional customers. Accounting and inventory applications moved to the desktop; service priorities shifted from centralized storage and access to communications and integration. A first step toward meeting these priorities was a campuswide network and, by 1990, most universities either had such a network or had plans for one. The Internet created the opportunity for electronic mail, the "enabling application" that further pushed demand for network access.

Library automation also reached a critical juncture at the turn of this decade. Many institutions had automated during the integrated-systems boom of the early 1980s, and those first-generation systems were now due for replacement. Initially wary of computers, librarians now had a taste for them and wanted to supply automated access to a wider range of data, especially journal citation data. The CD-ROM revolution, although generally taking place on local area networks, clearly pointed to an almost unlimited range of automated information resources. Most important, the accelerating growth of campus networks linked to the Internet led to ever-increasing user demands for remote access.

In short, by 1990 or so, libraries needed to expand their services in ways that required deeper technological expertise than they possessed. Computing centers, for their part, were freed from traditional tasks by the microcomputer and had the time to devote to library needs. They also operated the communications infrastructure libraries wished to exploit. These trends pushed the two academic centers into each other's arms. On some campuses, there was a merger—sometimes led by a librarian, sometimes by a systems professional.

## A Brief Narrative of the Distributed Library Initiative

The recent history of MIT libraries and the campus computing center (called information systems, or IS) illustrates these trends. The libraries installed their first integrated system in 1984; by 1990, that system had reached its limits in size and functionality. It had been extraordinary when purchased, but technological change had outmoded the original proprietary hardware, which emphasized dedicated, polled terminals hostile to network communications. On the IS side, MITnet had been an early member of the Internet family and provided a firm foundation for universitywide connectivity. "Athena," the students' computing environment, for example, was a famously successful project providing distributed services to more than 1,500 Unix workstations.

However typical MIT was, as far as we can learn, no one ever seriously considered merging IS with the libraries. Actually, we sought a marriage rather than a merger—a real partnership that would allow each organization to bring its specific expertise to the problem of networked information. We wanted this partnership to grow simultaneously and organically at all staff levels—to foster a convergent understanding of goals, values, and methods on both sides.

Planning for the partnership started in 1990 at the highest administrative levels, with Marilyn McMillan, IS's director of information systems planning, and Greg Anderson, the libraries' associate director for systems and planning, meeting to discuss their organizations' mutual interests and goals and later arranging for larger meetings with other administrators in IS and the libraries. Those meetings led to a basic formulation of the respective strengths of the two organizations: The libraries determine content; IS provides infrastructure. On one side, the libraries were organizationally and intellectually better suited for judging the content of networked information— they had established methods for keeping current with the curriculum, for monitoring trends in campus research, and for understanding the goals of scholarly communication. On the other side, IS was organizationally and intellectually prepared to provide the expertise and tools required for operating and maintaining the infrastructure to deliver the information the libraries selected. Moreover, IS could integrate the delivery of this information into the MIT computing environment.

It became clear, however, that the provision of substantial amounts of networked information would require more effort than either organization was then prepared to supply on its own. At that point, Jim Bruce, vice president for information systems, and Jay Lucker, director of the MIT libraries, realized that ongoing strategic contact was required to make the partnership critical to both organizations. This led to the establishment of the first formal policy-making collaboration, The Libraries/Information Systems Steering Group, which soon became known by its e-mail address, LIBTALK. It set out to create a strategy for providing electronic library services to the MIT community—and the world—that developed into a project known as the Distributed Library Initiative (DLI). LIBTALK agreed that the partnership would be both long term and central to both organizations. It would be guided—but not driven—by specific, current projects. LIBTALK then initiated a process of mutual education at all staff levels.

Technical staff from both organizations met for the first time in 1991. Libraries staff presented a history of library automation, a brief introduction to the MARC record structure, and an explanation of the concept of authorities. IS staff explained network services, the Athena computing environment, and security protocol. These meetings continue to this day but in a different format. Now they are lunchtime talks with open attendance and both organizations urge all staff to attend. Presentations have ranged from a detailed explanation of the Z39.50 protocol, to a discussion of copyright issues in the electronic forum, to talk about current projects. (The technical group became known, as LIBTALK had, by its e-mail name—ELIBDEV—for Electronic Library Developers.)

To foster working relationships, IS and the libraries initially worked on a few small projects. OWL (Online with Libraries), for example, was a jointly developed, Athena-based online reference service. At about the same time, the "library menus" appeared on Athena. These pull-down menus led to a variety of information services available either online or in the libraries' paper collections. On a broader level, we began examining infrastructure issues. The Z39.50 protocol was key to our plans and, in 1991, representatives from IS and the libraries joined the Z39.50 Implementors Group, an international forum of developers for the nascent Z39.50 protocol.

As such small projects proliferated, the partnership saw the need to coordinate the various activities. A second formal group was created (again named for its e-mail address—DLICC—for Distributed Library Initiative Coordinating Committee). In addition, the Laboratory for Computer Science research group Library 2000, headed by Professor Jerome Saltzer, was keenly interested in electronic libraries, and members of this group joined the coordinating committee. To help with copyright issues, the Intellectual Property Counsel became a regular attendee.

For major projects, the membership of the coordinating committee is now quite flexible, though a core group remains. As the two organizations worked together and learned more about each other, they sought out users to advise them on the creation of new services. For example, in 1992, the libraries and IS joined with the Committee on Academic Computing to present a DLI Day, which attracted more than seventy participants from across the university, including staff, researchers, faculty, and students. Small groups focused on specific information needs, opportunities, and constraints.

All this activity led to the eventual development of the DLI vision by the IS/Libraries Steering Group in 1993. This vision statement concluded with a vivid forecast of the DLI five years hence, for 1998:

> The way MIT and its people do research and pursue education will be revolutionized by enriched access to all forms of information at their fingertips. Sitting at a workstation in the classroom or laboratory, in the sorority, or in the airplane, anyone can retrieve, manipulate, interpret, and integrate information into their personal knowledge banks. They can easily move among personal, on-campus, and worldwide resources to find, evaluate, sort, and store information. MIT students, researchers, educators, and administrators, freed from the drudgery of information management, are now better able to work together in putting that information to use in the advancement of humanity.

With this vision as a guide, interest in access to networked information spread to the creation of still another formal IS/libraries group, the Network User Team (NUT). NUT's IS members include a programmer, a faculty liaison, and the manager of its Educational Planning and Support unit; NUT's libraries members include representatives of public services, collections, technical services, and library systems. This group manages new releases of existent applications, develops access to new resources, and coordinates technical support of applications and hardware with functional support of content and training. NUT's projects have included adapting each successive release of WILLOW, a Z39.50 client developed at the University of Washington, for use in making databases available over Athena; evaluating available interfaces for the online Oxford English Dictionary and implementing a Web version employing Open Text software; and providing ongoing support of networked information resources. Support to software is provided by the Library Systems Office and IS;

questions regarding intellectual content or training are handled by reference librarians and Athena faculty liaisons.

Currently, the steering group, the coordinating committee, and NUT are the only formal joint IS/libraries groups. However, nearly every new project creates ad hoc groups on varying levels of formality. Recently, we have experimented with software development by open invitation: Once a project is defined and a core team identified, meetings can be attended by any interested staff and the product goes through extensive testing and review. The core team formally answers each suggestion, explaining why each one was or was not adopted.

At about the same time (1993) that the steering group developed the DLI vision, it issued a general schedule of network development. Since then, DLI has been mostly on track. Working with the University of Washington and Stanford, for example, MIT created an early Z39.50 client (WILLOW) with code written by both IS (underlying protocol drivers) and library staff (MARC record management). The library Web soon superseded the library Gopher. We mounted our first local databases using BRS software, then migrated to OCLC's Newton; software was written to provide automated access to OCLC's FirstSearch databases through Athena; and a team of librarians and IS staff worked on Elsevier's TULIP project (delivering images of that publisher's engineering journals to the desktop using both WILLOW and the Web).

## DLI: A Social History

Sustaining our drive through the next few years is crucial to DLI's viability in the long run. At this point, it is fair to say that IS and the libraries have developed a fruitful, mutually respectful working relationship. From the beginning, both IS and the libraries consciously acknowledged the cultural differences of the two organizations while focusing on common goals. Although we always emphasized each other's professional expertise and distinct areas of competence, we also fostered "technology transfer" between the two organizations. Our plan was not to have one group adopt the culture and methodologies of the other but, rather, to let a third culture evolve out of shared philosophies and objectives.

Indeed, we consider that the awareness of cultural differences between the two constituencies, together with the decision to invest staff time in exploring them (as well as professional similarities), has been a key element in the success of the partnership. Another salient factor has been the active participation of upper-level administrators from both units in setting goals and priorities, concurrent with the participation of frontline staff in the actual design and delivery of services. These considerations, both formal and informal, have enabled groups in each organization to share their respective expertise, skills, and values.

A brief review of the literature on collaboration between academic libraries and campus computing organizations provides a broader perspective on how typical our experiences may be. In this literature, a great deal of analysis has been done on the pros and cons of merging such units. However, relatively little attention has been paid to the benefits of sharing cultures, or even to descriptions of the respective professional cultures.

David C. Weber points out that the library profession has a long shared history of standards, philosophies, and procedures whereas campus computing has a strong technical orientation characterized by a volatile entrepreneurial environment and rapidly changing technology.[1]

Sheila D. Creth, in a survey of discussions among library and computing administrators and managers, observes that campus computing staff come from a variety of backgrounds:

> Since they do not share a common professional and academic preparation, there is no socialization process for a computer professional prior to accepting a position in a computer organization. They considered this lack of shared professional philosophy and values to be a major contributor to an ethos in which individual action and thought is more highly regarded than a focus on the views, standards or values of the collective group. In contrast, this group of [computing] professionals considered that librarians with their similar educational backgrounds experience a process of acculturation in which they develop a shared philosophy and common values. Therefore, they are more likely to act within

the boundaries of accepted professional beliefs and behavior, being less likely to act independently.[2]

Creth's survey also dealt with the respective values of the two professions. Computing professionals were regarded as sharing a *technical* orientation, as encouraging entrepreneurial behavior, and as valuing creativity, whereas librarians were seen as having a *service* orientation, a consensual approach, and fiscal responsibility. Both groups were identified with a professional orientation of being focused on the world of information and the consumers of information, and of being concerned with their own institution (and hence, one may assume, with their local customers).[3]

As Kristin McDonough points out, we should distinguish "subcultures" and "vested interests" within and between both the library and the computing professions:

> There used to be talk of separate 'cultures' in our own profession, as exemplified by public services and technical services librarians. Today, technological advances have forced a crossover. . . . Another salient point is the competition that has existed on some campuses between administrative and academic computing. Rather than 'cultures,' might not the issue be the pull between vested interests?[4]

To expand our perspective of MIT's merger efforts, we interviewed McMillan and Anderson about the early stages of IS/libraries collaboration and later invited the participants of various joint efforts to a focus group. Overall, our colleagues confirmed the sense that MIT's experience corroborates many of the observations chronicled in the literature.

Looking back on the early stages of collaboration, Anderson and McMillan remembered that each organization expected to benefit from building a partnership with the other. Although both organizations hoped to be the primary provider of electronic library services over the network, IS had the technical expertise and the hardware as opposed to the libraries' well-established connections to instruction, scholarship, and MIT's academic life in general.

Ironically, each unit saw the other as being at an advantage politically. The libraries, were concerned that they would be absorbed and controlled by IS which, in turn, feared that the libraries had deeper service contacts across campus and could build powerful alliances demanding unsustainable services. Picking up on the "marriage" metaphor, Anderson and McMillan agreed that their organizations saw the possibility that the partnership would be a "deadly embrace" as each tried to leverage resources from the other while retaining complete control—ending with both parties squandering staff and financial capital on fruitless projects. To avoid that, they recognized that some kind of collaborative model would have to be developed. As they searched for the right model, they kept the cultural differences constantly in mind.

The initial focus was actually on defining the scope of the partnership; awareness of each other's organizational structure, and then the respective professional cultures, followed as the collaboration took shape. McMillan and Anderson arranged high-level meetings that avoided discussions about specific projects but, instead, focused on sharing organizational goals and values: What does your organization wish to accomplish, and what is important to you? The meetings were carefully designed not to raise expectations or to preselect outcomes. Clearly, McDonough's vision of a possible "pull between vested interests" was perceived in the formative stages of the libraries–IS partnership. The great extent to which this pull was overcome can be attributed to all parties having taken the time necessary to accommodate one another's organizational frameworks and to explain decisions in one another's terms. With the top management in the two organizations being committed to collaborative dialogue, the frontline staff who worked on specific products experienced a rich, creative tension rather than a clash of cultures.

The focus group we organized for this study was composed of libraries and IS staff, all of whom had been active in at least one collaborative project. We asked participants to comment on the two professional cultures of librarianship and computing. They perceived librarians as tending to be orderly, striving for perfection, and having a sense of responsibility to the public. IT professionals were regarded as being eager to make resources available—"willing to throw stuff out there," as one participant phrased it—but also inclined to assume that almost anything is subject to change. Whereas librarians were seen to believe that things should stay as they are (and this may explain their urge to "strive for perfection"), IT culture holds that change will probably be beneficial (an assumption that can backfire if customers are already satisfied with a service or product).

Despite that fundamental difference in outlook, the librarians valued certain attributes of their IS colleagues: flexibility and a positive orientation to change, combined with a task orientation and a focus on results. IS participants, in turn, appreciated librarians' respect for the past and their ability to apply lessons or knowledge from the past to the future. IS participants generally seemed to have gained from joint projects an appreciation of the depth of professional librarianship.

A group whose experience was distinctly more ambivalent was library systems personnel. This unit's dual role seems to have created ambiguity and frustration for its members—a sense of being caught between two cultures, each with a clearly defined area of expertise. (In future research, we hope to explore the cultural and professional dynamics of library computing units in academic libraries during the Internet era now under way.)

Denis H. J. Caro and Amarjit S. Sethi contend that of the factors that shape a technology plan or project, the social ones are more important than operational, technical, or economic ones.[5] McDonough agrees that "among the daunting challenges that lie before campus information providers, the human issue of cooperation is as important—and as thorny—as the technological ones of connectivity and networking."[6] MIT libraries and IS have avoided many of the notorious social-interaction pitfalls by acknowledging and fostering the human side of collaboration; by giving staff members throughout our respective hierarchies a chance to participate in planning and information sharing, both in formal and informal settings; and by encouraging the building of partnerships that are rich in personal satisfaction and not limited to tapping the knowledge of the individuals involved.

Nevertheless, this approach had some initial costs. McMillan and Anderson spent three to four hours preparing for every hour-long

meeting. They agree that focusing only on projects would have supplied more successes in the beginning. But it is by no means clear that quick successes would have fostered the deep working relationships the two organizations have achieved. These relationships have moved beyond the DLI into other projects, some removed from information retrieval. For example, IS invited library staff to join the task force charged with creating and maintaining software development methods at MIT. In addition to creating procedures for identifying and tracking requirements, the team examined software development tools and project planners. Library staff were asked to advise the reengineering of the IS help desk, and IS also chose a librarian to be the CWIS administrator. On the libraries side, IS staff now run all the major servers used by the libraries; they routinely offer security audits of library-operated systems. The libraries also make sure that all licenses go through the IS Intellectual Property Counsel.

## Conclusions

Traditionally, campus computing centers and libraries have had different "cultures" that emphasize rather distinct values and goals. MIT elected to build a long-term collaboration, a partnership that would require ongoing relationships at all levels of the two organizations. To accomplish this, it focused on brief, project-oriented tasks while building a work environment that directly addressed the issues raised by cultural differences. This approach, characterized by concurrent investments in specific projects and underlying working relationships, has resulted in an effective and productive partnership, highly valued by members of both organizations. Participants in our joint ventures have profited by a deeper understanding of the professional values of their counterparts, and the resulting services have benefited from respective strengths of our two professions.

NOTES

1. David C. Weber, "University Libraries and Campus Information Technology Organizations: Who Is in Charge Here?," *Journal of Library Administration* 9, no. 4 (1988): 5–19.

2. Sheila D. Creth, "Creating a Virtual Information Organization: Collaborative Relationships between Libraries and Computing Centers," *Journal of Library Administration* 19, no. 3/4 (1993): 120–21.

3. Ibid.

4. Kristin McDonough, "Prior Consent: Not-So-Strange Bedfellows Plan Library/Computing Partnership," ERIC/ED 364225 (Apr. 12, 1992), 10–11.

5. Denis H. J. Caro and Amarjit S. Sethi, "Technology Strategy: The Role of Strategic Planning and Monitoring Systems," in *Strategic Management of Technostress in an Information Society*, ed. Amarjit S. Sethi et al., (Lewiston, N.Y.: C. J. Hogrefe, 1987), 35.

6. McDonough, "Prior Consent," 4.

# Farewell to All That . . . Transforming Collection Development to Fit the Virtual Library Context: The OhioLINK Experience

*David F. Kohl*

T hroughout history, one of the dreams of scholars and librarians alike has been that longed-for library that has it all— the whole record of human achievement and thought. From the days of Alexandria, to the traditional riches of the Bodlian, to the powerhouse collections of the modern era at Harvard or the University of Illinois, the ideal has always been to have all the resources in one place, in one glorious, fabulous collection—a kind of library "Camelot," as it were.

Of course, it never happened, though the flame of hope burned brightly for a while during the extravagant growth in library collections in the 1960s. But more important, as the twentieth century wanes, the fundamental premises underlying that ideal have changed irrevocably. Increasingly, we have realized that the purpose of heaping up great stacks of books in one place was not an end in itself (prestigious though that might be) but, given the technology available at the time, it was simply the best way to provide relatively quick and easy access to those materials. With the maturation of the information revolution over the past decade, as well as prolonged inflation of material costs, it has become progressively clear not only that grand, single-site library collections are no longer an ideal method of providing access but that this whole approach has severe limitations and drawbacks. Research specialization and publication proliferation, overall decline of funding sources, and additional costs of electronic resources and services have collectively overwhelmed academic library budgets. Yet, as the traditional ideal of all-encompassing libraries has waned, the electronic era has given rise to new prospects for both comprehensive and cost-effective collection development.

Academic libraries of Ohio are in the forefront of a long-term process to restructure collection development models through a new kind of library consortium—OhioLINK (OL). As both a virtual library and a "just-in-time" collection, its organizational structure is based on a strategy of resource sharing through networked access and delivery systems so that materials housed in any location are equally available to everyone in the consortium on a timely basis. Thus, instead of having fifty-four autonomous library organizations with self-contained collections, OhioLINK develops and distributes its resources, as needed, throughout the state. The sheer strength and economy of this strategy is captured in the hypothetical case of attempting to create the equivalent of OL's twenty-million volume collection at each of the fifty-four member institutions at a cost (if it could be done at all) of $106 billion, compared to OL's three-year cumulative operating budget of under $10 million.[1]

OL's strategy of developing and sharing resources has depended on the creation of a distinct technological infrastructure and on a reassessment of print-age practices and norms, as well as those for electronic resources and services. To describe OL's restructuring of collection development, it is helpful to begin by outlining the relationship between infrastructure design and service philosophy.

## What Is OhioLINK?

Begun in the late 1980s, OhioLINK now includes all publicly supported institutions of higher education and the state library, as well as a growing number of private colleges. Its resources range from small community college holdings to those of Carnegie Research Universities I, from special collections to electronic databases. Its services extend to approximately half a million students and faculty at more than ninety sites, and its network presently handles more than 3,400 simultaneous users. More specifically, OL provides to each member institution on a round-the-clock basis access to:

- the library catalogs of all Ohio institutions of higher education, accessible from local library, office, or home computers;
- an aggregate collection of twenty million volumes, available within two days through patron-initiated circulation system requests;
- more than fifty commercial bibliographic databases (e.g., the Wilson line, Medline, ArticleFirst, English Short Title Catalogue, among others);
- fifteen full-text databases, including Hannah Online (Ohio legislative information), Chadwyck-Healy's Verse Drama and British Poetry, and Britannica Online;
- full-text articles from more than 300 PowerPages journals, 174 Academic Press journals, and 1,140 Elsevier journals;
- the Internet via both gopher and Web browsers.

The underlying network handles more than a million system searches and ten thousand patron-initiated interlibrary requests per week. On a more general plane, OL's organizational development reflects two complementary frameworks—one based on a new model of technological unity, the other on a radical reinterpretation of library cooperation.

## The Framework of Technological Unity

The vision that shaped OhioLINK's infrastructure was the implementation of the same hardware and software at all OL sites. Rather than attempt to link a diverse, historical crazy quilt of individual-institution automation choices through some interpreter (such as Z39.50), OL saw the overriding need for a common system of hardware and software. Libraries that had not been using the Innovative Interfaces system were required, at OL's formation, to shift to that system. Although those libraries experienced substantial change and some inconvenience in the late 1980s, the unified system clearly improved patron service and facilitated technological progress. More subtle, but equally important, in the early years of OL's organizational development, such technological unity delivered a message to patrons and librarians that they were part and parcel of a unified system. The resulting ease of use, the infrastructure's robustness, and its real and symbolic unity have been key factors in OL's success.

At the same time, this infrastructure was not meant to eliminate local library autonomy. It is essentially a "federal" system operating on two levels: Each institution's local system coupled to, yet on a different level from, the central network. This network has three main functions: (1) serving as a union catalog of all bibliographic and item-level records in the state, (2) operating as a switching station for libraries to distribute patron-initiated circulation requests, and (3) providing a common platform for electronic databases and Internet gateways. Each site's system handles local inquiries to the local catalog and is the originating site of all consortium item-records. This federal design keeps heavy local traffic at the local level while enabling seamless linkages to the central system or to other local systems. The seamless character of the infrastructure is enhanced by immediate, real-time record updates (e.g., a bibliographic record loaded locally is almost simultaneously uploaded to the central database) and also by the common search engine at all OL sites.

The ability of a patron to make direct book requests to any member institution has probably had the biggest impact on OL's service performance.[2] The library-to-library relationship for book borrowing is akin to that for library-branch borrowing in a traditional setup. An OL patron identifies an item he or she wants and, if it is not locally held, simply types his or her name, identification number, and home library for the book to be sent for pickup. Delivery between libraries is handled by a commercial firm at an average round-trip cost of 40 cents per item. Thus, inexpensive and rapid circulation transactions have replaced more costly and cumbersome interlibrary loan (ILL) procedures. Studies have shown that 87 percent of books requested through the patron-initiated circulation system are indeed available and delivered—with over 50 percent of the requests filled in two days and over 80 percent in three days. Such speed and reliability have been critical to the development of a sense among patrons and librarians alike that the virtual library is effective and worthwhile.

There continues to be concern in one area: browsing the stacks. As it turns out, the solution lies in how the problem is defined. As long as it was perceived as a need, primarily expressed by the faculty, to physically see and handle books, it remained a frustrating and difficult issue. In fact, few of the faculty were really lamenting the loss of a trip to the library during not always convenient open hours to wander through often poorly lit and dreary stacks to handle dusty books. What they were describing as they talked about seeing the size of the book, flipping it open and scanning the table of contents, checking the index, perhaps doing some spot-reading, was a search for information as to how valuable a particular book was likely to be for them. The problem with using the electronic database was not just a romantic longing for the physicality of the print materials but the relative poverty of bibliographic information. Although the same problem existed earlier with the card catalog information, faculty had learned to browse the local collection to supplement limited card catalog bibliographic information. Once we realized that within OL, or any virtual library, the change from a card catalog to an electronic catalog was not just substituting one component for another in the same system but, instead, represented the first step in implementing a whole new system—a whole new ecology, so to speak—the solution became not only possible, but obvious. We needed to add to the electronic bibliographic record as much of the information provided formerly by browsing as possible.

The first step has been to add commercial table of contents information. With the recent ability to hot-link MARC records, OL is also experimenting at some sites with book review links. The Chadwyck-Healy database of individual book index information offers possibilities for even further bibliographic enrichment. OL is hopeful, indeed reasonably confident, that such bibliographic advances, coupled with twenty-four-hour networked access, from home or office, to the online catalog will more than offset the tradition of having to be physically in the stacks to browse only a relatively small, local collection.

## The Framework of Radical Cooperation
Although the technical vision of a unified, yet federal infrastructure was significant for the development and acceptance of OL's virtual

library, even more important has been the radical redefinition of library cooperation among both librarians and university administrators. Traditionally, library cooperation had been confined to the periphery of operations—ILL, cooperative collection development, and reciprocal patron privileges—and represented whatever gestures of service or economy were feasible, given the autonomy of libraries and the primacy of their clienteles. Although local autonomy retains a marked importance in OL's federal system, the main framework of energy and activity centers on a conviction that local problems cannot be adequately solved locally but, instead, require the larger context of a consortium. In this perspective, cooperative arrangements are designed to reshape the very core of library operations in OhioLINK and its member institutions.

It means training local staff to be as responsible for serving consortium patrons as they are for serving local clienteles—for example, allocating staff and setting procedures to make two-day book deliveries a reliable routine. Radical cooperation also means occasional local sacrifices for the collective good; for example, the policy that article requests within OL's system are provided without normal ILL charges entailed a serious drop in the revenue stream for many medical libraries. Radical cooperation means that individual member institutions do not own a collection in the traditional sense but, rather, are stewards of collections for the consortium. In that regard, OL libraries provide access to local materials on the same basis for consortium patrons as they do for local clienteles.

## Collection Development in the OhioLINK Context

The evolution of OL's virtual system—based on a unified, yet federal infrastructure together with a radical reinterpretation of cooperation—has led inexorably to fundamental changes in collection development. Indeed, any effort to retain the tradition of autonomous, self-sufficient collections would have cut off practically all opportunities for the consortium to resolve once-intractable problems of resource costs and demands. OL's restructuring of collection development practices and norms falls under three rubrics: moving from ownership to stewardship; participating on the consortium level in the information revolution; and transforming the role of the local bibliographer.

## From Ownership to Stewardship

Because it enables academic libraries of Ohio to share materials almost as easily and reliably as if they were held locally, OL represents a truly feasible opportunity for coordinated, statewide collection development. In retrospect, it seems fairly obvious that such an approach to collection development must follow, not precede, the construction of a virtual library and delivery system. Until librarians and patrons are convinced by personal experience that the physical location of materials is largely irrelevant for their purposes, it is difficult to make the case for a genuine division of statewide (or regional) collection responsibilities. Once that Rubicon is crossed, however, significant opportunities for cost-effective resource sharing open up.

Although the new strategy of building collections on the basis of shared stewardship, rather than autonomous ownership, is still evolving, certain key points are emerging. The first point is that collection development is still an important local responsibility. This is philosophically obvious, in that a virtual library where everyone relied on someone else to do the actual collection purchasing, processing, and housing would be "virtually" no library at all. Unfortunately, in practice, philosophical clarity is easy to lose if some librarians, or especially university or college administrators, see system participation as a chance to solve local budget problems by relying inappropriately on common resources. Individual institutions cannot be allowed to "overgraze the commons." Sadly, the more successful OL becomes, the greater the temptation for administrators to neglect their local libraries—a sure recipe for eventual disaster. OL libraries, both individually and together, have had to remain vigilant and vocal to oppose such thinking. Especially in a shared system, each local institution retains responsibility for contributing appropriately to the common good.

A second point is that even with a quick, convenient, and reliable method of sharing resources, it seems likely that each institution will continue to need to identify and take responsibility for providing a core set of materials for its particular constituency. Heavily used core items should continue to be held locally. The key change is that responsibility for marginal, esoteric, or highly specialized research materials can be divided up—a kind of state Farmington Plan. Because it is no longer necessary (let alone feasible) for each institution to attempt to be self- sufficient in all areas, it becomes possible to replace superficial width across the subject spectrum with more narrowly defined, multiple, specialized collections at the research or comprehensive level. OL has found that using the RLG Conspectus to provide a detailed breakdown of present collection strengths around the state provides a helpful beginning. The important point to keep in mind is that the conspectus looks backward and that the issue here is future responsibility. In some subject areas where strong internal subgroups already exist (e.g., music and law), discussions are already under way to establish areas of subject responsibility for specialized collections within these broader areas. The goal of the exercise is to make sure that the composite of the specialized areas adds up to full coverage in all important subject areas. Early statistics indicate that the duplication rate among OL library collections—just over 40 percent of books being held in more than one library—is substantial enough to allow much more in-depth coverage if the funds could be reallocated. Clearly, there will be substantial political problems to overcome, with both local academic departments and colleagues around the state.

A third point is that cooperative collection agreements need to be relatively formal, written agreements, possibly with commitment at the provost or presidential level. Casual understandings do not provide the reliability needed for an institution to stop collecting in an area and rely on someone else's collection. Because librarians do not control their central funding allocations, it seems likely that the collection commitment must be at the institutional rather than library level. Clearly, in a situation of considerable mutual interdependence there must be strong and clear assurances of follow-through on the part of all players. Developing the mechanism for establishing subject-area responsibilities among the players and ensuring a serious commitment is likely to be difficult and politically complicated.

## Consortium Participation in the Information Revolution

Active involvements in the information revolution—partnering in the development of new tools and exploring new funding arrangements having economies of scale—compromise another broad agenda for bibliographers. With an aggregate collection development budget (representing members' combined spending) in excess of $25 million a year, OL attracts great interest from vendors. In 1994 (following eighteen months of discussion and negotiation with Chadwyck-Healy), OhioLINK purchased both the British Poetry and the Verse Drama databases for all consortium members—both present and future. The extraordinary cost of these databases to a single library (the British Poetry database alone was then selling for more than $41,700 per site) precluded their purchase by all but the largest and most affluent libraries. But by using OhioLINK to, in effect, negotiate a statewide purchase, the volume pricing allowed Chadwyck-Healy to offer a major discount and still feel satisfied that it was making a reasonable profit while simultaneously allowing even the smallest Ohio community college access to a major tool.

OL does not simply represent a large market; the diversity of its member institutions (in terms of size, mission, patron type, etc.) allows commercial vendors to test a product in different (subconsortium) market ranges. The longest development project has been UMI's PowerPages, which has full-text articles for about 600 journals. Providing this database as a stand-alone local system was fairly straightforward, although managing a jukebox farm of almost 1,500 discs required more technical attention than OL had anticipated. The real test, however, has been the multiple challenge of (1) integrating the database into OL's scores of local environments, (2) distributing it to myriad local printers and fax machines, and (3) automating printing and billing processes so as not to overinvolve local staff. Although still partly under construction, this aspect of OL's integration is already operational at most sites. (At the University of Cincinnati, for example, more than a thousand articles have been printed on busy days.) By this time, both UMI and Innovative Interfaces have had a rich experience to modify their products.

OL's partnership with UMI has also enabled librarians to learn much about issues of infrastructure and policy in the delivery of electronic information. A salient issue has been what is reasonable behavior when printing is "free." Although there is natural concern over an inconsistent policy of monographic materials being freely available while electronic materials have a print charge, it has remained important to discourage abuse in the latter medium. OL has found that when UMI articles are provided free of charge with pickup at the local circulation desk, about 15 percent of them are never retrieved. Further, a small fraction of patrons print as many as a hundred articles at one time from "free" databases. With some mechanism needed to institutionalize thoughtful choices, OL decided to charge ten cents a page for printing UMI articles but also to allow local institutions to subsidize their patrons. Thus, for example, a given library could allow patrons a hundred pages of articles free per semester but charge additional article pages each at the ten cent rate— thereby continuing, to some extent, the tradition of cost-free library resources while encouraging reasonable use of those resources.

## The Transformed Role of the Bibliographer

It is perhaps a paradox, though a deeply satisfying one, that with all the broad concerns for large-scale organizational development, a key player continues to be the local bibliographer.

Although the advent of OL has begun to substantially transform their role in the collection development process, individual bibliographers remain no less fundamental or important and, perhaps, have become even more crucial.

Their new role is a dual one within OL. Bibliographers have a major responsibility not only to fundamentally revise how they go about collection development but also to help construct the new organization within which they will need to work. A number of new assignments and changes of vision are required.

First, bibliographers are finding it necessary to fundamentally revise their understanding of their job. Collection mapping is becoming more important than simply collection building. In the true virtual library, collecting the materials all in one place is less important than knowing where all the needed materials are. It is very similar to the way we have traditionally talked about reference librarians. They do not need to know everything, they just need to know where to find everything. Similarly with the new bibliographers, they do not have to own everything just to know where to find everything. To construct this virtual collection, the bibliographer/selector starts not with the holes in the local collection or the amount of money available for purchasing materials but, rather with the needs of the faculty and students. The bibliographer then specifically determines how each needed element will be supplied—ILL, regional consortia, commercial vendor, local purchase, etc. Local purchase continues to be important, but it is no longer the exclusive or even central element in providing access to the materials needed by faculty and students for research and instruction. Purchase for the local collection becomes just one strategy among many for providing access to materials. This is a very different starting place and a very different task than we are used to for bibliographers/selectors.

Second, what is purchased locally follows a very different strategy than that of traditional arrangements. Rather than the need to cover all areas needed for local research and instruction, even if such attempts at wide coverage are limited and spotty, it makes more sense for the bibliographer (as mentioned earlier) to focus on maintaining a core collection with narrowly defined speciality areas collected at the research or comprehensive level. The problem with many of our traditional collections is that limited funds had to be spread over too broad an area with the result that in-depth research/comprehensive collecting was giving way to broad-based, rather mediocre collections. The key to success in returning to serious research collecting in narrowly defined areas, however, is that someone else must be collecting at a research/comprehensive level in complementary areas so that the full subject is covered in-depth. Third, bibliographers can no longer consider resources outside their immediate domain as being somehow peripheral. It is not enough to say to patrons that materials are "out there" and so they need not be collected locally. A critical new task of bibliographers is, rather than just to map the consortium collection, to make certain that what is "out there" is, indeed, accessible. This task involves keeping up with coordinated collection development groups, serial cancellation projects, commercial information services, and resource-sharing agreements. In that regard, OL has found that a new oversight group, called Cooperative Information Resources Management, has been a useful layer of organizational development.

A fourth point in the transformed role of bibliographers, so far largely unaddressed in the literature, is a tremendous need to provide ongoing education and training in technical areas. Apart from print-age subject expertise, electronic information requires increasing sophistication about both current limitations and prospective opportunities for networked applications throughout the academic institution. Traditionally, a bibliographer could purchase a book with the calm assurance that sunlight or electric light (the infrastructure of the print-on-paper world) would be available to the patron. Bibliographers must now consider not only content and visibility but also how electronic resources integrate with other resources and whether they all suit multiple platforms and delivery mechanisms. The staff of a consortium can lead the way in training bibliographers in this rapidly changing area.

Fifth, another largely unaddressed area has been the role of the bibliographer in explaining the virtual library to faculty and students. Although some features of OL, such as patron-initiated ILL requests, have generated much goodwill, there has been little follow-up discussion of their implications for resource sharing. The process of revising collection development statements (with a shift from collection building to collection mapping) will give bibliographers concrete opportunities to raise such problems and prospects with local stakeholder groups. We are just beginning along this new path, where much remains to be discovered.

## Conclusions

Over the past decade, OhioLINK has been a pioneering effort to resolve local academic library problems though statewide approaches. Development of its unified infrastructure and radical reinterpretation of interlibrary cooperation have been dual strategies to move beyond the outmoded notion of an all-encompassing local university library. Although efficient sharing of traditional materials is a necessary first step to establish credibility of the virtual library concept, the main power and significance of the virtual library will be unrealized without concomitant and fundamental changes in collection development. Overall, OL provides a truly new opportunity to successfully tackle challenges that had been intractable within traditional organizational structures associated with print-age norms of collection management.

## NOTES

1. OL makes available to fifty-four libraries a combined book collection of approximately twenty million volumes. A traditional strategy for autonomous local collections would have required purchase of 1.06 billion additional volumes (54 times 20 million minus the original 20 million). The hypothetical cost of acquiring such collections, let alone processing and storing them, would have been in the range of more than 106 billion dollars ($100 per volume times 1.06 billion volumes). In contrast, OL has made such a collection available to each of these institutions from a cumulative central budget of less than $30 million. Because nearly $20 million of this central OL money is devoted to capital purchases for local purposes (computers and software for individual campuses), the final amount of OL money is under $10 million.

2. Patron-initiated circulation within OL warrants further comment. Although still library-to-library borrowing, it is much easier and more transparent for patrons to use than a traditional ILL system. In ILL, requested materials have not necessarily been bibliographically identified, nor are their locations necessarily known. Furthermore, in ILL the participating libraries are autonomous—they might not have lending agreements, or they might impose charges. These considerations have made ILL a problematic endeavor. Patron-initiated circulation, on the other hand, deals with known bibliographic items in a unified infrastructure with interlibrary agreements already in place. Thus, any authorized patron has access to the materials with no more need of mediation than a work-study student to handle checkouts.

# Facing Change and Challenge through Collaborative Action: The CIC Libraries' Experience

*Barbara McFadden Allen and William A. Gosling*

I n a situation reflective of many changes in higher education over the past decade, the academic library community faces significant and intractable economic pressures that require completely new service models and budget strategies.[1] Current priorities include: elimination of unnecessary duplication of effort, consolidation of services and departments, and general downsizing of staff. Such pressures arise from the need to invest (and continually reinvest) in a network infrastructure capable of meeting ever-rising demands for digital information, as well as the lag in research materials budgets behind publication proliferation and price inflation.

Consider, for instance, that most branches of scientific publication show an exponential growth of about four to eight percent annually, doubling every ten to fifteen years. *Chemical Abstracts* took thirty-one years (1907 to 1937) to publish its first million abstracts; the second million, eighteen years; the most recent million, only 1.75 years. Essentially, more articles on chemistry have been published in the past *two* years than in all of history before 1900.[2]

Compounding such trends are changes in societal attitudes toward higher education in general, which will dramatically affect academic libraries. As public sentiment goes, so goes funding for public agencies. And private universities will not be exempt from this phenomenon, as such attitudes will affect the distribution of public monies to private institutions for research and other activities. A politics of survival will come into play as public university administrators react to the demands of a citizenry—an electorate—calling for financial accountability, more affordable tuition, and greater attention to undergraduate teaching and learning.[3] As federal research and development (R&D) monies dwindle, all academic institutions will be engaged in sharper competition for fewer dollars.

In this economic environment, universities and colleges are cutting low-demand and redundant programs while emphasizing comparatively strong ones.[4] The resulting academic restructuring will affect the ways in which librarians manage traditional collections, as well as build electronic information systems. Moreover, the growth of "electronic communities" of scholars, teachers, and learners generates increasing needs for remote access to information resources. Distance learning environments require continued investments in network and information infrastructure, putting new pressures on existing budgets. Consortia of universities are suited to deal with these initiatives and their costs through collaborative action. By drawing upon the expertise across a spectrum of universities, collaborative action can minimize obstacles and exploit opportunities. The Committee on Institutional Cooperation (CIC) is perhaps ideally suited to such collaboration, due to the broad scope of the consortium and to each member university's demonstrated commitment to deep levels of collaboration. An examination of the CIC's experience may be useful in understanding how such an organization can be an effective agent for successful change involving academic libraries.

## The CIC: Organized for Action

With headquarters in Champaign, Illinois, the CIC is the academic consortium of twelve major teaching and research universities.[5] Collectively, these universities engage in over $2.8 billion worth of funded scientific and engineering research annually, of which some $1.5 billion is derived from federal sources.[6] They employ more than 30,000 full-time faculty members and enroll nearly a half-million undergraduate, graduate, and professional students on their main campuses, conferring nearly ten percent of all master's and professional degrees and over fifteen percent of the Ph.D. degrees awarded annually in the United States.[7] Their libraries hold in excess of sixty million volumes and maintain more than 550,000 serial subscriptions.

Founded in 1958, the CIC is organized both horizontally and vertically. Its board of directors is composed of the chief academic officers of the member institutions, appointed by the presidents (who themselves meet twice annually). Over the years, nearly every academic and administrative unit within each of the twelve institutions has been involved in CIC programs, participated in cooperative groups and panels, or enjoyed other benefits of collegiality across the region. Cooperative ventures at all levels have arisen from these interactions, giving the CIC a four-decade history of effective voluntary interinstitutional cooperation among these large and well-funded universities. Ranging from no-cost student and faculty exchanges to multimillion dollar R & D projects, in areas from international agriculture to student aid, the programs of the CIC offer a clear demonstration that these institutions have developed mechanisms that enable them to accomplish collectively far more than they could ever achieve acting on their own.

The CIC has been governed by three founding principles:

1. No single institution can or should attempt to be all things to all people.

2. Interinstitutional cooperation permits progressive educational and experimental programs on a scale beyond the capability of any single institution acting alone.

3. Voluntary cooperation fosters effective, concerted action while preserving institutional autonomy and diversity.

The beginnings of what, ultimately, became the CIC Center for Library Initiatives can be traced back to 1992, when the members of the CIC called for an overall unifying strategy to address the many crises facing academic libraries: escalating costs for research materials, pressing needs for the application of new information technologies, space shortages, and budget constraints. In a conference of provosts and library directors that year, it was agreed that the libraries would collaborate in a strategic planning process to provide a framework for understanding and addressing these many issues. The essence of that plan called for greatly expanding levels of interdependence.

By the beginning of the twenty-first century, the CIC libraries will have a cohesive consortial organization guided by a vision of the information resources in the CIC as a seamless whole, whether those resources are developed or owned individually or collectively. Through shared planning and action, the libraries and their patrons will have equal access to the total information resources of the CIC. In addition, the libraries will provide the students, faculties, and staffs of the CIC universities with access to comprehensive resources throughout the world. Through collective leadership and cooperative action, each CIC library will realize extensive value-added services for its clienteles. The CIC libraries will be in the forefront of efforts to preserve, expand, and access both electronic information resources and traditional collections.

After adopting this strategic plan (which can be found in its entirety on the CIC's home page [8]), the presidents, chancellors, and provosts made a joint commitment to implementing the plan by creating the CIC Center for Library Initiatives, which opened in 1994. It is important to note that although all member universities support central office costs, each institution determines how—and to what extent—it will participate in any given project. Such flexibility allows participating institutions to contribute to those projects in which they have a particular interest, while choosing a lesser role in other activities. All universities contribute to the work of the CIC in selected ways, and all benefit from the whole of the activities undertaken.

Together, the CIC libraries are working to establish the definitive research library for tomorrow. This future cannot be defined with great confidence, but it seems clear that the foundation will lie in networked access to, and collaborative development of, vast stores of electronic information; deep levels of collaborative collection management of both traditional and networked resources; and shared decision making to achieve cost-effective and balanced growth through strategic planning. In short, this future will engage our universities in interdependent relationships increasingly driven by new technologies but all founded upon a shared commitment to meeting faculty and student research needs.

## Collaboration with Nonlibrary Partners

Because the CIC is organized as a consortium of *institutions* (as opposed to a consortium of *libraries*), there are ample opportunities for academic libraries to work with other key academic groups, such as the directors of campus computing centers, the university press directors, and other faculty and administrative units. Such interorganizational and interdisciplinary collaboration is manifest in several innovative projects. Preliminary meetings have taken place between the university librarians and the chief information officers to delineate challenges to providing desktop access to digital information. Actually, the needs of the CIC libraries underscore a number of projects that will be adopted by the chief information officers. For instance, the libraries have defined security and network bandwidth needs which are now at the heart of planning efforts aimed to bolster the telecommunications systems shared by the member universities. Other collaborative approaches would include independent budgeting strategies to augment local networks; shared public-service or "help desk" functions for users needing remote assistance in the use of electronic information resources; and joint development of the telecommunications and security infrastructure linking the CIC's local networks for desktop delivery of remote electronic resources.

Members of a CIC university press and university library planning group are exploring the potential for the development of a long-term collaborative program of electronic scholarly publishing. Such collaboration would minimize the investment and risk for each campus, while drawing on the expertise available across the consortium. In this area, the libraries have a salient new role in helping to formulate prospective economic models for the electronic production and dissemination of scholarly research. Many areas will be addressed through such pilots, including editorial content; technical, business, and marketing plans; and intellectual property rights. The proposed initiative points toward an important potential alliance between publisher and library, and could provide a test bed for the university community to facilitate scholarly communication.

The libraries are also assisting in the development of the CIC Learning Technologies Initiative to enable faculty to make better use of electronic communications, videoconferencing, computer networks, multimedia software, and other interactive learning technologies in the classroom. Faculty, technologists, university administrators, and librarians are all engaged in this effort, and emerging projects include active library roles in the delivery of information resources.

Similar partnerships among faculty, computing center staff, and librarians are emerging on each campus, strengthening the commitment to develop CIC cooperative models originating from both local and regional initiatives. Together, such boundary-spanning activities provide a range of opportunities for wide-scale experimentation. Each CIC member university draws on its own strengths, together with the human and material resources from the consortium, to build programs responsive to the changing climate in higher education.

## The CIC Virtual Electronic Library: Unifying Strategy for Collaborative Action

The Virtual Electronic Library (VEL)—a project supported by the U.S. Department of Education through a $1.2 million Title II-A grant—aims to allow any student, faculty, or staff member of the CIC universities to check out a book, print a digital file, listen to a sound recording, view a video, or access and use any of the myriad information resources owned or licensed by the CIC universities. By late 1997, Phase I of the VEL will be complete, including deployment of a state-of-the-art HTTP/Z39.50 gateway (OCLC's *WebZ*) in the thirteen CIC university OPACs, with concomitant patron request functions. This gateway will provide a single, customizable, graphical user interface enabling the patron to search simultaneously all consortium OPACs, to access locally mounted databases, and to place interlibrary loan requests.

The next phase of the VEL will build upon work now under way within the CIC libraries, collectively and individually, to provide access to digital information systems. Pulling together these disparate resources into the VEL environment will probably take some years. As digital resources increase in depth and breadth, CIC libraries will be challenged to provide reliable, easy-to-use access to this world of information. It will be important to design seamless access systems that not only extend traditional models of information access but also take advantage of new technologies to maximize the potential of digital information. Moreover, the access systems must interface with legacy systems, such as the vast array of bibliographic databases developed many years ago.

For any successful transition to the digital future, the CIC libraries must partner with computer scientists and engineers, as well as with campus computing facilities. Boundary spanning partnerships are essential to ensure the most effective and efficient means of providing the seamless access, bandwidth, storage, and security systems necessary for building and maintaining digital information systems. The VEL is the doorway to the vast resources of the CIC universities—whether those resources are print or digital—and is the umbrella under which the collaborative work of the CIC libraries takes place.

## Management of Traditional Collections

Although the CIC libraries have engaged in informal or ad hoc coordinated collection development efforts for years, especially in the purchase of large microform sets or very expensive individual items, each institution has retained its own specific print collection profile. Since 1994, however, the effort to create a VEL across the CIC has focused on a new plan for greater electronic leveraging of the vast print collection resources of member institutions.

This plan—developed in response to a request from CIC library directors for more systematic coordinated collection development within the CIC—proposes to move the member libraries inductively from a few carefully selected pilot projects to a more gradual and comprehensive program of coordinated collection development.[9] Pilot projects build upon existing relationships and enable the CIC to test and stretch the limits of cooperation while planning for models that could encompass ever-larger segments of the collective information resources.

A number of projects are now emerging. The music librarians are mounting a subject resources page on the CIC Web site. The pharmacy librarians have completed a project to identify foreign drug compendia held across the consortium and have established a cooperative policy for collective reference use of these resources. Participants in the linguistics pilot have gathered data about collection strengths, serial holdings, and expensive resources as a means of coordinating acquisitions, avoiding unnecessary duplication, improving reference services, and realizing cost savings. The geology librarians have established an e-mail list and are investigating the possibility of negotiating a CIC-wide license to a key geographic information database. Finally, the South Asia Working Group reports progress in many areas, notably in the establishment of the Urdu Research Library Consortium—including both CIC and non-CIC research libraries—to purchase and make accessible one of the world's finest collections of Urdu publications. In perhaps the boldest step, the Universities of Minnesota and Michigan are experimenting with the sharing of a South Asian area studies bibliographer.

Effective staff communication, often depending on personal encounters, is an essential ingredient for any kind of collaboration within and across institutions. The collection development officers (CDOs) set out to build a sense of common purpose early in the process of writing their 1994 plan for collaborative collection management through a series of face-to-face planning sessions, first to articulate a set of mission statements, then to hold meetings of peer bibliographers in six pilot areas. These meetings were important in engendering a sense of interinstitutional community. Follow-up plans and communications have been arranged through CIC private e-mail lists, conference calls, and peer meetings at national conferences. It is clear from these early efforts that cooperative collection management becomes more effective when it is managed on two levels with all of the staffs feeling that they are working with a peer group within the consortium at the same time that they are focusing on locally defined goals and objectives. A personal foundation is difficult to establish in a "virtual" environment, so careful attention must be given to establishing the right combination of face-to-face versus "virtual" encounters. In CIC's experience, face-to-face meetings seem most productive once a set of common objectives has been established through e-mail and telephone discussions within a given group.

An ongoing concern in this process of building collaborative arrangements has been the difficulty some staff have had at each library in thinking globally rather than locally. Selectors may be uncomfortable telling faculty that their library does not acquire material in a certain area because another CIC library does. Only when the library user sees that the materials are actually available on a timely basis will this general concern be overcome. Thus, patron-initiated request systems, consortium bibliographic controls, and daily courier service among the main campuses—all integral to an effective program of cooperative collection management—are being developed in the CIC virtual electronic library.

Although these programs offer a good start to a very daunting prospect—that of building a single, unified research collection for twelve universities—there is much work to be done with an urgent need for greater collaborative management of journals. Research has shown that even within an environment of cooperation, CIC libraries tend to cut the same journal titles, thereby decreasing the overall mix of available titles.[10] Through a coordinated effort—including shared serial records and cancellation data—the CIC libraries could, conceivably, ensure that the number of available titles remains very high, whereas duplicate subscriptions decrease. The CIC has begun to explore emerging technologies capable of linking disparate serials management systems to this problem, but no clear approach has been identified. This will require additional research and attention, and no doubt evolve only as a collaborative effort between serials librarians, CDOs, and automation staffs.

New ways of presenting the cooperative collection management model to each campus are also necessary. In part, CIC addresses this need through information releases targeted first at library staff, then at other groups on campus. Such communication is but one tool to build awareness, acceptance, and enthusiasm about the collaborative work of the CIC libraries. However, it will require time for the acceptance of this new service model, which represents a significant departure from the traditional model of institutional self-sufficiency (even though that was never fully realized). Moreover, a library staff must feel that both the library administration and university administration will support them and recognize this fundamental shift.

The area in which cooperative collection management has been most readily adopted within the CIC is in electronic resources, where there is no established culture surrounding such resources and a clear need for collaboration to both handle cost and share expertise. Moreover, consortium-networked applications provide broader access to electronic resources than could ever be realized with print-based materials—as long as licenses allow for such resource sharing.

## Licensing and Acquisition of Electronic Resources

Coordinated by the Task Force on the CIC Electronic Collection, collaborative acquisition of electronic resources has advanced at a brisk pace, with a policy now in place.[11] To facilitate the decision-making process, each CIC library has designated an electronic resources officer (ERO) to oversee the local response to any potential collaborative acquisition. In most cases, the CDO serves in this capacity, although in some instances the head of a digital library serves as the ERO. Negotiations are initiated in one of three ways: (1) from acquisitions already planned on an individual campus, (2) from discussions among subject specialists or other peer groups, or (3) through recommendations by the Task Force on the CIC Electronic Collection. Proposals are developed by the group or individual supporting the activity, then peers on other campuses are contacted to determine the level of interest for each particular resource under consideration. Specific recommendations following discussion of a proposal, once agreed upon, are forwarded to the EROs for consideration. The EROs coordinate local decision making with systems staff, budgeting offices, acquisitions, technical services, library administrators, and other key stakeholders on each campus. The final proposal, including a list of interested participants, is then forwarded to the CIC Center for Library Initiatives, and the center initiates the negotiation process with the vendor.

The existence of a central office for the consortium offers a distinct advantage to both vendors and member libraries. Several models for selecting and acquiring resources have emerged. In one case, the CIC—working with the University of Wisconsin-Madison (the host-server site)—negotiated with Beilstein to license the Crossfire database for the entire CIC membership. In another case, the University of Michigan collaborated with the American Mathematical Society to make the AMS MathSci back files and current data available through the University of Michigan online catalog for other CIC universities. In yet another case, the CIC coordinated an agreement between Encyclopedia Britannica and seven CIC libraries for access to Britannica Online. Through these and many other acquisitions, members have realized total cost savings (or cost avoidance) on subscription prices alone of nearly $1 million since 1994.[12] However, to support such acquisitions on a large scale, there must be a common set of understandings and expectations about licensing and contractual language in order to expedite the approval of these purchases and ensure that rights and protections under U.S. copyright law are properly asserted. The central office addresses these issues.

## Development and Management of Electronic Resources

The CIC is aggressively pursuing the creation of original digital resources (material uniquely held by a CIC library) and is also pursuing the development of projects intended to support the collaborative management of Internet and other nonunique digital resources. The Task Force on the CIC Electronic Collection aims to develop a planning framework that incorporates not just collections but also the necessary infrastructure and institutional support. This course of action will: (1) draw upon complementary expertises of libraries and information technology organizations on CIC campuses; (2) leverage existing institutional strengths; and (3) exploit opportunities for partnership with vendors, authors, and publishers of electronic and digital resources. Ultimately, all types of information structures (visual image, text, text image, audio, encoded text, multimedia, and spatial and numeric data) will be delivered across the CIC in a networked environment. Several pilot projects are leading the way toward this future.

One such project is the development of a CIC collection of electronic texts in the humanities. This digital collection will pull together disparate humanities e-text resources into a cohesive collection; give CIC faculty and staff experience in using such resources; and establish an identifiable "CIC collection" of humanities e-texts. An exciting opportunity is being explored that will link several CIC e-text production centers, enabling scholars and librarians to contribute new resources to the collection.

Another pilot project is the prototype CIC Electronic Journals Collection. The prototype system is available on the Web and is intended to serve as the foundation for a large-scale, fully managed collection.[13] The prototype includes some fifty electronic journals, with current bibliographic records, Web interface, and complete archival collections. The anticipated cost and labor savings by providing this service centrally—rather than duplicating the process of acquiring, cataloging, archiving, and maintaining such a collection at several libraries—is undoubtedly substantial. Although the prototype system may undergo restructurings, it is clear that the CIC libraries will stay on a collaborative track in managing their electronic journals.

## Preservation

The research library traditionally has accepted the role of steward to a large body of printed materials. This stewardship, by any definition, includes the retention of at least one copy of all materials acquired, with such retention necessarily including the conservation and preservation of these materials in order to meet the needs of the scholarly research community in perpetuity. Librarians are familiar with the race to preserve materials printed on acidic paper that is literally self-destructing. Even as librarians seek ways to protect and preserve these increasingly delicate print collections, preservationists are under great pressure to use their scarce resources and talents in the burgeoning area of electronic information resources.

In response to traditional preservation needs, the CIC is engaged in a series of multiyear preservation microfilming projects. Nine member libraries are participating in the current project, which involves microfilming some 8,743 volumes and conserving 699 other valuable volumes. Together, the materials preserved through this project represent carefully selected sources across the consortium of the essential ideas and expressions in a wide range of subject areas, including American fiction, German literature, Africana, and religion.

CIC preservation officers are also struggling with issues associated with the preservation of digital information. If a library saves files on floppy discs, for instance, what happens to those files when such discs are obsolete? Are computer discs of all types the "acid paper of the twentieth century"? How do you preserve the "experience" of interacting on the Internet today? Research and experimentation along such lines might best be accomplished in a collaborative environment, because digital information sources by their very nature are more easily "shared" than physical objects. The CIC library directors have appointed a CIC Task Force on Preservation and Digital Technology to foster intelligent, timely, and efficient consortium use of digital technology in preserving both print and electronic collections, as well as to increase access to them.[14]

## Lessons Learned
### Challenges
Copyright and licensing of electronic materials are of grave concern to librarians and should be to the academic community at large. Proponents of far-reaching changes to copyright law have suggested that special restrictions be placed on electronic resources; that there should be no such thing as "fair use" within the electronic environment; and that digital information should be made available through a cost-per-use model. If realized, such a restrictive approach to ownership and distribution of digital information would profoundly undermine CIC's ability to collect and share electronic resources, especially in a networked environment designed to serve the academic community. On a broader level, such restrictions would hinder the public-service mission of the university to provide information services to state residents and to society at large.

Another challenge before us involves distance learning. The CIC libraries must support all kinds of educational programs, including multicampus, remote-site, and other kinds of nontraditional programs that require regional networked access. How can libraries collaboratively develop "electronic reserve" services to support distance learning? Clearly, faculty and staff must be educated about certain limitations to such resource sharing under existing law, and libraries must endeavor to deal equitably with students, faculty, and publishers. Individual efforts on CIC campuses, now under way, may coalesce into models for collaborative action.

CIC members must also juggle their participation in many consortia (regional, statewide, national) when making local decisions on the collaborative acquisition of resources. OCLC and RLIN (as well as many commercial vendors) offer an abundance of electronic products for either document delivery or online access and downloading, as well as a growing number of full-text files. CIC libraries also belong to some of the strongest regional library consortia in the country, such as ILLINET and OhioLINK. Each library must coordinate local, CIC-wide, regional, and national acquisitions and services across these levels. This is a largely uncharted area that will require further exploration and experience before patterns of an efficient and effective decision-making process emerge.

It is arduous to change established cultures—even when the old culture was not successful in meeting known needs. Such cultural change in the library context involves reshaping ownership-versus-access patterns by reeducating faculty and users to the benefits of greater resource sharing, and by demonstrating the timely delivery of resources through either enhanced electronic document delivery or use of a rapid courier service. Faculty and research staff must be afforded on-site access to the rich collections held by the consortium partners as well. There is slow—but unmistakable—progress in shifting away from all old paradigms associated with print-based collection development.

Another outmoded paradigm is the print-based standard of the ARL's collection statistics. Until this traditional standard is reformulated to take into account other resources—especially in electronic formats—as well as new access services, and until it recognizes new parameters to evaluate the quality of collections, the old reliance on sheer numbers will continue to impede the necessary goals of cooperative collection development.

In the long run, CIC libraries will be constantly evaluating goals and programs with particular regard for a decision-making infrastructure that supports collaborative action without placing undue pressures on already overburdened staff. Pilot acquisitions programs have built a sound foundation of human networks, but taking the next steps toward full-fledged, as well as institutionalized, interdependence is a more difficult challenge.

## Opportunities
CIC experience suggests that other consortia have significant opportunities:

• to enhance service to the user;

• to leverage investments;

• to manage change proactively;

• to become a more integral part of intra- and interuniversity decision making;

• to experience professional development on a personal and organizational level.

To meet such opportunities, consortia might find it especially useful to focus on the following action-steps:

(1) Negotiate consortial agreements for collaborative acquisition of commercially licensed databases, access networks, and document delivery services.

(2) Establish interdependent collection development and preservation policies and activities based on models of cost-effectiveness.

(3) Build interdisciplinary partnerships, locally and regionally, for the creation of digital information resources.

Other consortia might also consider adopting the following core principles and values that the CIC has come to recognize:

• Every partner must perceive some real-world benefit from cooperation.

• A central administration for consortial programs is a visible symbol of interinstitutional commitment, vision, and action, and an important feature in a successful cooperative venture.

• The main focus is on enhanced access to, and delivery of, the right information to users.

• All cooperative collection management programs must operate within copyright law and licensing provisions, while forcefully asserting established rights and working to expand such law in the area of "electronic reserves" material.

• Each program must allow for varying levels of participation by different partners, at least for discrete projects.

• Parity among partners—a "trusted peer" relationship—is essential.

• There must be accountability to university administration.

• Communication—between the consortium office, member libraries, computing centers, campus administrations, and the faculty—

is critical to the success of endeavors for academic institutions as a whole.

• Face-to-face interaction is a necessary and vital counterpart to virtual communication in establishing and maintaining human networks.

• Cooperative ventures existing apart from a given consortium—on state, local, and regional levels—will have a continuing and probably complicating role in the local planning for members of the consortium.

• The consortium must provide a framework within which members can achieve both local and collaborative goals and objectives.

• The overall mission of any academic library consortium must be to provide better (faster, easier) access to more information resources for the faculty, staff, and students of its members.

## Conclusions

The pace of cooperation among university libraries began to quicken around 1990 when research libraries in the United States found themselves confronting an unprecedented array of problems, including rising user demands, escalating numbers of publications, and skyrocketing prices. At the same time, new and emerging technological advances had begun to change the scholarly and scientific landscape. Although their libraries were under great stress, the CIC librarians saw new opportunities to provide, through cooperative action, better service and greater access to information for the students and scholars they serve, while sharing the costs and work associated with these improvements.

The successful projects implemented by the libraries of the CIC universities are evidence that collaboration can be an effective tool in meeting and enhancing service needs, even—or particularly—during a time of great pressures. When the members of a consortium have embraced the concept of a single, comprehensive, distributed library based on interlocking collections across the member universities (as opposed to the traditional model of many autonomous libraries), the resources of the collective can be successfully opened up to the entire user population. Creative and flexible budgeting strategies in this environment allow members to tailor purchases in areas specific to the research domains of their universities while foregoing purchases outside those local domains. At the same time, budgetary restraints will further structure acquisitions along a continuum between ownership and access decision models. Licenses drawn for access by the entire consortium, rather than on a case-by-case basis, will be more cost-effective. In this vision, librarians collaborate with campus computing staffs and with university administrators to make strategic plans for networking electronic information across the academic institution. Clearly, pooling resources is a competitive advantage for research library services in the new millennium.

## NOTES

1. Anthony Cummings et al., *University Libraries and Scholarly Communication: A Study Prepared for the Andrew W. Mellon Foundation* (Washington, D.C.: ARL, 1992).

2. Eli M. Noam, "Electronics and the Dim Future of the University," *Science* 270 (Oct. 1995): 247–49.

3. Peter Schmidt, "More States Tie Spending on Colleges to Meeting Specific Goals," *Chronicle of Higher Education* 43 (May 1996): A23.

4. David W. Breneman, "Public Colleges Face Sweeping, Painful Changes," *Chronicle of Higher Education* 42 (Sept. 1995): B1.

5. The institutional membership of CIC includes the University of Chicago, the University of Illinois, Indiana University, the University of Iowa, the University of Michigan, Michigan State University, the University of Minnesota, Northwestern University, Ohio State University, Pennsylvania State University, Purdue University, and the University of Wisconsin-Madison.

6. FY93 R&D spending in science and engineering at CIC universities totaled $2.835 billion, of which $1.587 billion came from federal sources.

7. In 1993–94, CIC universities awarded 66,715 bachelor's degrees, 25,687 master's degrees, and 6,655 Ph.D. degrees.

8. The CIC home page is at: http://www2.cic.net/cic/ [July 20, 1997].

9. *CIC CDO Cooperative Collection Project: Report to the CIC Library Directors* is available at: http://www.cic.net/cdo.html/ [July 20, 1997].

10. Tina E. Chrzastowski and Karen A. Schmidt, "Collections at Risk: Revisiting Serial Cancellations in Academic Libraries," *College and Research Libraries* 57 (July 1996): 351–64.

11. All reports of the Task Force on the CIC Electronic Collection are available at: http://www.cic.net/cic/pub.html/ [July 20, 1997].

12. A more complete description of the CIC licensing process is found in the proceedings of "Licensing Electronic Resources: State of the Evolving Art," a conference sponsored by the ARL, Dec. 8–9, 1996. A summary of the proceedings is available at: http://arl.cni.org/scomm/licensing/sum.html [July 20, 1997].

13. The CIC Electronic Journals Collection is available at: http://ejournals.cic.net [July 20, 1997].

14. Information regarding the CIC Task Force on Preservation and Digital Technology is available at: http://www.cic.net/cic/cli/imaging.html/ [July 20, 1997].

# Shaping Consensus: Structured Cooperation in the Network of Alabama Academic Libraries

*Sue O. Medina and William C. Highfill*

igher education in Alabama evolved within a framework that stresses local autonomy and individualism. Absence of a history for united statewide efforts forced leaders of academic institutions to operate in a highly politicized arena, depending more on effective lobbying with the state legislature than on academic programs or state needs to effect progress for their institutions. Few incentives encouraged them to work together as long as the Alabama legislature rewarded political acumen over state need.

In the fragmented higher education environment that characterized Alabama, academic librarians were relatively isolated. Few cooperative programs had been initiated among institutions or libraries. Use of interlibrary lending, the most traditional form for sharing resources, was minimal. Librarians from different institutions seldom met except through participation in state library association activities. There was little, if any, communication between librarians at privately supported schools and those at publicly supported institutions. No mechanism existed for discussing issues of mutual concern, much less for planning coordinated responses to issues affecting their libraries.

By the late 1970s, Alabama's low per capita income, regressive tax structure, and absence of home rule for raising local taxes had contributed to very low funding for services administered by local, regional, and state levels of government. Deficiencies in critical revenue supporting traditional government services led to discussions of such topics as the large number of academic institutions, the quality of education, unnecessary replication of academic programs, and the need for the state to utilize limited financial resources more effectively.

To respond to such issues, the state's coordinating and planning agency for higher education, the Alabama Commission on Higher Education (ACHE), invited an advisory Council of Librarians to review the status of Alabama's academic libraries. The report of its work, *Cooperative Library Resource Sharing among Universities Supporting Graduate Study in Alabama*, found that the state's libraries lagged far behind their peers elsewhere in book and serial collections, staffing, facilities, use of technology, and access to external resources.[1] The report pointedly stated that Alabama's academic libraries lacked sufficient resources to support graduate education and research. Further, it stressed that institutions offering graduate education could not continue to maintain the illusion that high-quality education could be provided within the existing paucity of library resources.

It was apparent that adequate financial resources would never be available for individual institutions to correct the deficiencies highlighted by the study. Consequently, the report recommended the establishment of a statewide network to implement ways in which the academic institutions might coordinate activities that would result in sharing library resources among all institutions. Support for this recommendation by university presidents and ACHE resulted in the creation of the Network of Alabama Academic Libraries (NAAL) in 1983. For the first time among Alabama's academic institutions, a formal organizational structure fostered cooperation.

General members of NAAL include both publicly and privately supported colleges and universities offering graduate education. Each general academic institution and ACHE name a voting representative to the network's governing body. General members are assessed an initial membership fee; there are no annual membership dues. A nonvoting cooperative membership category has been established for libraries not affiliated with educational institutions but which hold research-level resources or are state-level agencies responsible for co-ordinating library services within the state. Cooperative members do not receive network funds except as part of special projects or as reimbursement for services rendered to general members. Program funds are appropriated by the state legislature to ACHE, which serves as fiscal agent and houses the NAAL office.

## Defining the Organizational Role of NAAL

The term *role* has been used to define the part played by an actor in a performance. In social science disciplines, the term describes the be-havior of individuals who occupy positions in the social structure. The concept generally characterizes the behavior of an individual in a position or setting with reference to the expectations of others for that position or setting. Most definitions of role assume the existence of consensus regarding expectations. Divergence in expectations for individuals, however, may result in conflict because of the pressure created by incongruent or countervailing forces.

Organizational theory, unlike role theory, lacks well-defined con-cepts of role. Research on role has been concerned primarily with *intra*organizational issues, the role of the individual within the orga-nization. There is little empirical research on how an organization's role is defined; yet, the term is used frequently in an effort to describe image, goal setting, and performance of an organization vis-à-vis the other organizations in its environment. As in the case of roles of individuals, conflict can result from incongruent expectations placed on the organization.

The organizational role played by NAAL emerged from the ex-pectations of others. Responsibilities of the new network had to be carefully delineated with regard to the state's colleges and universi-ties. The initial charge grew from *Cooperative Library Resource Shar-ing*: "to establish a network through which sharing of academic li-brary resources would be coordinated to strengthen academic research and graduate study." Acceptance of this charge presupposed a change in the status quo. Responsibility for library quality had always been the exclusive domain of the individual institutions. How would the institutional representatives to NAAL define the consortium's role relative to those of the parent institutions?

Actions required for the formal establishment of NAAL, negotiation of the details of its governance and its relationships to ACHE and its several advisory councils (such as the Council of Presidents), and development of governing documents (bylaws, agreements) were exercises necessitating individual institutional change to support the goals of the new network organization.[2] Once network organizational issues had been resolved, the next impact of NAAL on the organizational identity and structure of its individual members occurred through the application of technology to library functions. Until the formation of the consortium, the majority of the academic libraries did not participate in OCLC. Network planners agreed that a machine-readable online database would be essential if NAAL were to initiate specific collaborative activities. Consequently, requisites for NAAL participation included membership in OCLC (for most members, this took place in summer 1994) and an enduring commitment to contribute current cataloging records to the OCLC database.

Acceptance of these requirements enabled all members to participate in the highly structured training program offered by the Southeastern Library Network (SOLINET), a regional OCLC broker; over time, this greatly facilitated the cooperative efforts of NAAL. Changes introduced by online cataloging were made as painless as possible by experienced SOLINET staff. Member librarians managed the process of changing to online cataloging without precipitating radical upheaval in their libraries. Acceptance of OCLC cataloging standards also meant that NAAL did not need to negotiate agreement on standards for Alabama contributions to the online database. For NAAL, this gentle initiation into the world of library automation opened doors of opportunity for members and lowered resistance to the introduction of technology for other library functions. It also demonstrated that member institutions would change their practices to ensure participation in, and commitment to, a statewide program.

The first project initiated by NAAL, creating a statewide online database for the holdings of all members, did not infringe markedly upon organizational responsibilities of individual members. Network funds were awarded to institutions to support retrospective conversion of bibliographic records for circulating monographs. Librarians in each institution planned their retrospective conversion project to fit existing workloads and patterns. Although the resultant machine-readable database advanced NAAL's goals, it also contributed to each library's efforts toward automation. Thus, members recognized that a mandate of an external organization did not necessarily conflict with the needs or priorities of local institutions but, rather, facilitated meeting those needs and priorities.

The significance of the retrospective conversion project lay not only in converting cataloging records into machine-readable format but also in the substantial commitment demonstrated by member institutions to the success of the network. Because state funding was not sufficient to permit completion of the machine-readable database within the five years considered essential for the inception of additional cooperative projects, each institution redirected a portion of its own funds to meet this deadline. These were institutional funds new to the library, not taken from other library programs. Once again, the members demonstrated a willingness to modify their individual programs to meet goals established for the statewide program.

Retrospective conversion was accorded highest priority for NAAL because the statewide online database would form the foundation for future cooperation. Successful completion of this project, the first NAAL effort requiring organizational cooperation, did not necessarily guarantee the success of other endeavors. It did, however, provide a touchstone that augured well for future prospects.

NAAL representatives knew that the retrospective conversion project had a finite completion schedule. At the end of that time, other cooperative programs had to be in place if the network were to continue forging its role as a cohesive agent. These had the potential of creating conflict between statewide goals and those of an individual institution. Areas of conflict could emerge from efforts to identify particularly weak collections, reduce unnecessary duplication among collections, and share library materials statewide.

## Achieving Behaviors Contributing to Cooperation

Traditionally, librarians have been rewarded for their contributions to the institution in which they are employed. In academia, promotion and tenure recognize an individual's contributions toward meeting university goals. Participation in NAAL, however, required support of the goals of an external organization. Moreover, these might appear at times to conflict with university goals.

After the creation of the statewide database (forecast for completion by 1990), NAAL ranked cooperative collection development and the physical sharing of materials as its major emphases. NAAL representatives began discussing the implementation of a cooperative collection development program, even though they knew several years might transpire before such activities were actually begun. Librarians would be required to forego the traditional focus on a single collection housed in one place and embrace a newer construct of statewide resources accessible to any student, faculty member, or researcher, regardless of the location of the user or the material. Concepts from organizational theory were used to effect change in the behaviors of the NAAL participants. Instances of their use are described below.

The first representatives to NAAL came from different levels in the academic hierarchy: university presidents, academic deans, a vice president for financial affairs, and librarians. These individuals had little experience working in groups in which membership was so diverse. This composition, the upper-level administrative responsibilities of a number of the representatives, and the size of NAAL made frequent or lengthy meetings difficult. Still, as the network program evolved, members needed to develop and support local institutional policies or procedures that would contribute to the statewide purposes of NAAL. Voting representatives would have to make informed decisions, yet meetings of the plenary body did not allow enough time to address complex issues and relationships underpinning each action. Two strategies were adopted to manage this problem: an annual planning retreat for NAAL representatives, and the appointment of standing committees to formulate recommendations considered for adoption.

### Annual Planning Retreat

Because NAAL members were dispersed over a large geographical area, representatives had few opportunities to work together. Among Alabama academic institutions, rivalries for financial resources, students, faculty, and institutional recognition, including intense athletic competition, were legendary and long-standing. These adversarial stances, though not actually menacing, had to be confronted in order for NAAL to achieve a common vision and coordinate shared action. A desired outcome in establishing NAAL was the development of a unity of purpose to support actions necessary to accomplish behavioral changes. To achieve this unity, individual representatives to the consortium had to learn to recognize the abilities of other members to contribute meaningfully to efforts of the group, to trust others to behave ethically, and to rely on the commitment of their colleagues to meet obligations made to NAAL.

An important organizational development tool in changing role perceptions and individual behaviors is an activity commonly called a retreat. NAAL adopted this tool to ensure that every representative would participate in formulating network policies and programs. Careful preparation of the agenda and format for the annual retreat has promoted the cohesiveness essential for an effective organization. From the initial retreat in April 1988, the agenda has been designed to build a sense of common intent, to assess the network's efforts to meet its purpose, and to explore new approaches for statewide cooperation.

The retreat is held at a Gulf of Mexico resort that offers the advantages of pleasant weather and off-season rates along with adequate meeting facilities and support services. Because the site is some distance from any participant's library, workaday distractions are minimized. The retreat and related social activities encourage positive interpersonal relationships necessary for effective collaboration. For new representatives, it affords a comfortable introduction to the group.

Most agenda items derive from the work of NAAL standing committees. Status reports for the various programs are reviewed, and recommendations for continuing projects or proposals for new activities are explored. Representatives are encouraged to contribute ideas about programs and to suggest new ideas. Possible solutions are discussed thoroughly. If additional research is needed, appropriate committees are asked to continue working on the topic under review. Time set aside for small groups allows participants to continue to examine those topics that especially engage their interest.

By design, votes are not taken during the retreat; those occur later at the annual business meeting. Absence of formal action encourages spirited discussion and stimulates consideration of various scenarios. Alternatives may sometimes appear impractical but frequently provide a basis for new solutions. Because no formal votes are taken, adversarial debate does not occur. No one needs to persuade others to support a particular position. All ideas are received without judgment, opening the way for hidden, but strongly held, positions to surface and allowing modification and judicious compromise, if needed. Representatives are informed about issues underlying a recommendation before they are asked to vote on implementation.

Retreats typically offer individuals an environment in which to respond to change. For NAAL, this meeting is also the source of change. It promotes a unifying and cooperative spirit for contemplation of issues on the basis of statewide need and solutions. Possible points of conflict between a given institutional priority and a NAAL program can be analyzed before the program is pursued formally for adoption. Informal, but structured, engagement of representatives in conceptualizing and crafting the consortium program helps minimize conflict as change occurs.

### Standing Committees

NAAL established standing committees to explore issues and prepare recommendations for consideration and approval. The work of the Collection Development Committee served as the model for other standing committees, such as those for resource sharing and electronic access. Membership of the Collection Development Committee was drawn from institutional representatives and librarians with expertise in collection management. It was charged with identifying or creating an appropriate model for statewide coordinated collection development. Committee members knew that several years could be allowed for this program to emerge; consequently, early meetings were given to philosophical reflections about the nature of Alabama's libraries and the need for support for graduate education and research, especially as these related to the state's economic development. The committee also identified emerging cooperative collection development projects throughout the nation and evaluated their utility for application in Alabama.

The Collection Development Committee set a high standard. Its deliberations were marked by discussion supported by research and logic, a focus on statewide issues and needs, and an absence of parochial agendas. This professionalism was demonstrated by the network's success in changing from a highly politicized model which had not rewarded cooperation to one that stressed collaboration. Availability of network staff to record and distribute detailed minutes helped ensure that members (all volunteers with full-time positions in their own libraries) could use meeting time productively.

As the complexities of NAAL programs have increased, standing committees have spawned subcommittees to facilitate completion of their assignments. For example, a subcommittee of the Collection Development Committee focuses on the role of the network in serials coordination, especially as budget constraints force cuts in subscriptions and electronic formats become more readily available. The committee structure has proved to be an important organizational development tool in advancing NAAL.

## Building a Collaborative Model for Collection Development

A primary responsibility envisioned for NAAL was to optimize academic library resources by implementing a statewide program to eliminate or markedly reduce quantitative and qualitative collection deficiencies in resources supporting graduate education and research. At the time this responsibility was being translated into program activities, no suitable model for cooperative collection development could be found in which participants included publicly and privately supported institutions or institutions ranging in size from comprehensive universities granting doctoral degrees to a small, single graduate program school.

Concern for cooperative collection development in Alabama coincided with the emergence of the same issue nationwide. In the 1980s, librarians began to engage in extensive discussions about cooperative collection development to facilitate a new focus on sharing resources. Nationally, a plethora of workshops addressed training needs. Articles mushroomed in professional literature, often concentrating on defining this new specialty.

Collection Development Committee members worked to forge an effective statewide policy. Thorough discussions in their frequent meetings assured familiarity with the issues, problems, and benefits of alternative policy recommendations. Because the committee began working several years before funds became available for cooperative collection development, there was no pressure to rush a policy to adoption. Distribution of background papers for comment by all NAAL members along with consideration of proposed cooperative collection development policy at the annual planning retreat helped provide voting representatives with information necessary for informed analysis and later action. As a result of this unhurried pace of deliberation, areas of potential conflict could be managed. Network members, as active participants in program design, were able to adapt their institutional structure to accommodate NAAL goals and program priorities.

## Managing Conflict

The process of building a collaborative model for collection development opened several possible avenues for disagreement. Potential existed for NAAL to create or magnify conflict between statewide goals and institutional purposes, between library faculty responsible for collections and teaching faculty relying on the collection for instruction and research, and between librarians responsible for working with the NAAL program and other librarians struggling to maintain the daily institutional workload.

To ensure that dissension did not arise, NAAL worked deliberately and carefully on its collection development policy. By engaging librarians from every member institution in discussing various options, NAAL was able to explore in depth those areas where future difficulties might lie. Success in meeting the statewide goals of NAAL required library faculty and staff in all NAAL institutions to realize that they were not working in isolation, that academic institutions within the state shared a common future, and that all were buffeted by the same educational, political, and economic forces. Also, they needed to believe that the program they were helping to create would improve the quality of resources and services available to their own library's users. Only through this recognition could librarians concur on a common vision and propose collaborative means to achieve it.

One threatening source of conflict in the cooperative collection development program was the necessity of identifying deficiencies in collections. Although librarians might sense intuitively the gaps and shortcomings of their collections, it was discomforting to them to consider that NAAL would reveal these deficiencies publicly. Awareness of specific deficiencies in individual collections was critical because deficiencies anywhere within the state negatively affected the total information resources available. Although all institutions had suffered the same historical funding insufficiencies and weaknesses in individual collections had taken years to develop or resulted from hastily implemented new academic programs, any acknowledgment of deficiencies might, by inference, be viewed as a criticism of current librarians and their stewardship of resources.

## Designing a Statewide Program

Before committing funds to strengthening the aggregate of information resources by acquiring specific titles, NAAL required factual data on which to base decisions. Documentation of inadequacies in library resources was essential as justification for continued state funding through NAAL. To select an appropriate methodology for this documentation, Collection Development Committee members reviewed extant and emerging collection assessment methodologies. No single model could be adopted intact for Alabama's purposes. Eventually, NAAL utilized components of the RLG Conspectus, especially a concept of enlightened self-interest and descriptions of collection levels.[3] Of paramount importance to NAAL, though, was the value placed by RLG Conspectus methodology on the judgment of the librarian completing an assessment. By stressing that librarians in each institution would compile and review raw data and interpret the meaning and value of those data to substantiate strengths or weakness, NAAL was able to overcome objections to sharing the results of collection evaluations. Availability of funds for acquisitions to correct deficiencies also served as a powerful incentive in overcoming librarian reticence to evaluate collections and share findings.

Early deliberations focused on procedures for selecting subjects and libraries to receive NAAL funding for improving statewide information resources. Although some proposed a central decision to select as few as five subjects linked to statewide economic development initiatives, the committee agreed that the network should underwrite some collection enhancement activities at each institution. NAAL adopted the idea of "enlightened self-interest" as the basis for selecting subjects for network funding for acquisitions. This acknowledged that librarians in each institution could best identify areas needing to be strengthened. This would reinforce an essential principle of cooperation: All partners must benefit from cooperative activities.

As a consequence of the application of enlightened self-interest, each institution now identifies the academic program area, or areas, it will stress during its participation in the Cooperative Collection Development Program. Diversity among collections receiving financial support occurs without NAAL's requiring each institution to identify a unique subject. When more than one school has selected the same or a very similar program for its NAAL collection development effort, institutional plans have reflected different facets of the programs. For example, projects to enhance resources for teacher education have emphasized educational administration, learning disabilities, or early childhood education. The plans have also varied by acquiring related source materials such as American literature rather than pedagogical materials. Thus, diversity occurs without the imposition by NAAL of restrictions on selection.

The collection development program is not, however, without some selection limitations. For example, NAAL funds cannot be used for acquisitions supporting academic programs that have been approved for less than five years or supporting an area for which a new degree is planned (e.g., a Ph.D. where previously only a master's degree was offered). Approval for new programs requires institutions to furnish adequate information resources and services. Ensuring these for newly approved or proposed academic programs remains strictly an institutional responsibility.

Lack of an external mandate for choosing subjects in which to acquire materials with network funds, and the resulting freedom of choice afforded to institutions, helped build trust in network goals. By funding an institution's proposal, rather than dictating choice of a subject, NAAL underscored the value it placed on members' judgment.

In its collection development program, NAAL did conspectus-type checklists to assess member collections' strengths and weaknesses. Two problems became apparent: Few libraries assigned individuals or teams any coordinating responsibility for collection development, and few librarians felt comfortable with such responsibility. NAAL libraries had to adapt and overcome these problems.

### Adapting Member Structures to Accommodate Network Goals

NAAL's delineation of collection development activities included traditional functions such as selection, acquisition, assessment, gifts and exchange, conservation, preservation, and weeding. Further, the statewide program encompassed cooperative activities, such as creating union lists, which served as an adjunct to strengthening local collections. Recognition that each institution needed to codify its collection development functions had a major impact on the organizational structure of member libraries.

Few NAAL libraries had written collection development policies. Only one library had consolidated traditional functions into the coordination responsibility of a collection development librarian; others had vested this oversight with the director. Most had apportioned traditional responsibilities to several librarians, and some institutions relied on teaching faculty for most or all selection decisions. Formulas for allocating funds to academic departments for acquisitions frequently handicapped librarians trying to acquire materials on the basis of student needs or use, especially in emerging or multidisciplinary fields of study.

Availability of network funds for acquisitions supporting a closely coordinated and well-managed statewide program required changes within NAAL libraries. Because the Cooperative Collection Development Program followed an annual planning cycle requiring proposals for funding, end-of-year reports, and continual project management, each library had to designate a collection development librarian as its NAAL liaison.

Among the primary reasons that libraries change organizational structure are to balance workload, coordinate similar functions, improve efficiency, and upgrade services. Designating a collection development liaison addressed most of these organizational needs as well. For example, because participation in the network program increased workload, activities were reallocated to achieve balance. Similar functions, defined as part of the statewide Cooperative Collection Development Program, could be coordinated more effectively if one person had responsibility for them. One result of applying NAAL's assessment methodology was a more efficient match between acquisitions and instructional programs. Enriching individual collections by the infusion of new funding for acquisitions strengthened the quality of information available to researchers throughout the state. Ideally, changes in local library structure to accommodate the NAAL program would ultimately balance workload, coordinate similar functions, improve efficiency, and upgrade services in the local library.

## Improving Expertise and Enhancing Status

NAAL recognized the need for Alabama librarians to learn from the efforts of their colleagues engaged in cooperative efforts throughout the nation. Reports of cooperative projects, notable for experimentation with new ideas and methodologies, often do not appear in professional literature. Therefore, it was vital that Alabama librarians attend conferences and workshops in which they could engage in discussions with their peers who were striving to implement cooperative collection development programs in other consortia. To promote professional interchange, NAAL funded a small grant program, $500 per institution each year, to pay travel and registration fees for participation in out-of-state workshops. Grants could not be used to attend general library conferences but could support participation in programs such as preconferences of annual ALA meetings, Institutes on Collection Development sponsored by the Association for Library Collections and Technical Services, and North American Serials Interest Group meetings. One librarian applied the grant to enroll in library science classes on preservation and archival management. In addition, at an Alabama Library Association annual meeting, NAAL sponsored a keynote address emphasizing the growing importance of cooperation in collection development. It cosponsored a three-day conference on collections management at the University of Alabama Graduate School of Library and Information Science. NAAL also sponsored a number of training programs exclusively for its members. These reviewed collection assessment methodology and its application to further the goals of NAAL.

As NAAL librarians became familiar with cutting-edge collection development practice and theory, and, in fact, helped hone that edge, their expertise elevated their stature on their home campuses. In role theory, accumulating expertise is one of the ways in which individuals attain status, thus enhancing their roles among their peers. Two other elements combined to improve the status of liaison librarians: participation in the Cooperative Collection Development Committee, and development of grant proposals subsequently funded by NAAL.

The Cooperative Collection Development Committee drew its membership from librarians named as liaisons for the Cooperative Collection Development Program. Reading literature and discussing findings related to committee projects also contributed significantly to the skills and knowledge of the newly designated liaison librarians. The NAAL director served as staff to the committee and researched topics as requested, for example, preparing literature reviews for studies of overlap and duplication, bibliographic control and use of microform materials, and for use of periodicals to provide guidance in predicting obsolescence.[4]

The requirement for collection management information on which to base the committee's recommendations led to NAAL's first research project. To respond to the charge that statewide coordination reduces unnecessary duplication among library holdings, the committee supported an analysis of overlap by ascertaining levels of duplication among the education collections of NAAL members. The study found a high rate of uniqueness (51% of the monographic records analyzed represented items held in only one location). Also, a low rate of duplication, an average of 2.6 volumes per title, was found.[5]

One of the initial concerns leading to the creation of NAAL had been reducing the perceived, but unverified, level of duplication, and this study provided objective data to assure legislators and administrators that duplication was not, in reality, a serious problem. Participating in a major research project linked to the political issues associated with NAAL heightened the collection development librarians' understanding of the complexity surrounding a statewide cooperative venture.

Methodology of the statewide program required each member to submit an Institutional Plan for Collection Development to NAAL for funding. At first prepared annually, each plan included the findings of a collection assessment and set forth procedures for correcting deficiencies identified as a result of that assessment. Because NAAL funds were allocated as grants to the institutions, collection development librarians were often required to work with an institution's office for grants and contracts. These librarians learned new skills in writing grants and administering externally funded projects, and enjoyed a status similar to that afforded other teaching faculty who attract grant funds to the institution. NAAL's ability to award grants to colleges and universities helped reinforce its role in its evolving relationships with these institutions.

Although NAAL representatives had been concerned about the possibility of conflict with teaching faculty who were acknowledged experts in their academic fields, growth in the expertise of librarians deflected any serious problems. In time, even in those institutions in which teaching faculty had carefully protected their prerogative to select titles for the library, librarians were increasingly entrusted with those decisions.

## Influence of Technology on Future Cooperation

The ever-changing technological environment mandates modifications in NAAL's efforts to coordinate resources and share materials. Adoption of "Information Retrieval Service Definition and Protocol Specifications for Library Applications" (Z39.50) by the National Information Standards Organization in 1988 advanced the possibilities for interconnectivity among disparate systems. Principal advantages afforded by this technology are the ability to query online public-access catalogs using the sophisticated search and retrieval software of local library automated systems, to examine other locally developed databases, and to share resources in formats other than print.

After NAAL installed linking software for eight NOTIS sites, interlibrary loan librarians found that using the linked system to verify availability status (e.g., on shelf, in circulation, at bindery) and serial holdings which are maintained in greater detail on local systems than in the Alabama union list on OCLC greatly facilitated interlibrary lending. In addition, greater detail of local holdings records led to discussions of the need to promote use of linked systems for interlibrary loan and to reexamine participation in union listing through OCLC.

The ability to share electronic databases, especially those containing full text, resulted in a major revision of NAAL's collection development program. In 1996, NAAL initiated a pilot project that uses collection development funds, previously allocated to institutions for acquisitions of print resources, to license online access to a general periodicals index with full-text articles for 650 of the 1,500 journals indexed. As a result of the evaluation of the project, NAAL is developing criteria for choosing and implementing shared databases and new guidelines for cooperative collection development. These criteria will consider the need to maintain print resources even when digital versions are available. An expected outcome of this effort will be a model for making collaborative decisions for serials retention and cancellations.

Other forces having impact on NAAL are the rapid development of distance education opportunities and the requirement to assure off-campus students access to information equal to that of their on-campus peers. Formulas for funding allocations to individual institutions of higher education in Alabama, based on full-time equivalent enrollment, contribute to competition rather than cooperation in providing services. However, the ease with which students can access library catalogs and shared databases calls for a rational statewide approach to providing information services, regardless of institutional affiliation. Finally, technology has promoted changes in user behavior, and NAAL needs to respond by providing electronic messaging so that users can submit information and borrowing requests directly to remote libraries known to hold needed items as well as develop a means to deliver information to sites without traditional libraries.

The vision of a statewide virtual library challenges the traditional identity of academic institutions and raises questions about the responsibility of individual institutions for providing services supporting their students' information needs. Alabama librarians do not have to grapple alone with these questions; through NAAL, they have forged an effective mechanism for finding solutions.

## Physically Sharing Materials Statewide

A fundamental principle of NAAL is that the total academic information resources of Alabama should be available to any student, faculty member, or researcher regardless of the location of the information or the user. Although cooperative collection development added a relatively limited number of new materials to the collective holdings, the willingness and ability to share their total library resources are factors that improved the effectiveness of all members in serving their users. Cooperative collection development without efficient sharing would be of little benefit beyond the holding library.

A major test of the commitment of members to NAAL was their willingness to make the local institutional changes necessary for a strong statewide resource-sharing program. To accomplish this, members waived all fees for interlibrary loans, charging neither their own users nor those of other NAAL members. They now lend all circulating materials to other NAAL members on the same basis as they lend them to their own users. They give priority to each other in handling interlibrary loan requests. To ensure that resource sharing is effective for students, especially those at schools on the quarter system, they expedited delivery. With state and federal funds, members installed telefacsimile equipment for transmitting copied materials; established a ground-based courier service using commercial delivery services; and, as Internet connections grew, began installing ARIEL workstations. New technology enabled local automated systems to be linked into an online interactive network that users could browse remotely. This linked-systems network also made possible the sharing of electronic databases, including those offering full-text documents.[6]

Changes in traditional interlibrary loan services, especially the ability to deliver requested materials quickly, also changed procedures and volume of activity in most NAAL libraries. Interlibrary loan departments achieved increased recognition as the number of transactions grew by over 600 percent from 1985 to 1995. The departments expanded and accepted new responsibilities for coordinating document delivery, pushing their purview beyond traditional interlibrary loan.

With the expanded utilization of electronic formats, especially the addition of databases containing full-text documents, the responsibilities of the collection development, interlibrary loan, reference, and automation librarians are melding. In NAAL's experience, "specialists" in these areas expect to have a role in choosing electronic materials because that choice affects aspects of the work of each. For example, collection development librarians might choose a particular electronic product to complement gaps in the collection. Interlibrary loan librarians might choose a product to expand the range of available materials and avoid ever more costly fees and copyright royalties. Reference librarians might choose an electronic version because it offers more efficient searching strategies for users. Automation librarians might want only products that can be supported easily by existing infrastructure. None of these librarians chooses alone. Increasingly, organizational structure must accommodate the blurring of lines defining responsibilities to ensure the most effective and efficient services for library users.

## Summary
An important contribution of NAAL, as is true of any sizable consortium, is developing and sustaining a model for collaborative decision making. Libraries are increasingly interdependent. The isolation of previous decades, which encouraged unilateral decision making, has vanished. The decisions individual librarians make by adding new materials, expanding technology, choosing electronic formats, and, regrettably, cutting budgets affect all consortium partners. In this environment, building a successful model for collaborative decision

making is the single most significant contribution of the Network of Alabama Academic Libraries to its member institutions.

## NOTES

1. *Cooperative Library Resource Sharing among Universities Supporting Graduate Study in Alabama* (Montgomery, Ala.: Alabama Commission on Higher Education, 1982).

2. Sue O. Medina and William C. Highfill, "Effective Governance in a State Academic Network: The Experience of the Network of Alabama Academic Libraries," *Library Administration and Management* 6 (winter 1992): 15–20.

3. Paul Mosher, one of the architects of the RLG Conspectus and an early consultant to NAAL, noted that institutions participate in cooperative ventures for the benefits accruing for their users. Not all cooperative ventures can assure immediate tangible benefits for every participant, but institutions subscribing to a concept of enlightened self-interest recognize that cooperative ventures benefiting the group also strengthen individual members.

4. The committee's discussion of the place of microforms in the state-wide program resulted in the compilation of a union list of major microform sets held by Alabama's academic and research libraries, *Alabama's Major Microform Collections*, enlarged and revised by T. Harmon Straiton Jr. (Montgomery, Ala: Network of Alabama Academic Libraries, Alabama Commission on Higher Education, 1991), 3 volumes. Straiton maintains and updates the union list on the Auburn University Libraries home page (http://www.lib.auburn.edu). To facilitate sharing, NAAL pays to add holdings symbols to OCLC for microform set analytics when machine-readable records become available for sets held by a NAAL library. For information about this project, see Sue O. Medina, T. Harmon Straiton Jr., and Cecilia Schmitz, "Major Microform Sets: The Alabama Experience," in *Advances in Collection Development and Resource Management,* ed.Thomas W. Leonhardt (Greenwich, Conn.: JAI Pr., 1995), 79–100.

5. Fred Heath, "An Assessment of Education Holdings in Alabama Academic Libraries: A Collection Analysis Project," in *Cooperative Collection Development: Proceedings of the June 1991 ASCLA Multi-LINCS Preconference*, comp. Diane Macht Solomon (Chicago: Association of Specialized and Cooperative Library Agencies, 1992), 37–65. The literature review prepared for the Cooperative Collection Development Committee was

subsequently updated and published as Sue O. Medina, "Duplication and Overlap among Library Collections: A Chronological Review of the Literature," in *Advances in Collection Development and Resource Management*, ed. Thomas W. Leonhardt (Greenwich, Conn.: JAI Pr., 1995), 1–60.

6. The NAAL Resource Sharing Program is described in Sue O. Medina, "Improving Document Delivery in a Statewide Network," *Journal of Interlibrary Loan & Information Supply* 2, no. 3 (1992): 7–14; Sue O. Medina, "The Network of Alabama Academic Libraries: Effective Document Delivery in a Statewide Academic Library Consortium," *College & Research Libraries News* 51 (July/Aug. 1990): 640–43; Sue O. Medina and Linda Thornton, "Cannot Supply: An Examination of Interlibrary Loan Requests Which Could Not Be Filled by Members of the Network of Alabama Academic Libraries," *Journal of Interlibrary Loan, Document Delivery & Information Supply* 6, no. 4 (1996): 11–33.

# Directed Technological Change in the Florida Community College System

*Derrie B. Roark*

t has been noted throughout this book that technological change has outpaced the organizational development of academic institutions and their libraries in the 1990s. This chapter describes how leaders in community college library and learning resources (LR) centers have assisted their institutions in technological adaptations that are geared to organizational change. It focuses on the impact of two concurrent processes—statewide library automation and regional accreditation—on the restructuring of LR programs in Florida. The implications of this experience for the general role that community college libraries can play in the development of their parent institutions are summarized.

## Introduction

Hillsborough Community College (HCC), located in west central Florida, serves 45,000 students on a complex of four campuses, each having a library/LR center. With a total program staff of forty-three, thirteen are faculty or professional positions. The program includes library and media services, satellite telecommunications, support for distance education, and technology planning.

The organizational structure of the LR program at HCC is fairly unique. The chief administrator is a staff officer (not a line officer) who heads the district LR office, which oversees centralized technical, media, and computer services. However, each of the four campus library/LR centers reports directly to its dean of student services. A campus library/LR center is charged with the implementation of collegewide policy; the district administration overseeing HCC's four campuses and those of neighboring colleges is not involved in the implementation process but does set policy, procedures, and timetables.

District oversight and campus autonomy make strange bedfellows. However, as HCC has participated in the development of a district-level instructional technology plan, its LR program— the linchpin of that plan—is viewed as a model of centralized training and purchasing. In that regard, planning from above has benefited both the LR program and its academic institution. Change, which sometimes must be imposed from above, is easier to accept from below if done across the board. At the same time, HCC's general experience suggests not only that strong coordination is necessary to ensure that technological development is done expediently but also that staff input and two-way communication on problems and processes are needed to make the whole process socially acceptable.

Directed technological change can also focus a college on the relationship between the particular needs of staff, faculty, and students, on the one hand, and the organizational design of an LR program, on the other. For instance, if a goal is networked access to information, planning and budgeting may call for a certain distribution of computers collegewide. Although feelings among LR staff of not being completely in charge may lead initially to frustration, such feelings can be overridden by the benefits that centralization brings in the way of shared priorities and matched equipment allocations. Overall, three factors have shaped HCC's organizational development in the adoption of new information technologies: (1) a statewide library automation project, (2) regional accreditation criteria for instructional technology, and (3) the general structure of the college's LR program.

## Statewide Library Automation

Florida's automation of higher education was initiated in 1982 with the adoption of the NOTIS system at the university level. Automation of the community college system, however, did not begin until 1991 with the adoption of the DRA system. By 1994, all sites at the twenty-eight community colleges were connected under the organizational auspices of the College Center for Library Automation (CCLA); by mid-1996, they had completed the connections for cataloging and the next year for circulation and serials management.[1]

With the advent of the CCLA statewide system, each community college LR program has been required to participate on CCLA's advisory board, to oversee state projects, and to appoint staff to liaison positions between the institution and the CCLA central office. A liaison may serve on a general regulatory committee (e.g., hardware, technical services, circulation, or public services) or on a more specialized standing committee (e.g., bibliographic quality control, resource sharing). Because the automation project was mandated by the Florida legislature, each community college was able to achieve fairly rapid technological progress without competing (politically or fiscally) with other college priorities. CCLA provided equipment, wiring, installation, training, and support. LR centers eventually adapted staff functions to the statewide system after a review of each college's policies and procedures.

The technological development of LR centers was thus shaped by state requirements for library automation. For example, the state mandated that community colleges approve a stronger policy on borrower privacy; that the interlibrary loan policy include student privileges; that staffing patterns be reviewed for work flow efficiency and cost-effectiveness; that reciprocal borrowing privileges within the state be given priority; that all library catalog records be included in the statewide system, with quality controls; and that cooperative collection development agreements become institutionalized. With resource sharing a major component of CCLA's philosophy, it became necessary to find staff time and alternate funds to process interlibrary loan requests; local sacrifices were made by cutting some unnecessary procedures (such as covering book jackets and making print copies of item-records).

Gradually, learning resources staff and library faculty across the state have come to rely on and trust other state-trained LR staff, as well as CCLA decisions made for the state LR programs as a whole. The professional staff who participated on CCLA's advisory board thus became the core of leadership within the state's LR community. CCLA projects put those local librarians in the forefront of a relatively new technological process in Florida's system of higher education. It was inevitable, then, for some librarians to become leaders in the development of technology within their respective institutions.

## Accreditation and Institutional Effectiveness

Hillsborough Community College was reviewed in February 1996 by a team of library and education specialists to assess its progress in meeting resource and service criteria of the Southern Association of Colleges and Schools (SACS). To prepare for the visit, the library and LR program had a preliminary review, by various college committees, based on the HCC strategic plan. Technology has become an increasingly significant part of SACS's criteria to develop an institution's research and curricular programs in conjunction with library resources and services. The criteria require an institution to develop a technology plan with input from key constituencies, to conduct periodic evaluations of that plan, and to incorporate those evaluations into a broader assessment of the institution's overall strategic plan. However, the accreditation criteria do not stipulate specific performance goals for particular information technologies, nor do they amount to a "cookbook" approach to organizational restructuring. Rather, the criteria call in a general fashion for the articulation, implementation, and evaluation of certain "principles of institutional effectiveness." Following are examples of this loose-in-principle, tight-in-local-application character of the criteria:

Institutions should supplement their traditional library with access to electronic information. Where appropriate, institutions should use technology to expand access to information for users at remote sites, such as extension centers, branch campuses, laboratories, clinical sites, or students' homes. The institution *must* provide evidence that it is incorporating technological advances into its library and other LR operations.

Although the diversity of educational programs and goals will be a major determining factor in the selection of information technology resources by an institution, there *must* be a reasonable infusion of information technology into the curricula so that students exit with the fundamental knowledge and basic ability to use these resources in everyday life and in future occupations. Institutions *must* provide the means by which students may acquire basic competencies in the use of computers and related information technology resources. A reliable data network should be available so that students, faculty, and staff may become accustomed to electronic communication and familiar with accessing national and global information resources. There *must* be provisions for ongoing training of faculty and staff members so that they may make skillful use of appropriate application software. These requirements apply to all programs wherever located or delivered.

The dual mandates of institutional effectiveness and technological advancement offer libraries and learning resources programs a salient opportunity to provide leadership for the institution at large. Because all of Florida's LR programs are now automated whereas many of its community colleges have had little or no technological development outside the library, they have had an important head start. Nearly all LR administrators, having been involved in the statewide library automation process, acquired an in-depth understanding of organizational redesign. With the CCLA office having served as a resource to community college libraries for hardware specifications, training programs, and other work flow transitions, an LR administrator tends to be viewed as having valuable and even unique experience in technology planning and development. Moreover, the SACS accreditation criteria support an LR administrator's prospective leadership role at the colleges. Even if not leading the development of an institution's technology plan, an LR program can use such criteria to enhance its own position to be the main provider of resources and services in support of the curriculum.

For example, because accreditation criteria require that students demonstrate competency in the basic use of computers, an LR program can have a main position in formal programs of information literacy and in credit courses on electronic information. Or, if not accorded faculty status, librarians can use accreditation criteria to justify library instructional programs becoming part of the academic system. (That may be a long-term goal. At HCC, for example, librarians with full faculty status have the opportunity to teach courses for academic credit, yet only one actually does so.) The essential point is that by generalizing what has worked well within libraries to assist educators and students, librarians have much to offer the larger institution in its attempts to foster social adaptation to new technology in the workplace and in the curriculum. For example, many of Florida's community colleges have placed the planning and implementation functions for instructional technology and distance learning within the institutions' respective LR programs.

## Organizational Restructuring of Learning Resources Programs

The organizational restructuring that has evolved within the HCC Learning Resources Program (as well as within each campus LR Center) has become evident during the 1990s in manifold ways. Some staff gained their first experiences in academic-level meetings and state-directed sessions; all staff use electronic communications for daily information sharing; and the training role of the HCC district office has strengthened as LR staff require new skills. Overall, a certain trust has developed between campus staffs and the district office as LR centers have become regarded by their campuses as initiators, rather than followers.

Campus LR centers have thus thrived with oversight. Although some staff still interpret it as "control," oversight enables an efficient redistribution of newly upgraded hardware to centers that demonstrate increased levels of staff expertise. Community college administrations, for their part, appreciate the accountability that CCLA imposes on the library and LR center staff because it reduces campus competition for technology-related funds, provides better library budget lines in the bureaucracy, and carries some assurance of quality control.

With the rising level of staff expertise, the college initiated a classification study of the paraprofessional employees in the LR program. That led to a restructuring of grade descriptions and specifications to strengthen the educational and experiential qualifications of entering paraprofessional staff, generally requiring more of a blend of library work and computing skills.

More important, HCC's eight reference librarians had been functioning as both members of the faculty and managers of the LR program. In order to provide the time necessary for the library faculty to develop professionally—in terms of computer expertise, library instruction, reference, collection development, and collaboration with teaching faculty—the college has created a new position of campus LRC manager to handle administrative duties.

## Summary and Observations

HCC's experience indicates a natural progression for an LR program to be called upon to initiate, or at least to participate in, the development of a collegewide strategic technology plan. Library automation has been fairly rapid and successful, occurring almost completely in the first half of the 1990s. Roles of both professional librarians and LR paraprofessionals have expanded. The regional accreditation criteria have bolstered technological development and facilitated the budgetary process on campus. Library faculty have gained valuable experience in state liaison positions and advisory boards, so it is now common for instructional technology and distance learning to be placed with LR organizations. Against this background, many of Florida's community colleges have had relatively little technological development or organizational restructuring outside the library/LR center. Accordingly, some of Florida's LR deans and directors, having taken up the challenge, are viewed on campus as change agents. They are active on the state level in initiating resource sharing, reciprocal borrowing, and cooperative collection development agreements, as well as in collaborative teaching and distance-learning projects. After all, their libraries have already been restructured to meet both statewide library automation and regional accreditation goals.

Rapid technological change is now commonplace. Organizational structures and social adaptation must keep pace. Institutions cannot thrive in the electronic era with industrial-age attitudes, policies, and procedures. As Florida's community college experience demonstrates, organizational development can be anticipated and planned as a centralized, top-down process of technological restructuring.

## NOTE

1. Paul McGinniss, Pete Tanzy, and Beatrice Smith, *Technical Feasibility of a Statewide On-line Catalog under NOTIS* (Tallahassee: Florida Instructional Resource Network, Florida Department of Education, 1988), appendix B; Jose Marie Griffiths and Lawrence W. Lannom, *Plan for Library Automation for Florida's State Community College System: 1989–1994* (Rockville, Md.: King Research, 1989); *The Path to LINCC System Implementation* (Tallahassee: College Center for Library Automation, 1992); *Library Automation of Florida's Community College System: Status Report, 1995–96* (Tallahassee: College Center for Library Automation, 1996).

# Restructuring the University of Vermont Libraries: Challenges, Opportunities, and Change

*Rebecca R. Martin*

Approaching the twenty-first century, higher education is being restructured by fairly recent shifts in strategic planning processes, professional identities and roles, and technological capabilities. Indeed, rapid and transforming—apparently never-ending—change has become a dominant paradigm for information organizations in this era.[1] Challenges and opportunities for academic libraries in this transition area include:

• an increasing emphasis on networked access to information resources, within the broader context of the emerging virtual library;

• an expanding role for library faculty and staff in teaching users how to identify, select, evaluate, and retrieve information resources relevant to their needs;

• an enhanced capacity for the library to create, organize, and disseminate select sets of electronic information (e.g., gateways to Internet resources);

• ongoing development of core collections to support university curricular programs and research needs within the constraints of publication proliferation and price inflation;

• a growing responsibility, in alliance with the computing center, to provide a network infrastructure to support academic programs;

• a continuing reassessment of services that may be strengthened or diminished according to changing user needs, or streamlined or consolidated to improve organizational productivity;

• a flexible faculty and staff, developing new skills throughout their careers.[2]

Although by no means unique, the University of Vermont (UVM) is a salient example of a library system engaged in such restructuring efforts which may be of interest to others.

## UVM: A Propensity for Change

UVM libraries have been at the forefront of technological change over the past decade. Although late to join the movement in the 1970s to the Library of Congress classification scheme, they reclassified collections while simultaneously moving all operations to a fully integrated online system in 1986.[3] Library faculty were early leaders in the introduction of computer disc technology to reference services at that time, and also in the creation of Internet gateways in the early 1990s.[4-5] Active collaboration with the university's computing and information technology division has been a critical component of these developments.

UVM is a small research institution with strong liberal arts and professional programs at the undergraduate and master's levels, an array of doctoral programs in the sciences, and a highly regarded medical school.[6] Three libraries form a system that serves a student body of approximately 10,000 students: the Bailey/Howe Library, the Dana Medical Library, and a small chemistry/physics branch library. Media services were added to the administrative responsibilities of the library director in 1987. UVM libraries have enjoyed strong financial support from the university and, although funding has been decreased over the past decade, the libraries have been protected in significant ways from universitywide budget reductions. The system has collections of more than one million volumes, employs a staff of thirty librarians and seventy paraprofessionals, and serves as the only research library for the state.

Of modest institutional size lending itself to moderate change, and with a library faculty having a record of innovative work in information retrieval, UVM libraries have been moving cautiously, yet steadily, toward new organizational models. The principles for the libraries' strategic plan, first drafted in 1993, reflect this propensity for change:

> Our organization must be dynamic, proactive, adaptable, and creative in response to our changing clientele, workforce and environment. Technology is constantly changing and is playing a larger role in collections, services and operations of the libraries. . . .[7]

Such principles and propensities for restructuring in a moderate key are described below in terms of organizational reforms, new professional roles, and planning strategies—all within a framework of seizing "windows of opportunity."

## Organizational Structures

In 1991, UVM libraries took the first step away from the traditional public services and technical services divide that has characterized academic library organizations for the twentieth century. The Bailey/Howe Library was eventually reorganized into three divisions, each with a public-service component: Information and Instruction, Collection Management Services, and Research Collections.[8] That shift had a number of designs: (1) to underscore the importance of a public-service commitment to all aspects of library work; (2) to incorporate the formerly freestanding Media Services; and (3) to enact the concept of collection management as an all-encompassing process, from the point of an item's identification for acquisition through its life on the shelf.

When these new divisions were established, a conscious decision was made by the library administration not to impose a particular set of conditions or techniques from above but, instead, to allow new approaches to evolve, depending on particular needs of the individual programs and the orientations of their respective heads. Over time, however, there has been a definite movement from hierarchical structures to more flexible patterns of management.

## Medical Library

The Dana Medical Library, a semiautonomous unit with a full range

of public and technical services, redesigned its organizational structures and functions over a period of several years, experimenting
with various methods and techniques. Drawing heavily from
trends in the health care sector, the current organization represents a melding of three approaches: matrix management, which
centers on function-based teams; total quality management
(TQM), which emphasizes user satisfaction through continuous
reappraisals of services; and the clinical–academic department
model, which places library faculty, as relatively independent individuals, in the roles of teaching, research, and service. Each of these
approaches is characterized by a reduction in hierarchy and a concomitant emphasis on collaboration.

Taken together, these approaches have reshaped not only professional and staff roles in the Dana Library but also organizational
planning methods. Library functions are arranged in a matrix of processes, with overlapping teams and coordinators assigned to each activity. Decision making and policy formulation rely heavily on user-
satisfaction and quality-improvement techniques, with a holistic systems perspective on problem solving. Dana Library faculty serve as
subject specialists and liaisons to the one or more departments in the
health profession schools and in the medical center.[9]

The planning process that led to these changes was characterized
by active involvement of all library faculty and staff at each stage. The
small size of the medical library was an important factor in this approach, for it enabled UVM libraries to try out new ideas and projects
on a limited scale. Eventually, a series of successes there generated a
sense of ownership in the process of change for the UVM system
as a whole. Although overall staffing has been reduced, new services have been created and certain traditional services have both
increased and improved. The redevelopment of services has depended on the packaging of a number of change processes: streamlining operations, restructuring organizational relationships, dis-
continuing some lesser-used services, and redesigning all programs
around TQM techniques.

## Collection Management Services

This division was created after a major organizational review and restructuring of the Bailey/Howe Library in 1993. Based on a plan by the five faculty members in the new division, six overlapping teams were created from traditional acquisitions and cataloging departments to form the Collection Services Group. This group set out to learn new technologies for materials processing, to identify interrelated processes of acquisitions and cataloging, to encourage staff development of new skills and roles, and to open up more communication channels across all functional areas in the division. Each of the teams was assigned a coordinator from the library faculty, with most staff serving on multiple teams.

Two technical-service aims overlapped nearly all teams: reducing the number of times materials are handled, and increasing the quality of acquisitions information in the online catalog. After nearly two years in operation, this restructuring process reduced cataloging backlogs by more than half and made the division more flexible for tackling other special-work projects. A steady stream of materials (at levels comparable to those handled under the previous organizational structure) is now being processed by fewer people.

## Access Services

In 1995, the interlibrary loan (ILL) office and the circulation department were reformed into a single new unit, Access Services, within the Collection Management Services Division. Those operations were combined to develop greater organizational depth and flexibility for handling an ever-increasing volume of ILL requests. For some years, library user requests for materials at geographically dispersed locations have increased 10 to 20 percent, owing largely to the steady growth of networked bibliographic databases and other electronic information resources. This unit has grown in staff size on the document delivery side. All circulation activities, ranging from student assistant duties to high-level staff assignments, have undergone a kind of cost-benefit analysis, with manual tasks being streamlined, coordinated, or automated. Such measures aim primarily at generating the internal resources necessary to develop and support a more fundamental capability of networked access and delivery services, such as patron-initiated ILL requests that would require less mediation by the library and be more convenient for the user.

## Diffusion of Innovation

Changes in the organization of the remaining divisions in the libraries—Research Collections, and Information and Instruction—have been less striking. Both continue to have hierarchical structures. Still, some diffusion of innovations from other divisions has begun to occur. In the Research Collections Division, the government documents department and the special collections department have drawn closer by practicing team-based management and experimenting with cross training and staff sharing. In the Information and Instruction Division, altlhough the old norm of independent professionals within autonomous departments prevails, the reference department has been experimenting with the faculty model of a rotating chair, as well as a more representative team approach to management.

## Professional Roles

Although organizational structures have been redeveloped, even more fundamental shifts have begun to occur in professional identities, orientations, and responsibilities. The major role of the libraries, as always, is to provide convenient, broad-ranging access to information and scholarship. However, technological changes in the nature of resources, services, and supporting library operations have actually had concomitant effects on the ways UVM has designed new professional roles.

## Reference

The focus of reference service throughout the UVM library system has increasingly become one of teaching electronic information retrieval skills and critical evaluation of identified sources. Although the libraries' on-site collections have remained essential to this endeavor, the burgeoning Internet and proliferation of new databases, especially on Web sites, have rendered the online catalog and the local materials it represents as just one of many information resources available. Library faculty thus have an ever-expanding role in teaching users how to identify, select, evaluate, and retrieve resources relevant to their needs. In addition, library faculty have increasing opportunities to team teach in interdisciplinary programs with faculty in other colleges and schools, particularly in the areas of informatics and information literacy.

An important element of this new reference paradigm has been the decision to place as many electronic resources as feasible directly in the hands of users. To that end, UVM has encouraged library faculty to make substantial professional commitments to the development of information gateways in the online catalog, on the campus network, and through remote access. Such gateways provide transparent access to scores of geographically dispersed databases, multimedia resources, full-text files and data banks, and Web tools. A certain level of systems expertise on the part of library faculty, with assigned responsibilities for the design and maintenance of gateways, has been an essential requirement for this paradigm shift. Collaboration with colleagues in campus computing has proved increasingly important to stay abreast of new network tools.

## Collection Management Services

As noted above, a central feature of the Collection Management Services Division has been to design operations in terms of the concept of continuum, a resource having a life from the initial point of its identification and acquisition—through cataloging, processing, housing, and use—to the final decision to preserve the item or remove it from the collection. This approach has streamlined operations (e.g., reducing the number of times a given item is handled). All staff involved now make decisions regarding materials and their records with this continuum in mind (rather than in response to a discrete process). Taking greater advantage of technology to expedite processes and being careful not to retain outmoded manual principles and routines in an automated environment have been twin goals.

Financial constraints, along with the need to redeploy limited staff, have stimulated such alternative approaches to collection management services. Staffing levels in this division have been reduced as the libraries' principal focus has been directed toward reference services associated with electronic resources and gateway systems. Inevitably, local collections have a somewhat peripheral, less-urgent position now than in the past. Creating more comprehensive, as well as accurate, access to materials in an online catalog environment has displaced the production of "perfect" catalog records on two levels: as a professional workaday norm, and as an organizational resource stricture on the budget. In that regard, UVM Libraries have begun to outsource the cataloging and physical processing of materials received through approval plans.

## Planning Frameworks

Restructuring UVM libraries has been an ongoing activity integrated with a broader reorganization of the academic institution as a whole. In 1992, the university president initiated a general strategic planning effort with overarching themes for academic programs.[10] The central position of the libraries was not only established then, but library programs were to be exemplars of the kind of excellence which the president's plan promoted.

In 1993, a planning team (of four library faculty and four staff) was appointed and chaired by the library director to build on the university's impetus and develop a five-year strategic plan for the libraries. The mission statement was rewritten, statements of new principles and timeless assumptions articulated, and strategic goals established. At each stage, drafts of the components of the plan were widely shared for discussion. The provost, the faculty advisory committee, and campus computing provided important reactions to early drafts. A year later, the basic document had been adopted with some action steps already taken.[11] This strategic plan (which has been updated once) has served in some areas as a fairly specific agenda for short-term goals (e.g., the development of a document delivery service) and in other areas as a rather loose framework for long-term change processes (notably, the reorganization of Collection Management Services, which had begun years before and later became an exemplar of change for the university).

Another campuswide planning effort, focused on information technology, began in 1995 with active librarian involvement. Many of the tenets of change already incorporated in the libraries' operations, principally the increasing shift to electronic information and the growing role of library faculty in teaching information literacies, were incorporated into the university's strategic plan.[12]

Decision making with regard to implementation of the strategic plans has actually taken different forms. Some restructuring of resources and services has consisted of collaborative efforts by staff members across different divisions. Examples of such broad participation include the extensive development of information gateways to electronic resources, the growing teaching role of library faculty, and the team-based management structures in collection services and in the medical library. Other decisions—usually bearing on specific work processes, reallocation of staff, and redirection of major operations—have required more administrative and budgetary direction by top administration. In that regard, the inevitable choices necessary to redistribute limited resources in order to undertake new initiatives are necessarily the responsibility of library administration. Inevitably—and despite general agreement on principles and directions—some resource and staffing decisions were resisted at first. In each case, the rationale for the decisions was fully discussed with those affected, but the role of the staff in making the ultimate choices was limited primarily to consultation.

## "Windows of Opportunity"

With planning for change being an ongoing feature of library administration at UVM all during the 1990s, various restructuring efforts have been implemented incrementally. The primary approach has been one of articulating a mission or redefining a function, focusing on problems and prospects for change, and then seizing opportunities as they arise. There is no specific blueprint nor firm timetable for reorganization. For example, the impetus for the general reorganization of the divisions of the libraries in 1991 was the resignation of the systems librarian and the retirement of the long-standing assistant director for technical services. Vacancies at all levels are viewed as opportunities to question the status quo and to redeploy resources. Other changes have been initiated by a particular need to reduce a budget line, by an urgency to offer a particular service, by the changing institutional framework to support a new information technology, by an availability of special funding in an area, or by some other "window of opportunity."

Being prepared to make decisions against a background of rapid technological changes, institutional plans, and static or declining resources has been key to achieving continuous evolutionary progress for UVM libraries throughout the decade. The importance of readiness for choice opportunities is clearly recognized in the principles of the libraries' strategic plan:

> Budgetary and other environmental constraints force us to set realistic goals and expectations, evaluate new and existing programs against our mission, assign priorities, focus our efforts, become more efficient, work cooperatively within our organization, create or find alternative approaches, and find new sources of funds. Budget constraints should not mean maintaining the status quo; we must continue to move forward and develop in new directions.[13]

Although the reality of a turbulent environment is readily acknowledged by library faculty and staff, reappraisal of traditional precepts and practices can be difficult. With individual roles and assignments in transition, certain other areas of the restructuring process—notably, organizational communication, staff development, and stress management—take on increasing importance at times.

## Overview
This case study is essentially a work in progress for a library system still undergoing fundamental change on many fronts. Although the newly developed organizational structures and professional roles have been designed to fit UVM's environment, the underlying approach to change (rather than specific developments) may well relate to other settings.

Susan A. Lee's description of cognitive complexity, in which strategic vision provides a compass but not a road map, is a relevant model for vision, flexibility, and risk taking.[14] In the context of the strategic planning process, specific short-term strategies and tactics are continually modified in response to changing opportunities and information. Uncertainty is an ever-present component of this approach to change, as it must be, but the resulting adaptability makes creativity and innovation realistic goals.

Somewhat differing organizational models within UVM's library system have allowed for varying degrees of organizational and staff readiness for change, as well as for flexibility in plans and programs. Experimentation with new approaches has been necessary—some approaches have been discarded. Organizational learning evolved as UVM modified models and techniques found in the management literature to its own environment. Evolutionary restructuring has become an ongoing activity and refining it an almost familiar process.

Although change of this order never becomes easy for those involved, the inevitable stress has come to reflect a rather healthy phenomenon, what Peter M. Senge calls "creative tension," which arises from the gap between vision and current reality.[15] Senge uses the metaphor of a rubber band stretched between those two points, with current reality being either pulled toward the vision or held back by the status quo. Whenever we attempt to restructure resources, services, or roles, current priorities and assignments form our daily reality. In keeping with Senge's metaphor of a rubber band, we should work to ensure that the creative tension moves current reality toward our vision, rather than giving sway to present pressures that would hold us back. Overall, with this process being one of evolution, it may not be possible to pinpoint where the present ends and this future begins. Still, the outlook is very promising if we can accumulate expertise as we restructure our organizations by seizing "windows of opportunity," by staying abreast of technological advances, and by strengthening our relationships with the academic institution at large.

## NOTES

1. Rosabeth Moss Kanter, Barry Stein, and Todd Jick, comps., *The Challenge of Organizational Change: How Companies Experience It and Leaders Guide It* (New York: Free Pr., 1992).

2. Libraries and Media Services, University of Vermont, *Scenario 2000* (1995).

3. Suzanne Massonneau, "Reclassification and Barcoding: A Unique Opportunity," *Collection Management* 13, nos. 1–2 (1990): 15–37.

4. Nancy L. Eaton and Nancy Crane, "Integrating Electronic Information Systems into the References Services Budget," *Reference Librarian*, no.19 (1987): 161–77.

5. Lyman Ross et al., "The Role of Academic Libraries in the Dissemination of Scholarly Information in the Electronic Environment," in *Computer Networking and Scholarly Communication in the Twenty-First Century University*, ed. Teresa M. Harrison and Timothy Stephen (Albany: State Univ. of New York Pr., 1996), 369–82.

6. The University of Vermont's Carnegie classification is Research II.

7. Libraries and Media Services, University of Vermont, *Strategic Plan* (1994), 9.

8. These divisions include: Information and Instruction: Reference, Media Resources, Chemistry/Physics Branch, and Outreach; Collection Management Services: Collection Services (acquisitions, collection development, cataloging, circulation, and interlibrary loan); Research Collections: Government Documents & Maps, Special Collections, and University Archives.

9. Julie Johnson McGowan and Elizabeth H. Dow, "Faculty Status and Academic Librarianship: Transformation to a Clinical Model," *Journal of Academic Librarianship* 21 (Sept. 1995): 345–50.

10. University of Vermont, *A Framework for Change: Final Report of the President's Commission on Critical Choices* (1993).

11. Libraries and Media Services, *Strategic Plan*.

12. University of Vermont, *Doing IT at UVM: A Strategic Plan for Information Technology at the University of Vermont* (1995).

13. Libraries and Media Services, *Strategic Plan*, 5.

14. Susan A. Lee, "Leadership: Revised and Redesigned for the Electronic Age," *Journal of Library Administration* 20, no. 2 (1994): 17–28.

15. Peter M. Senge, *The Fifth Discipline: The Art and Practice of the Learning Organization* (New York: Doubleday, 1990).

# Rethinking Public Services at Harvard College Library: A Case Study of Coordinated Decentralization

*Caroline M. Kent*

H arvard has not been immune to the enormous environmental changes that have taken place in the academic library world in recent years. Although its finances are more stable and much more generous than those of most other academic libraries, the Harvard College Library (HCL) has also had to contend with escalating materials and benefits costs; the necessity of networking and its accompanying costs; shrinking pools of available staff for new initiatives; a huge, ever-changing staff training crisis; and all of the problems accompanying a large organization's need to change its methods and staff quickly.

Finding solutions to such problems requires that different parts and levels of any organization work together effectively. In an institution that prides itself on independent action, the achievement of consensus (or even respect for majority rule) can seem almost impossible to achieve. This chapter argues that HCL's experience in restructuring its highly decentralized administrative model may be a microcosm of how academic libraries will face the problem of collaboration on a national scale.

## Harvard's Tradition of "Organized Anarchy"
Of all American academic libraries, Harvard's system is probably the best qualified to represent a model of "decentralization." Sidney Verba,

who is both a well-known political scientist and the Carl H. Pforzheimer University Professor and director of the library, often remarks that the Harvard libraries' organization resembles the Southern Confederacy of the last century. In our worst moments, however, we may more likely take after the German feudal states! Each of the faculties (e.g., medicine, law, or divinity) has its own library, and the directors of those libraries answer to the deans of their schools, not to the university library director. The university library director chairs the Harvard University Library Council, which comprises all of the directors of the libraries of the different faculties and looks for ways to coordinate the various libraries' activities. Agreements are struck, "treaties" are signed, and collaboration and parallel activities engaged in—sometimes. When cooperation is not achieved, everyone smiles politely and tries again for collaboration at another time.

In all of Harvard, the Faculty of Arts and Sciences (FAS) presents the most distinct model of "organized anarchy." FAS's largest library unit, HCL, includes the following eleven major libraries: Widener (graduate social sciences and humanities), Lamont (undergraduate social sciences and humanities), Hilles (undergraduate social sciences and humanities), Cabot (undergraduate sciences, and graduate math and statistics), Kummul (geological sciences), Fine Arts, Music, Houghton (rare books and manuscripts), Tozzer (anthropology), Littauer (political science and economics), and Harvard-Yenching (Far Eastern languages and literatures).

HCL contains a major portion of the university's libraries' holdings—seven to eight million of the almost thirteen million volumes total. Despite its size, HCL does not control all the FAS libraries: Under the direct jurisdiction of individual FAS departments, museums, and research centers are approximately forty more libraries, ranging from a single, unstaffed room of books to the Ernst Mayr Library of the Museum of Comparative Zoology with a staff of eleven and a collection of more than 250,000 pieces. These forty-some FAS libraries have tacit representation on the University Library Council by the director of HCL, but their activities, budgets, and collections are independent. It would be logical to assume that because all FAS libraries nominally report to the director of HCL, they would act in an orderly fashion. Sometimes that is the case, other times not.

## "Every Tub Stands on Its Own Bottom"

HCL's decentralization is not accidental: It is a true reflection of the organization of Harvard University as a whole. Harvard's cultural climate of independence has a way of asserting itself everywhere. Since early in the nineteenth century, one of the traditional and covering principles of Harvard has been the phrase "every tub stands on its own bottom." This means that each administrative or academic "tub" (unit) must generate its own income and is responsible for paying its own expenses (the bottom line); or, as economic historian Seymour Harris defined it: "No college is responsible for the solvency of another, nor is the university."[1] (The use of this phrase is so ubiquitous that most Harvard administrators will recognize its shortened form of "ETOB" on memos.) This culture inevitably reproduces itself as it attracts like-minded librarians, administrators, and scholars, all of whom carry on the tradition. Bureaucratic-minded administrators sometimes find Harvard's environment incredibly frustrating and are confounded by how decision making often slips away from them. Programmatic progress becomes dependent on the power of personalities, the quality of minds, and, when available, the goodwill of individuals.

At the same time, the decentralization and independence of the Harvard libraries have resulted in great richness for our users. If a department or center felt ill served by the existing organizations, or if faculty and researchers simply wanted their resources very close to hand, they could start a library and hire a librarian! The department then had to support that facility and staff financially but, traditionally, no effort was made to prevent the creation of such collections. This, of course, made for certain duplications in the collections. But Harvard's wealth rendered that a relatively slight concern except for the most expensive of titles. The result for the experienced user was easy availability of their most desired, specialized titles. This tradition continues with Widener Library still getting requests from groups of scholars for new subcollections (intellectual "boutiques") in buildings where they will be most readily available to scholars and students. So, the Sanskrit scholars and the paleographers might want their materials in restricted-access rooms, or the Celtic scholars might want their periodicals shelved in their seminar room.

Such "organized anarchy" has worked to the advantage of the user except in one salient area—library public services for the collections. Here's a true-to-life example of what a Harvard library user can experience: A senior undergraduate concentrator in history is in the midst of writing an honors thesis. The topic is interdisciplinary, so the student must use the collections of five of the Harvard libraries frequently. She must remember from which of the five she checked out the 150 books in her room because she must make sure to renew all of them on different schedules. Some libraries allow the student to call book renewals in, but Widener (which holds the major history collections) requires her to haul her 100 or so books back every month to renew them. She has to carry a different photocopy card for each library she uses, but in her case that's only five, so she does not feel too bad (she knows people who carry ten). She must remember, that if she needs reference help in the evening, Widener reference is not open after 7:00, although she can usually find someone in the undergraduate libraries to help her—provided her question is not related to Widener's collection.

HCL has traditionally had abnormally low public services staffing. In 1989, when I became head of research services in Widener—then a collection of 3.4 million volumes—there were five full-time reference librarians (a number more fit for a four-year liberal arts college library with fewer than a million volumes). Circulation staffs fared somewhat better (although Widener still has no evening or weekend supervisor on duty; students are assigned this role). And anyone who used Harvard interlibrary loan (ILL) units will attest to how slow they had once been—the result of low staffing levels and little administrative support.

Also, the various service units often had very little to do with each other. Following Harvard's tradition of independence, every circulation department had its own fine structure, loan periods, and so forth. Reference desks existed in some libraries, but not in others. Some reference departments had active research instruction programs, whereas others would not even engage in building tours. As for ILL, some libraries did it and some did not—like circulation, every library was free to develop its own charge and loan policies.

In a library where collections were valued above all other considerations, confusion for users was regarded as an acceptable situation. Even public services personnel, when faced with the threat of a lower materials budget, would often defend (albeit resentfully) the lack of expenditures in service areas. In many U.S. academic libraries, reference librarians enjoy a certain level of institutional prestige and respect; at Harvard, they traditionally have been the least-recognized group of librarians. Staff grumbled about their lack of standing and support but simultaneously enjoyed enormous freedom of action in their independent "tubs." But all of the tubs, universitywide, began to sink with the advent of shared automated systems and networking.

## Shooting Fish in a Barrel, or Sinking the Tubs

A presumption of total organizational and fiscal independence and decentralization can only work at a university when there are no development and supportive costs that the community must share. Networking and networked resources, which require collaborative efforts and payments, made Harvard's administrative model vulnerable to failure.

Ironically, the general problem that Harvard's principle of ETOB represents—how to distribute both costs and income to the individual units that incur those costs and generate that income—had inspired in the 1980s a theory of financial organization in higher education called *responsibility center budgeting* (RCB). Now, in the 1990s, Harvard had to discover how ETOB (or what had been adapted as RCB at some other academic institutions) fits into the networked environment.

RCB links immediate program management with meaningful authority over resources as a way to shift incentives for cost-effective performance down the organizational hierarchy. But when RCB is implemented at an institution, it is important to exert enough central control so that unwarranted duplication and misuse of fiscal control do not occur. If this method of budgeting is not directed carefully, "it can result in dissension, discord, distortion, dissonance, disaster and doom."[2]

"Doom" is a strong word, but being forced to share can certainly lead to "discord and dissonance" at Harvard. Responsibility center budgeting was not "implemented" at Harvard. Instead, it grew out of the institution's history and unwittingly inspired a general model adapted at other academic institutions. Certainly, there was little in Harvard's past to facilitate the kind of central support necessary for effective development of a computer network. Poorer units, which traditionally had great difficulty in supporting themselves, were forced to choose between either not automating or begging for central support, even though they knew that support would be translated into political as well as economic debt.

Some units risked sinking into debt to the institution for the sake of being networked, whereas other units remained unnetworked until very recently. Moreover, there was no effective central networking group; instead, each unit undertook the effort on its own. Academic computing (the Office of Information Technology), which had maintained the old mainframe systems and had *tried* to implement centralized networking, became an easy target for administrative takeover. As Harvard's networking situation became increasingly confusing, and as the role of the network in the university's enterprise grew in importance, "who owns the fiber" emerged as a major institutional issue: who installs, who supports and, most important, who pays.

This universitywide struggle to be networked presented fundamental problems for the libraries. Technical support was clearly needed for computing, but of the scores of libraries on campus—some with virtually no organizational infrastructure—which ones had the "right" to own the fiber or, conversely, an obligation to pay for it? Even more significant was how the fight for fiber affected the delivery of services. Implementing campus networks was extremely difficult when your fiber was "owned" by multiple administrative units. If you needed fiber pulled across a road to a library, it could take years to figure out who was financially responsible to do that. One departmental library remained unnetworked for two years: The fiber came to the wall of the library, but the fiber was "owned" by another academic department that had no interest in sharing it with the library.

Public services personnel were pulled into this struggle whenever they sought to find the right help and support arrangements for the users of the libraries, whose questions ranged from "How do I get access to HOLLIS at home?" and "Why don't you have the MLA on a network?" to "Why isn't my building networked?" Reference librarians found themselves lending their e-mail accounts to frustrated users, hooking up modems for them, and giving them advice on software purchases.

The university libraries, despite their history of decentralization, were making serious headway in learning to cooperate for the implementation of HOLLIS (the online library system). Starting in the early 1980s, the libraries had begun to develop distributed funding arrangements for its support. In that framework, very disparate libraries came to various agreements on HOLLIS's development. As time passed, the learning curve of cooperation got trickier when other databases were loaded either in the HOLLIS environment or made accessible through HOLLIS Plus, the system's networked gateway. Groups of Harvard libraries had to agree on a funding model based on use: HCL might pay 40 percent, the law school 20 percent, the Kennedy School of Government 10 percent, and so forth. Although there were times when the libraries were cranky with each other over the time it took to develop distributed funding models, the effort was succeeding. No longer was each library "tub" standing on its own bottom. The libraries were developing their cooperative framework into a model that the rest of the university would have been well served to pursue.

### "What to Do, What to Do" or, "How to Avoid Hand-Wringing"

Why did this essay start with the traditions and cultures of Harvard University as they surround its libraries? The answer lies in a basic idea, one that applies to any library embedded in a university: *When instigating change, respecting an institution's culture results in forward movement; not respecting it, in stalemate or decay.* Restructuring an organization, therefore, depends on understanding what your institutional culture and values are, and figuring out where you intend to go and how you can get there without violating revered norms. In other words, any library wanting to determine its own future must engage in some sort of formal planning with an eye on local traditions. Planning is important in any institution. For Harvard in the age of the network, it is critical that planning occur, and that the deliberation process be inclusive and widespread. All players must be engaged and invested in the results in order for the institution even to hope for cooperation. That is not a reflection on staff members' willingness to cooperate but, rather, on certain tensions between operating units which represent the independent desires and demands of their respective faculties and funding agencies.

There were actually three different planning efforts that went into redefining public services at HCL. First, an informal effort was begun with the appointment of a new associate college librarian for public services in 1988. Second, a formal, librarywide strategic planning process took place at the request of the newly appointed director of HCL in 1991. And third, a formal planning effort specifically for public services became part of a broader move toward a "gateway" library in 1993–1994.

## Beginnings of Change in Public Services
In 1988, Lawrence Dowler was appointed associate college librarian for public services (of HCL). Recognizing the increasing importance of service in the upcoming decade, he immediately sought ways to reorganize public services in Widener and throughout HCL. The changes made within Widener were structural in nature: Seven former divisions were reorganized into three large departments: Research Services, Access Services, and Government Documents and Non-Book Formats.[3] Within each of those units, internal reorganizations also took place.

Although having direct managerial control over the public services units of Widener, the associate college librarians (of HCL) have an ambiguous relationship with the outlying units. Associate college librarians oversee their respective areas throughout HCL's libraries, but individual departments in the libraries answer to the heads of those same libraries, who in turn answer to the director of HCL. Inevitably, the associate college librarians are left with an arsenal of "c" words: communicate, collaborate, cooperate, coordinate.

Such managerial ambiguity led to the formation of a new coordinating committee in the spring of 1988, the Public Services Issues Committee.[4] Although the committee did not include every HCL library, it was fairly representative. After an early agenda-setting meeting, the following concerns of the various public services units emerged: poor communication; lack of information; problems with particular service areas (reserves, ILL, security); conflicting policies; and problems with special-format materials, particularly with regard to a consistent technical approach for the delivery of technically dissimilar bibliographic databases.

By 1991—on the eve of formal, systemwide strategic planning—the committee had evolved to a point where greater numbers of people needed to be engaged. Consequently, it expanded into three new structures: the Public Services Advisory Committee, which was the services administrative advisory group to the associate college librarian for public services; the Council for Reference and Research Instruction; and the Access Services Council. This concurrent internal reworking of public services units with the changes taking place in HCL's central administration was fortuitous. Public services staff since 1988 had been rethinking their roles within the library and with their users. As no other single library group, they were ready for, and committed to, broad change.

## Strategic Planning at the Harvard College Library

In 1990, shortly after his appointment as director of HCL, Richard De Gennaro engaged the library in a formal, inclusive strategic planning process.[5] It included task forces on services, collections, intellectual access, space planning, and staff and organizational development. From their deliberations came *Commitment to Renewal: A Strategic Plan for the Harvard College Library*, in 1993.[7]

Because the reorganization of public services was already well under way when this formal planning effort was announced, HCL's public services staffs were particularly enthusiastic. They did carry, however, a heavy history of being underfunded and understaffed (at the time of strategic planning, there were only twenty professional staff members spread over the eleven HCL public services units). This history left those staff members both willing to cooperate and collaborate with each other but unsure of their relationship to higher administration. But the following strategic goal was set: "Help students and faculty to achieve maximum benefit from library services and resources by making use of the library more convenient and efficient." Such a statement would be self-evident at many universities; at Harvard, it was radical.

Much to the shock of public services staff, the administrators listened to them. Over the next several years, the number of professional positions associated with public services units rose from twenty systemwide to thirty. New initiatives, often arising from the public services councils, received fair consideration. In addition to those new positions, support was received for modernizing book retrievals from remote storage, for establishing a document delivery system, for building an electronic classroom, and for creating several coordinator positions below the associate college librarian level.

## The Gateway Concept

Early in 1992, following a recommendation in the original strategic plan, HCL engaged in a planning effort that was devoted to public services. In response to the needs for renovating the Lamont Library and for addressing, more broadly, the effects of technology and networked resources on public services units in HCL, conceptual development of a "gateway" library began:

> Gateway is a metaphor for access to knowledge and evokes the image of crossing a threshold and entering a dramatically expanding world of information and learning; the library, as gateway, is the means by which students and faculty will locate and use this information. The gateway we envision is the constellation of services, the organization required for providing these services, and the spaces dedicated to student learning.[6]

The working groups in this public services planning process included more than a hundred staff members throughout HCL. They were organized into several task forces and working groups. Some task forces had broad charges; other working groups, created to address particular problems, had very specific charges. All of them produced a large number of recommendations, such as an ongoing program of user needs assessment, an improved document delivery facility, more widespread technological support, and a larger service staff. [8]

Concurrent with the gateway planning process was a universitywide effort to create a statement of organizational or community values. Articulating such a statement can be an important institutional step if it raises tacit assumptions to a conscious level where they can be discussed and validated. This was undertaken by a group known as the Steering Committee on Staff and Organizational Development, in 1993–1994. Although the effort to get any community engaged in defining its values can result in cynicism, that committee—by thoroughly involving a substantial majority of the community—managed to produce a statement reflective of HCL's explicit and implicit values. Seemingly obvious phrases, such as "serve our community" and "provide access to a broad array of information sources," all rather novel for Harvard College, were essential to validate the public services staffs' interest in developing plans for the future. [9]

The gateway planning, which was wholly focused on library services to users, and the statement of community values were, together, the final validation of public services in HCL. Reference, research, access, and interlibrary loan staff could finally feel that those issues they had always regarded as being so important were, indeed, widely regarded as central to HCL's mission.

## The Future

Is there something in Harvard's struggles that has some utility or application to other libraries? It is undisputed that Harvard has the largest number of noncentralized libraries among U.S. universities. And no library administrator reading this has any intention of developing such an extremely decentralized administrative model! Most libraries have regarded service as central to its mission for decades; Harvard is a Johnny-come-lately in that respect. Can our peculiar history, therefore, have relevance for any other library system?

I would argue that it does, for an important reason: With the increasing prevalence of networking, the greater ease with which we distribute remote resources, and the pressures in many educational systems to engage in remote teaching, HCL's emerging model for planning and collaborating among disparate players may be a microcosm of how academic libraries will have to deal with each other on a national scale. Collaboration, team building, elimination of unnecessary bureaucracy, respect for institutional culture—these are all key processes for restructuring academic organizations.

In saying all that, however, I do not mean to imply that HCL has solved such problems to anyone's satisfaction. Still, we have clearly demonstrated that continual attention to our current position relative to where we intend to be (that is, strategic planning) is helping us cope with the lag of organizational development behind technological change. Do not make the mistake of feeling too much self-satisfaction over *our* struggles; you, or the next generation of library thinkers, may well face essentially the same struggles of how to get along in the networked environment.

## NOTES

1. Seymour E. Harris, *Economics of Harvard* (New York: McGraw-Hill, 1970), 226.

2. Edward L. Whalen, *Responsibility Center Budgeting: An Approach to Decentralized Management for Institutions of Higher Education* (Bloomington: Indiana Univ. Pr., 1991), 156.

3. In 1995, a fourth department, Interlibrary Loan and Document Delivery, was created.

4. Committee participation at Harvard is very important (although often frustrating). The solution to many problems can only come by putting all the right players in a room, closing the door, and hoping that the conclusions and agreements arrived at will actually stick after the individuals leave the room.

5. The strategic planning process has been well described by Susan Lee, "Organizational Change in the Harvard College Library," *Journal of Academic Librarianship* 19 (Sept. 1993): 225–30.

6. Harvard College Library, *Commitment to Renewal: A Strategic Plan for the Harvard College Library* (Cambridge: Harvard College Library, 1993).

7. Lawrence Dowler, ed., *Gateways to Knowledge: A New Direction for the Harvard College Library* (Cambridge: Harvard College Library, 1993), 4.

8. Harvard College Library, Gateway Planning Committee, *Final Report* (Cambridge: Harvard College Library, 1994), 3–4.

9. Harvard College Library, *Values Statement* (Cambridge: Harvard College Library, 1995).

# Adapting Organizational Structures in Technical Services to New Technologies: A Case Study of the University of Nebraska-Lincoln Libraries

*Joan Giesecke and Katherine Walter*

C hanges in the organizational structures and professional roles of technical services librarians at the University of Nebraska-Lincoln (UN-L) may be of interest to other libraries. Administrators, faced with shrinking budgets and increasing demands for user services, must decrease the cost of processing materials and increase the flexibility of their organizations. They simply can no longer afford or justify traditional technical services departments that are unable to process large backlogs, let alone new materials, in a timely manner. To outsource the cataloging and processing of materials, to purchase electronic bibliographic records, and to limit local editing are attractive alternatives to the stereotypically large, but unproductive, technical services department.

At the same time, it is not uncommon for libraries to reallocate staff from technical services to public services to support new programs for patrons, such as electronic reference services and Internet training for students and faculty. This staff reallocation process has been facilitated by the rising costs of monographs and serials: As libraries shift from ownership to other methods of access, there are fewer new materials to be cataloged and processed. Overall, technical services departments are under fire to increase efficiency, speed production, and reduce costs—as well as to help out in public services. In this changing environment, technical services librarians must carve out new organizational structures and roles if they are to retain a high professional standing in their organizations.

The university libraries of UN-L have a staff of about 150 full-time equivalents supporting the university's tripartite mission of teaching, research, and service. Over the past five years, the traditional hierarchical structure has evolved into a much more flexible model. Although the library system retains departments, decision making across the organization is usually made on a programmatic basis. Changes have been gradual but systematic, incorporating both technical and public services departments. Of primary interest here, technical services librarians have influenced organizational structures and program designs by identifying unique areas of professional expertise and marketing them to the administration. As a result of their efforts, the framework of the organization has become more fluid, with less emphasis on old reporting lines and more emphasis on new interactions between public and technical services. Such flexibility in structures and roles has made it much easier to reach creative solutions for coping with new technologies and the changing environment.

## New Technologies, Old Structures

A continuous improvement program for technical services was begun after the implementation of an integrated library system (Innovative Interfaces) in early 1990. In seven months, technical services advanced from a primitive circulation system and database to a fully automated environment with acquisitions, cataloging, circulation, database maintenance, serials, and authority control modules all in place. Work flow was necessarily invented and modified on an ad hoc basis as each module was implemented. By summer, all modules were up and a general review of work flow was needed. This process began with a small team interviewing staff to draw flowcharts, then integrating the charts into major processes or functions that might be streamlined across work units. The act of simply asking staff how they did their work led them to examine the systems and processes on their own and to begin to see the redundancies that had accrued. The next step was a series of time studies of automated tasks to identify other inefficiencies. However, despite all these changes in processes and study of work flow, technical services generally operated under the old organizational structure. Automation had come about without much change in the traditional reporting lines or missions of each unit.

## A New Course for Public Services

With implementation of the integrated library system, patron demands on public services increased dramatically. By 1994, circulation had risen 5 percent, reference questions 36 percent, and interlibrary loan borrowing 20 percent. To address this situation, public services librarians evaluated the impact of the integrated system on nine key services. In general, the study showed that patrons were pleased with the expanded access provided by an integrated library system and wanted to see additional customized services added to the libraries, particularly in the area of document delivery. To address the need for more flexible services patterns, the librarians concluded that different organizational structures and roles would be necessary to bring about participatory management of the changing service programs. The new structures took the form of four coordinating units: an Electronic Resources Program Group, an Access Program Group (interlibrary loan and document delivery), a Library Instruction Program Group, and a Collection Development Committee. The libraries began to implement many changes based on the recommendations and decisions of these four teams, which initially would include only public services librarians.

## A New Awareness in Technical Services

Although work was increasing in public services, it was beginning to decrease in technical services. The number of monographs purchased declined as the purchasing power of the library was reduced by inflation. With fewer new books to process, technical services began to work on a number of database cleanup projects and other long-standing projects. Because those projects were not as crucial to the libraries as meeting the demands of the patrons, the dean of libraries announced the need to move six to nine positions from technical services to public services.

As noted above, technical services librarians had continued to follow traditional approaches to their roles in the library during the early automation years. By spring 1993, however, they realized that they were left out of many decision-making opportunities in the libraries. With the growing emphasis on direct-patron services, public services librarians were learning how to influence the future direction of the libraries while technical services librarians perceived that their own skills were being overlooked.

Accordingly, technical services librarians called a meeting with the associate dean for collections and services and their department chairs to discuss this situation, beginning with the need for stronger distinctions between professional and support staff work. They noted that support staff could handle most of the production work. Some of the prospective professional roles identified included: to provide language and subject expertise for translation and cataloging, and to serve as resource people for other staff; to concentrate on cataloging original materials; to write documentation; to provide specialized training services; to be on librarywide committees; to initiate projects with other libraries; to participate in policy decisions; and to be more engaged in problem solving for the library at large.

At the meeting, they also discussed the possibility that all cataloging might be done from a few major centers but concluded that national standards are not sufficient to eliminate the need for local practices. Thus, for titles that may be treated as either monographs or serials, cataloging practices will vary according to different emphases of local collections; some access points or headings will similarly reflect local user needs. Also, bibliographic records may not be available on a timely basis from a central source (e.g., GPO cataloging records, which are usually made available on tape within six months after pieces have arrived). Although support staff know local practices and can verify if a heading, for example, is valid, they are not trained to interpret cataloging rules or to identify better headings. Professional catalogers pointed out that they understand complicated applications of rules, as well as new trends in cataloging. They create and influence the development of databases; provide access to electronic materials; and understand how information is packaged. All such skills, they argued, were too important to be overlooked in the new downsized, technological environment.

## Restructurings

Later in 1993, technical services librarians were eager to join the public services program groups in librarywide decision making. Those groups, however, were not prepared to open their memberships. The associate dean suggested, as an alternative, that technical services librarians look more broadly at creating new roles for themselves in the library at large. In 1994, they developed a general proposal based on an overview of trends and developments in their field (e.g., the continuing importance of local rather than national practices; the rising importance of electronic formats). This proposal outlined not only new skills but also long-term career opportunities. It was initially formulated from individual assessments of significant or desired elements and tasks in a restructured environment. Not surprisingly, there was a great deal of variety in those job designs and career plans. Although catalogers generally figured on spending most of their time on cataloging, they also wanted to participate in such areas as collection development, computing operations, distance learning, or public relations. In all, twenty-eight specific interests were identified. The common denominator was "involvement in decision making." Given the range of interests, the final proposal included several job and career models.

The first of several actions to bring the proposal into effect was a study to identify where technical services librarians had been devoting their time and attention, and how those patterns might be reallocated to new activities. Another study was to learn how decisions are actually made in the organization. With this background information, a collective "Technical Services Librarians Position Paper" was sent to the dean of libraries.

The main new role envisioned is one of greater involvement with information technologies through the creation of catalogs and databases for the campus network. Another is consulting work for academic libraries or affiliates in the region. (For example, UN-L technical services librarians have presented workshops on cataloging for NEBASE, Nebraska's OCLC affiliate network.) Additional consulting services involve authority work and certain areas of individual expertise (e.g., music cataloging, preservation planning, and grant writing). The position paper included the suggestion that technical services librarians with language or subject expertise assist public services librarians with collection development, reference, and liaison responsibilities.

Even as the position paper was being developed, the associate dean took some initial steps. One was to support the enlargement of membership of the Administrative Group (formerly the dean, two associate deans, and department chairs) by creating a rotating (three-month) position for a nonadministrative librarian—with the first appointee being a technical services librarian. A similar step was to persuade each public services program group to create a member-at-large slot, as well as to have the general memberships selected jointly by the department chairs of public services and technical services.

The position paper was clearly the impetus of this extension of public services' structures and roles to technical services librarians. Catalogers became responsible, for example, for the creation of bibliographic records for Internet resources in the library gopher. This task (once handled by the automated systems office) involved them in collection development matters of access to electronic information: which resources to add, how to choose the best path for accessing a database, how to describe such resources for patrons.

In recent years, technical services librarians have continued to take on new roles. These include managing the outsourcing contract for the cataloging of special materials; cataloging electronic journals, Web sites, and other Internet resources; and facilitating the shift from gopher access to Web access of information. Thus, technical services librarians now participate in the development of policies and procedures to incorporate new technologies into collections and services.

## A More Flexible Organization

Change is a constant of this era. At this writing, librarians at UN-L face the challenge of working in an environment where the university is merging libraries, computing, and telecommunications into a single information services organization. This restructuring has altered some of the management models in the libraries: Administrative committee structures have flattened, and the once-separate public services and technical services departmental committees have been merged into joint groups to handle issues affecting the library as a whole. In technical services, an enlarged Operations Group (department chairs, firstline supervisors, as well as some rank-and-file librarians) now meets to discuss librarywide work flow issues and procedures. Other organizational changes are inevitable as technical services librarians continue to remind us that they need to be represented in decision-making bodies and that they have valuable skills for the organization.

In conclusion, technical services librarians must redefine their roles in an era in which their traditional work is in decline. Outsourcing, purchasing of cataloging tapes, receiving online catalog records—all such cost-effective changes bring into question the position of the technical services professional. Career development becomes a real concern as technical services librarians foresee the traditional intellectual aspects of their work dwindling. Although technology does not replace the intellectual work that technical services librarians do, they must—as we discovered at UN-L— take the initiative in reestablishing their own futures. These librarians, once relatively isolated, have broadened their professional roles to reference, collection development, automated services, and bibliographic instruction. Those newly won roles are crucial: They create improved access to collections and enrich the librarians' careers.

## Further Readings

Eskoz, Patricia A. "Catalog Librarians and Public Services—A Changing Role," *Library Resources and Technical Services* 35 (Jan. 1991): 76–86.

Gorman, Michael. "The Corruption of Cataloging," *Library Journal* 120 (Sept., 1995): 32–34.

Kelley, Bill. "Outsourcing Marches On," *Journal of Business Strategy* 16 (July/Aug. 1995): 38–42.

Ogburn, Joyce L. "An Introduction to Outsourcing," *Library Acquisitions: Practice & Theory* 18 (winter 1994): 363–66. Note: This is one of four articles on outsourcing in this issue of *LAPT*.

Waite, Ellen J. "Reinvent Catalogers!," *Library Journal* 120 (Nov., 1995): 36–37.

# Benchmarking and Restructuring at Penn State Libraries

*Gloriana St. Clair*

This paper discusses how the technique of *benchmarking*—comparing local practices with best practices—can make a restructuring program easier, more credible, and more effective. During the 1990s, librarians have shown increasing interest in mechanisms of organizational change such as benchmarking because higher education, as a whole, must either restructure to meet new challenges or stagnate. This chapter blends an account of benchmarking initiatives at Penn State Libraries with broader assessments of this approach to restructuring academic libraries. The discussion proceeds in twelve sections: rationale for benchmarking, selection of a benchmarking team, determination of appropriate and meaningful measures, planning the strategic process, justification of the planning process with university administrators, discernment of best comparators, collection of data, development of questions as a brainstorming activity, preparation for the trip, report of results, redesign of the local process, and conclusions.

## Rationale for Benchmarking

Benchmarking is a quality assessment tool that operates effectively in a strategic planning environment. Etymologically, the term *bench-*

*mark* comes from a surveyor's mark to establish elevation. In business, and particularly in total quality management (TQM), a benchmark means a standard of excellence against which other similar outcomes are measured or judged.[1] For higher education, several ideas are often pulled together in the use of the term. The most inclusive one is *assessment* of different ways to determine the effectiveness of programs. Two related ideas are *process benchmarking* to compare processes and *comparative analysis* to improve results. Comparative analysis focuses on *what* was accomplished, whereas process benchmarking examines the work flow to help a planning unit improve its effectiveness and/or efficiency.

In the literature on TQM, William Grundstrom describes benchmarking as "the practice of being humble enough to admit that someone else is better at something, and being wise enough to learn how to match and even surpass them at it."[2] That suggestive approach may be particularly useful for those librarians who resist benchmarking efforts for fear that their operations are not optimal. Such resistance stems from two powerful sources—pride and fear of change.

## Selection of a Benchmarking Team

The link between benchmarking and strategic planning is crucial. Benchmarking programs must be directly related to the organization's strategic objectives. Consequently, a benchmarking team should include persons who understand both the specific processes being benchmarked and the broader objectives of the library together with its parent institution. Such persons should also have extensive professional contacts, imagination, and an ability to explain the benchmarking project to administrators, faculty, and staff.

Authority and ability to move a restructuring project through the organization are perhaps the most important keys to success for a benchmarking team. The team may choose to work with a process improvement team after an initial decision has been made about which processes appear in greatest need of benchmarking. That team would help assess how best to implement the results of a benchmark process into the organization. Benchmarking requires that the owners of the process (those who do it daily) be empowered to change it. TQM models recommend a team composed of practitioners with a high-level sponsor to provide political and economic resources for project implementation.

A general problem or area being benchmarked usually involves more than one work flow process. For instance, if a college were to read in the Higher Education Data Sharing (HEDS) data that one of its comparators was able to add a book to its collections for $10 a volume while its own cost was $26 a volume, the investigation of that differential would lead to different areas of the library—collection development, acquisitions, cataloging, and circulation. The comparison of figures would constitute *comparative analysis*, and the affected work within each library area would be continuous *process benchmarks*. A team with administrative leadership and membership from all those areas would coordinate the project.

DuPont Corporation, which has a well-developed benchmarking program, suggests an average of five months per project, with key players spending 20 percent of their time on the project. Penn State Libraries' experience shows that, for two or three months a year, at least one member spends 20 to 25 percent of time on benchmarking and three (or so) other team members about 10 percent of their time. The trip to investigate another institution is actually a minor part of the team's time. Overall, about a third of the team's effort will be for planning, another third for integrating results back into local practices, and the final third for completing the process of change, including initial efforts to re-shape the organization's culture.

## Determination of Appropriate and Meaningful Measures

The search for best practices is time-consuming and therefore expensive. As noted above, areas selected for benchmarking must be important in the organization's strategic plan. Confusion among assessment, comparative analysis, and process benchmarking are likely to arise. Any of these approaches can lead to organizational improvement but, for the purpose of restructuring, process benchmarks are the most useful because they (1) specify a best practice that is clearly superior to local practice and (2) provide a clear direction for implementing it into the local organization.

In the example of HEDS data on the cost of adding a book to a library collection, comparative analysis will point to one or a few cost-reduction areas, and the process benchmark will indicate how the lower-cost institution manages such cost-effective work flows. The higher-cost institution would either restructure certain processes to match those of a lower-cost institution, or justify its higher cost by acceding to various claims by staff that (1) outputs are of higher quality; (2) inputs, such as salaries, have greater value; or (3) the local process is somehow a unique condition. However, an administrator should beware of resorts to "uniqueness" because they tend to be tied to a reluctance to change, rather than to any justified need for higher costs.

In a related fashion, staff members and immediate supervisors rely on three tactics to avoid process benchmarking. First, trying to steer benchmarking away from their own areas (the "uniqueness" argument). Next, after a cursory comparison (sometimes even using published data), contending that their operation is underfunded, thus bound to fare poorly in a benchmark. Finally, engaging in prolonged debates about what is an appropriate methodology. A library administration intent on restructuring must simply persevere in the face of all such defensive tactics. The opposite situation occurs when supervisors, instead of avoiding scrutiny, want to select an area that they believe will make them look good. Although that could lead to some ego gratification, such an expensive benchmarking effort would not contribute to meaningful change. The goal of benchmarking projects should not be to show superiority of performance but, rather, to show scope for improvement. (A caveat is that a goal of restructuring is often not to improve a process but to shift resources from one area to another, as academic libraries are now looking to save money in collection management, and particularly in technical services, to reinvest in digital library projects.) Many universities and their libraries have a set list of institutions for comparison. However, for the particular strategic processes selected, such a list might not include the best comparators. When restructuring, the library should find the best practices in each area of change.

## Planning the Strategic Process

In many institutions, restructuring will be accomplished through an established cycle of strategic planning. Basic strategic considerations should guide all initiatives, including benchmarking. First, benchmarking selections should reflect key issues from the mission statement, strategic plan, or some other organizational framework. Second, the areas selected must be measurable. Third, an institution undertaking its first benchmarking exercise may prudently avoid areas of known resistance unless it is clear that those areas desperately need restructuring. Prolonged debates over appropriate methodologies indicate poor prospects for fundamental change (e.g., because reference service generally has a long history of unsettled scores in the literature and contentious relations with the faculty, it may prove difficult to benchmark). All in all, first benchmarking projects should be visible and have a high probability for success.

At Penn State, the first benchmarking project was part of a strategic plan requirement of all colleges and campus units. The libraries' benchmarking team initially chose a project focused on faculty productivity, as that is a source of staff pride. However, we realized later that, although our own productivity might compare well with other libraries, it would not compare well with that of Penn State colleges. Although this decision might imply the kind of avoidance behavior noted above, it boiled down to a realistic assessment of the difference between service-oriented library faculty productivity and research-oriented academic faculty output, which has highly visible publication outcomes.

Many of the colleges at Penn State planned to benchmark a large variety of different areas—twenty or thirty, with seven or eight different comparator universities. The libraries ended up selecting just three areas for benchmarking: electronic resources, because the strategic plan predicates an electronic future; human resources development, because individual learning is essential to an electronic future; and interlibrary loan (ILL) borrowing, because the access paradigm is a key strategy. (Some asked why we would focus just on borrowing instead of on both ILL functions of borrowing and lending. We responded that lending is not strategic for Penn State users: From a faculty/student point of view, the libraries lend only so that they can borrow—and, of course, to be good citizens.)

That process of selecting benchmark aims took several weeks. The basic principles—be strategic, plan to improve, and envision next year's plan—have been critical to success. During the first year of benchmarking, the library's lack of a strategic plan hampered the effort. For example, one librarian reported difficulty in selecting processes to benchmark because the library had no strategic plan. In essence, a planning unit must have an agreed-upon direction, if not a plan, before selections about appropriate benchmarks can be made.

## Justification of the Planning Process with University Administrators

One of the keys to benchmark planning is that members of the team communicate not just with others in their field but also with local administrators on why particular areas were selected. Drawing generally on DuPont planning materials as guidelines, Penn State Libraries made the case for the ILL borrowing benchmark project with discussions of (1) the need to increase access to other collections when decline in the library's purchasing power diminished the strength of local collections and (2) the apparent room for improvement found by comparison of Penn State's ILL to other ILL operations. Although justifications vary according to particular benchmarks, the essential point is that some cogent explanation must be offered for the strategic importance of each process selected. In addition, the knowledge or interest of an audience is a salient consideration for any benchmark (or strategic) plan. Planning units often exhibit a propensity for jargon and detail. It is important to clarify and simplify benchmarking plans, because university administrators and faculty, not just experts in the same field, are directly involved.

## Discernment of Best Comparators

After selecting the benchmarking team and the processes to be measured, and justifying those decisions in terms of the institution's strategic plan, the next step is to identify the best comparator organization. The initial choice is whether to limit the search to other libraries or to seek a generic comparison in another industry. Until processes have been compared outside the industry type, the best comparators may not have been located. Companies use lists of best practices and information about winners of Baldrige awards to identify possible comparators. (Baldrige winners pride themselves on their willingness to share information about best practices with others.) Similarly, articles in library literature will often suggest which libraries are significant in certain areas.

Staff will likely raise arguments about the comparability of benchmarking results that came from a comparison with a different type of institution. As with claims about institutional uniqueness and quibbles over methodological approach, such arguments probably reflect a resistance to change. Of course, the more analogous a comparator organization is to the group undertaking the benchmark, the easier it will be to persuade the group to change. However, if a generic comparator provides a truly superior process, then it is worth the effort to persuade staff to use it. For example, because one of Penn State Libraries' benchmark areas, human resources development, centers on training and we knew from attending TQM meetings that some engineering companies had well-developed programs, we put them forward as possible comparators in that area. And in the area of electronic resources, we had thought we could rely on just other libraries but, in a follow-up benchmark the second year, we decided to benchmark our providing support for remote users by visiting IBM.

For any organization, networking is the main way to find out who are the best in areas of interest. We began the process of identifying all library benchmark comparators by asking colleagues around the nation who they thought had the best programs in particular areas. In order to find the best comparators for ILL borrowing, we developed a different decision matrix of identifying borrowing units with the same number of requests placed on both OCLC and RLIN.

## Collection of Data

Before a planning unit can develop a list of questions about another institution's processes, the unit must understand its own process and the needs of its customers. Institutions that practice TQM will already have analytical tools at hand, whereas those not engaged in

TQM may do training or reading on such techniques as flowcharts, control charts, and customer surveys. The TQM team at Penn State for improving ILL borrowing used many of those techniques. It began with a telephone survey of selected customers, followed by a short, paper-record analysis of current users. These data were put into a Pareto chart which demonstrated that getting materials in a timely fashion is the most important ILL feature for customers. Although over 80 percent of customers indicated satisfaction with a ten-day response time, the team sponsor (the dean of libraries) challenged the team to strive for a five-to-seven-work-day goal.

In order to compare its outcomes with those in other libraries, the team developed other flowcharts. From paper files, it found that the average ILL borrowing turnaround time in 1994 was twenty-one working days—far longer than customers desired. With the help of a statistical specialist from the university's TQM center, the team continued to track its performance. In 1995, it was able to reduce delivery time to fifteen days; current delivery is, on average, ten days.

Although the main flowchart still reflects a great deal of complexity, the number of process steps has been cut a third. The team continues task analysis by sharing charts with best comparators to determine other steps that can be eliminated or modified to make benchmarking outcomes more equivalent.

## Development of Questions as a Brainstorming Activity

Questions for the comparator about the process being benchmarked may be developed by either the benchmarking team or a process team. Any set of questions may take two to three hours to formulate; it should be tested with colleagues, refined—and then answered by the originating organization because it is essential to know local practices when exchanging information with the benchmarking partner. Steps for brainstorming a set of questions include:

• Write down questions without regard to order.

• Ensure that all members of the team agree on the meaning of each question and the definition of each term.

• Group the questions around steps in the process.

• Prioritize the questions and determine their sequence.

• Test the questions under the interview or investigative conditions in which they will be used.

• Modify the questions based on the results of the test.

• Be sensitive to wording and cultural differences when the respondent and the interviewer have different backgrounds.

• Answer the questions yourself.

Used as a platform for the dialogue with the other institution, the question set allows the benchmarker to delve into layers of the best-practice operation. Refinement of questions may be augmented by preliminary minitours of, and handouts from, the comparator institution.

In general for comparative analysis, many questions can be answered from standard sources, such as statistical publications of the ARL or of the ACRL. What the process should focus on, however, is not simply what the result was but how it was achieved. Questions should have that methodological point of view. Libraries are generally quite free about sharing information on operations, and we encountered no problems of confidentiality.

## Preparation for the Trip

The character of a trip to a generic enterprise is quite different from a trip to another library. Companies that are practitioners of renowned quality in one form or another are accustomed to both seeking best practices and receiving visits. Dates and length of visit are discussed (along with any special requirements for visiting a manufacturing plant) and a list of questions sent ahead. The process of scheduling the visit with another library should be as easy, but libraries tend to ask many more questions than do manufacturers about the nature of the benchmarking project and about interview scheduling. On one Penn State Libraries trip, a corporate contact was forthright about the quid pro quo, wanting to know what training programs the university has available and whether they were open to outsiders. The benchmark team will, of course, invite those with whom it benchmarked to visit them and may expect other libraries to inquire about its experience.

## Report of Results

Because the benchmarking team must communicate with various audiences, several different reports, with varying emphases, need to be written. The overall product for Penn State Libraries' annual report is actually a compilation that pulls together three or four of the most important ideas from a benchmark process and explains them in terms of organizational and parent institutional advantages, barriers, and costs. The team implementing the benchmark will make use of a much broader range of information to implement the changes, but the rest of the organization needs only to focus on overall improvements.

Unlike a typical faculty committee report, the library's product should be a table of actions for the organization. Because the team will have worked with a sponsor along the way, it should have already developed coalitions of supporters and strong prospects for implementation. The academic institution makes a strong general commitment to the project, whereas the library administration gives detailed and directive guidance to the unit being restructured. At least some members of the unit should be on the benchmarking trip to enable them to see an alternative process firsthand and thus gain greater commitment to the changes proposed. However, it may not be possible for the whole team to make the trip, given the costs as well as some inconvenience to the comparator organization. An alternative is to invite someone from that organization to visit the local workplace and to discuss the restructuring process. Telephone or conferencing (such as PicTel) offer other alternatives for communicating with a larger work group.

## Redesign of Local Processes

A typical difference between academic committees and TQM teams is that the former produce reports that tend to be shelved whereas the latter make enduring improvements in work processes. Yet, the resistance from units facing a benchmark restructuring can be visceral. Employees will fear for their jobs, their schedules, their established procedures, their work space, their benefits, their prestige, and so on. Such fears can build into a range of barriers to redesigning things. Typical barriers are the "not-broken" syndrome, innumerable requests for detail, pronounced misunderstandings, hurt feelings, slow response times, and exaggerated claims of uniqueness.[3] Benchmark communications—assurances, explanations, and directives—must be repeated in a variety of different ways and contexts.

Incremental change is not the only means available to remedying a shortfall from the best practice; a complete restructuring (or reengineering) of a process may be necessary. Outsourcing is the greatest response to a shortfall between local and best practices. For example, the University of Alberta Libraries recently outsourced cataloging to a Canadian vendor. Their studies showed that 40 percent of such costs would be saved by outsourcing and that half of those costs could have been saved by simplifying their own cataloging processes, for an accretion of "special needs and handling" had driven internal costs up. That phrase and those figures have had a marked influence on a Penn State group currently at work on an outsourcing project.

In the area of ILL borrowing, Penn State Libraries are awaiting the results of a project, called the Virtual Electronic Library (VEL), by the Committee on Institutional Cooperation (CIC), a consortium of twelve major midwestern universities. An objective of this project is to enable library patrons searching the catalogs of other CIC institutions to initiate their own ILL requests. The VEL group believes that a five-day turnaround time will be necessary to maintain credibility with CIC teaching and research faculty. Continuous improvement of Penn State's ILL borrowing process might meet the five-day standard someday, but displacing the TQM model in this area would appear to be more cost-effective and expedient. With CIC interlibrary borrowing shifted from the traditional model to the circulation model, all users of the thirteen institutions would be like local borrowers for each library. The outsourcing approach requires that we throw out the old model and start anew.

## Conclusions

Benchmarking is a complex process requiring a genuine search for improvement on the part of the initiating institution. A significant investment of time must be made to identify strategic areas for benchmarking, select individuals to participate in the benchmarking process, determine appropriate and meaningful measures, justify the processes selected, discern the best comparators, collect significant data for comparison, make the trip, and introduce the changes back into the organization. Although some processes will lend themselves to continuous improvement, others may require fundamental restructuring or even outsourcing. Work redesigns, whether incremental or radical, must be fully implemented in the organization before the project can be judged a success. Thus, although the formal benchmarking process can occur rather rapidly, the changes that benchmarking introduces into the culture of the home institution can be profound.

Although benchmarking is complex, it can be summarized in terms of four primary elements:

1. *Be strategic*: Align benchmarking objectives with strategic directions.

2. *Be humble*: Select a process that needs improvement.

3. *Choose a process*: Make sure the area being investigated qualifies as a process.

4. *Plan to succeed*: Pick a strategic area in which significant improvement can occur.

Taken together, these elements can make organizational restructuring efficient, effective, and credible.

*Acknowledgment: Research and editorial assistance by Karen L. Gerboth, Sondra K. Armstrong, and Susan L. Walker.*

## NOTES

1. The standard text on benchmarking is Robert C. Camp's *Benchmarking: The Search for Industry Best Practices That Lead to Superior Performance* (White Plains, N.Y.: Quality Pr., 1989), which uses a model to describe the benchmarking process. Many companies have published manuals about their procedures for doing benchmarking studies, and a variety of articles are available in business literature. However, exhaustive reading in the area is not necessary and may lead to study without action.

2. William Grundstrom, "C+Q+P/M=Benchmarking: TQM and Academic Libraries," in *Total Quality Management in Academic Libraries: Ini-*

*tial Implementation Efforts: Proceedings from the 1st International Conference on TQM and Academic Libraries* (Washington, DC: Office of Management Services, Association of Research Libraries, 1995): 131.

3. Jerry W. Young, "Building Support for Change, A Workshop for Leaders at Work," in *Work-Session Workshop for the Academic Council of Penn State University Libraries,* workshop presented by Stable Change Consulting, Nov. 30–Dec. 1, 1995, 84.

# Restructuring Liberal Arts College Libraries: Seven Organizational Strategies

*Peggy Seiden*

D iscussions about digital libraries over the past decade have generally focused on content and design issues—with relatively little attention to the kinds of organizational changes that enable academic libraries and their users to take full advantage of electronic resources and services. In the mid-1980s, Pat Molholt, Patricia Battin, and John R. Sack were among a number of writers who popularized the concept of the digital library as a networked scholar's workstation through which researchers could meet all of their information needs without leaving their office.[1] In 1989, Nancy Evans and Mark Kibbey fleshed out the concept in an article entitled "The Network Is the Library," which described Carnegie Mellon University's efforts to begin building the infrastructure to support such workstations.[2]

These writers' ideas have helped to shape our profession's ultimate vision of a wholly digital information environment. Although such a digital future may still seem a long way off, in a few professions and disciplines (e.g., law, medicine, business, physics) this vision is closer to a reality. However, most academic librarians in the mid-1990s have taken a more conservative stance: that the overall information environment will remain distinctly heterogeneous in the foreseeable future, defined by a growing number of digital collections with a continuing demand for print materials.

The point is well taken but, given the diversity of academic library users, it bears closer scrutiny. For undergraduate students, whose information needs and research behaviors are not particularly specialized or exotic, the balance of reliance on print versus digital materials may be undergoing a significant shift. The recent proliferation of full-text article databases covering core scholarly and popular journals and the growth of the World Wide Web have combined to create a digital environment that undergraduates gravitate toward for doing research. Even when librarians and faculty try to dissuade students from overreliance on the network, many students start and end their research at the computer. For a large number of undergraduate students, *the network is the library*.

This fundamental shift in students' patterns of library use has put considerable stress on the traditional organization of library public services in recent years. In response, libraries have developed a variety of strategies. This chapter focuses on seven organizational change strategies I identified in a spring 1997 survey of the Oberlin Group, a consortium of seventy-four liberal arts college libraries across the country. Some of the discussion centers on my own institution, Skidmore College, which *Yahoo!* magazine cited as among the most wired institutions of higher education in the country.[3]

## Impact of Technological Change on Public Services

Like many small colleges, Skidmore would not be considered among the early adopters of information technology. But the rate of use of technology for personal, research, and curricular needs began to increase rapidly about 1993. In part, the growth in the use of technology can be attributed to the development of resources such as the Web. Yet, Skidmore accelerated the process by establishing a Summer Faculty Institute that year. Since then, nearly 40 percent of the faculty have participated in this program, which has a broad focus on information technology applications in the curriculum and in both undergraduate-level and advanced research.

Skidmore chose to approach student computer literacy indirectly—through course-integrated applications—rather than through any specific requirement that could be met through a single course focused on computing skills. Its summer institute provides faculty the opportunity not only to learn about new technologies but also to begin redesigning their courses to take advantage of these technologies. Although it is difficult to ascertain the number of courses that use technology, demand for electronic classrooms and computer projection has far exceeded the availability of such spaces on campus. Applications in support of the curriculum include student Web sites as course projects, Web-based research, participation in Internet discussion lists or newsgroups, online bibliographic and full-text databases, commercial software, as well as courseware such as the Daedalus program for writing or Mathematica for calculus.

The level of computer experience among incoming classes is also rising dramatically. A survey of first-year students found significant increases among those who stated that they were already using e-mail, the Internet, or word processing at least once a week. For the entering class in 1996, e-mail use was sixfold higher (7% to 44%) than the entering class in 1994, Internet use tenfold higher (2% to 20%), and word processing a third higher (60% to 80%). Thus, arriving students are better prepared to take advantage of a rapidly expanding collection of digital resources on the campus network. Although Skidmore did not initially embrace CD-ROMs with the alacrity of many other academic institutions, by 1990 the library was providing full-text articles through UMI's ProQuest Business Periodicals database. In 1993, the library joined the Lexis/Nexis academic program, which quickly became a core service (business and government are two of the college's largest majors). Currently, students do over 5,000 Nexis searches per month (the equivalent of over one million dollars of commercial-rate search time). In 1995, the library purchased Expanded Academic Index Full-Text, which has become the usual starting point for research projects. The library has continued to build its collection of full-text journal databases through Project Muse, JSTOR, and Academic Press IDEAL. In addition, the library provides networked access to FirstSearch, a half dozen Silver Platter databases, Current Contents, Cambridge Scientific Abstracts, Mathematical Reviews, and Periodicals Contents Index, and is implementing a CD-ROM server to make available previously stand-alone databases, such as America: History and Life. All in all, the library provides at least one major index/abstracting service for each academic department in the college.

The scope of the impact that these digital collections have had on undergraduate students' information-seeking behavior was elucidated by a study conducted from 1994 to 1996. The study observed the following behavioral patterns and attitudes:

• Undergraduate students, driven by time pressures and seduced by the convenience of "one-stop shopping," rely increasingly on full-text databases and the Web—to the near exclusion of other valuable resources in other formats or media (notably print).

• Students frequently start and end their research at the computer.

• Students are either unaware of, or choose not to use, non-computer-based abstracts and indexes, thereby missing other valuable sources that fall outside either the scope or time frame of computer-based sources.

• Students have difficulty discerning qualitative differences among various digital sources of information, a problem exacerbated by the homogeneous access through a single computer or interface.

• Increasingly confounded by the expanse and heterogeneity of the information environment, undergraduates seek to simplify it by limiting their searches to familiar sources.

• Most undergraduates never move beyond the novice stage; although some may become more or less expert in searching a particular database, they do not exhibit expertise in their overall information seeking.

This study reveals a significant gap between undergraduate students' reliance on the networked environment and their true understanding of it. As the complexity of the information environment grows, their need for help in using the library effectively increases.

In light of this problem, it is not surprising that an exit survey of 1996 Skidmore seniors showed, for all areas of computer use, students feeling less comfortable with, and wanting more instruction in, library applications. However, what *is* surprising is that, despite a doubling of the number of library instruction sessions from 1994 to 1996 and the concurrent development of a workshop program, students indicated that they had learned how to search chiefly in one-on-one sessions with a reference librarian. Of course, questions about how to access a database frequently turn into prolonged reference consultations. When one adds a large number of questions on e-mail, newsgroups, printer problems, and general network problems to these research-related inquiries, it becomes clear why support needs require a restructuring of library public services.

Yet, higher education is facing a time of stagnant personnel growth and few institutions are able to obtain new budget lines for additional staff. Steven W. Gilbert, director of technology projects at the American Association for Higher Education, draws an important distinction between this decade and the next one. Up to now, most colleges have done reasonably well supporting the "early adopters," the first 10 to 15 percent of the faculty to use information technology in their teaching. Gilbert notes that the level and quality of support that was adequate for the first five percent of the faculty is probably strained dealing with 15 percent of the potential faculty-user pool and will not scale up for the next 70 percent of the faculty.[4] Thus, an information technology support crisis looms on many campuses—university and college. Median overall staffing in the Oberlin Group of liberal arts college libraries is twenty-five, with the median number of librarians nine and a half. With such modest personnel resources, how can college libraries support the technological needs of not only the relatively limited number of faculty but the student body as well? Although some libraries in the Oberlin Group continue to make do in their traditional organizational structures by tacking new responsibilities on already overburdened staff, other libraries have demonstrated considerable determination and inventiveness in redesigning their organizations, which better enables them to embrace and exploit new information technologies. The essential approach has been one of creativity, flexibility, and trial and error. These college libraries have demonstrated a willingness to try different solutions and to abandon those that are not successful—a risk taking which, however prudent and necessary, is atypical of much of higher education.

In my informal survey of the seventy-five members of the Oberlin Group, spring 1997, one third responded. These identified, collectively, seven organizational change strategies to leverage existing staff resources in support of the digital library:

1. reorganizing or redesigning staff positions;

2. developing cross-functional teams;

3. modifying reference desk staffing patterns;

4. increasing the use of undergraduate students to support information technology across campus;

5. extending or formalizing relationships with campus computing and/or media services;

6. collaborating with faculty to address changing information literacy needs;

7. developing consortium relationships with other colleges.

## Reorganizing or Redesigning Staff Positions

A common first step to dealing with rapid technological change is to create a specific position to deal with the new service and/or format. Such a position mitigates the stress on others to adapt the new technology single-handedly by establishing a change agent who can foster the processes of diffusion and integration within the organization as a whole. To deal with the increased need for public-service technology support, many libraries have established a position called either an electronic resources or electronic services librarian. Although now a fixture in a number of libraries within the Oberlin Group, it has rarely been the product of a new budget line. Rather, it tends to be redesigned from a former position in public services, or is part of a broader convergence of technical services and public services. For example, Earlham College redesigned a reference slot to create the information technology/reference instructional librarian position, which is responsible for Web-page development, equipment, and software support, and is a focal point for staff development in the area of information technology.

Years ago, such positions assumed near-total responsibility for reference databases. However, once the volume of electronic resources rose and the role of such resources was no longer tangential to the research process of the majority of the library's clientele, all reference librarians have had to be responsible for supporting users of these resources. Thus, whereas a first step may involve *centralization* of the new function in a redesigned position, the next step becomes *decentralization*, or *distribution*, of the now-manifold function among similarly redesigned reference positions. In some instances, such decentralization extends to technical responsibilities as well as to selection, support, and instruction. For example, at St. John's/St. Benedict's College, all public services staff maintain the CD towers. Moreover, in a number of colleges, positions outside public services have undergone a technological broadening. For example, the head of technical services at Skidmore is responsible for all processes related to electronic serials—from contract negotiation and collection management to campus publicity. Other colleges have redesigned, instead, a collection development position to be the manager for information resources, including electronic serials and databases.

Decentralizing, or distributing a technology support function to a larger pool of library staff, generally depends on the extent to which the intellectual content of a given resource (to be delegated to everyone in public services) can be separated from the underlying infrastructure.

Although academic libraries now expect a certain level of technical expertise from their reference staff, a single individual—the systems librarian—usually retains responsibility for maintaining network servers, software, and the overall configuration of the public workstation environment. Actually, some college libraries have only recently added the position of systems librarian. Because of the facile nature of turnkey library systems, they could rely on their technical services departments, with campus computing centers maintaining the infrastructure. The addition of the systems librarian position rather late in the game is a reflection of the increasing complexity of the networked environment since 1993 or so.

The progress of decentralizing responsibility for digital resources, which requires public services staff to take on a broader and more specialized workload, usually requires, in turn, a restructuring of other parts of the organization to relieve public services of some former duties. At Skidmore, the library upgraded an interlibrary loan (ILL) assistant position to a professional level (though not one requiring an M.L.S. degree) in order to free the head of public services of routine management of interlibrary loan. Oberlin College moved both ILL and government documents from reference department management. A few colleges, such as Willamette and Albion, have begun using paraprofessionals to assist in public services—a strategy for which Larry R. Oberg, library director at the former, has been a strong advocate.[5] Along the same lines, Skidmore is training circulation staff in reference databases to provide support when the reference desk is not staffed.

## Developing Cross-Functional Teams

One survey respondent observed that "we seem to do a lot with committees and task forces rather than investing everything in single positions." This statement reflects a second organizational change strategy—the development of cross-functional teams. Such teams bring together traditionally disparate processes and individual expertise within the library or from other organizations on campus. (The latter type of team, mainly involving library and computing center partnerships, is discussed in a later section.) The two most commonly mentioned "teams" by survey respondents were an electronic resources committee (chiefly to make selection and processing policies) and a Web design committee. For example, Smith College has an Electronic Resources Working Group with responsibilities for coordinating and resolving problems ranging from acquisitions and systems support to public services; and Colgate's Electronic Products Evaluation Committee is responsible for evaluating and selecting all computer-based resources. Some colleges, however, retain a form of *decentralized* responsibility that might be called the *committee-of-the-whole approach*. At Skidmore, for example, recommendations for acquisition of resources (in any format or medium) are solicited from the community, and purchase decisions are made by all librarians (with the subject specialist's input carrying extra weight). However, Skidmore chose the cross-functional team approach for its library's Web-page development rather than to charge any single individual with that task. Its Web team (composed of the systems librarian, the head of public services, the cataloger/database maintenance librarian, the library director, the humanities/special collections librarian, and the interlibrary loan supervisor) decides the look and feel of the library's home page, as well as its intellectual content. Two members of the team have an important liaison role in serving on the campuswide Web committee.

## Modifying Reference Desk Staffing Patterns

Among the few models of restructuring staffing patterns for the reference desk, perhaps the best known is the Brandeis model, in which graduate students are trained to handle basic reference queries while referring research consultations to professional staff. Virginia Massey-Burzio in *Rethinking Reference in Academic Libraries* (a workshop eventually held at three universities) wrote that this model was developed to address the practical demand brought on by electronic information technologies that challenged "our most cherished service beliefs." She noted the salient problem of public services burnout: "Being warm and friendly with long lines at a reference desk while trying to man a constantly ringing phone and fielding questions about a paper jam is stressing out even the most saintly reference librarians."[6] However, liberal arts college libraries have generally rejected the Brandeis model. Apart from practical considerations, such as the absence of graduate students who staff the reference desk in this model, it is a philosophical matter. For college libraries, the reference desk retains its traditional and cherished role of a *classroom*, the place where librarians engage in the central function of academia—*teaching*.

Still, given the practical issue of growing demand on the reference desk, several of the Oberlin Group colleges are experimenting with new service patterns. To extend reference hours, Wooster College has implemented a variant of the Brandeis model—tiered services—by utilizing undergraduate assistants during certain hours to handle basic questions while referring more sophisticated problems to a backup librarian. Wooster is now considering moving to a complete referral-based model. Other colleges noted that they have extended reference hours and moved to double staffing in order to cope with increased demands for support. Although one can project that increases in individual workload will begin to take its toll on public services librarians, few colleges have undergone major restructuring to redistribute overall workload. Most changes appear to be incremental, and many colleges still rely upon meeting these increased needs by adding part-time librarians to their reference staffs.

## Undergraduate Support of Information Technology

With a local library school to facilitate double staffing of the reference desk, the sheer number of public microcomputers (seventy) in the library has necessitated the creation of additional personnel resources not only to cope with the usual technical problems but also to provide—in the future—a basic level of support for library databases.

The use of undergraduate students for elementary reference work is not an altogether new strategy. It has recently received attention because of some highly visible, successful programs—for example, at the University of Southern California, undergraduates perform "triage" in the "information commons" of the new undergraduate library.[7] Also, Gilbert has been promoting this general approach in his Teaching, Learning, and Technology Workshop (for the American Association of Higher Education). He points out that undergraduates now tend to have better skills and more knowledge about new information technology than do most faculty and staff.[8] In a networked campus environment, the use of students has a broader benefit: The development of a trained cadre can assist remote users in dorms, public workstation clusters, and classrooms. Because only a fraction of the growing numbers of digital library users will actually be on the physical premises, peer-to-peer instruction becomes increasingly important. At some campuses, each dorm has a resident support person. Initially, that position was usually created to help with network connections and basic applications but, as noted above, Skidmore envisions extending the responsibilities to cover elementary library database queries.

Nearly all of the Oberlin Group respondents to my survey indicated that they are coming to rely on undergraduates in new ways to support information technology. Apart from the library reference area, a common responsibility is Web-page and gateway maintenance. Nonetheless, greater integration of undergraduates into public services remains controversial. One college library director pinpointed a common concern in noting that "students have just enough knowledge to be dangerous." Any solution to managing this concern depends on training, but that is not easy. Typically, students can handle basic tasks but lack sophistication in search strategies and a good enough understanding of the information environment to have an intuitive grasp of when a question should be referred to a reference

librarian. Even more critical are public-service attitudes and communication styles befitting anyone in a user-support role. Only a strong
student assistant preparatory program can possibly seed the campus
with students adequately trained.

Undergraduates are not an unlimited resource. The pool of work-
study dollars is finite and getting additional work-study hours can
put the library in a tug-of-war with other units on campus. At William Paterson College, funds to pay for information assistants come
from a modest student fee.[9] However, smaller colleges may not have
a student body large enough to make such fees sufficient. Nor is
there much enthusiasm in the mid-1990s for increasing fees in academic institutions, regardless of size. Thus, although Skidmore was
able to implement an information assistant program in part because
of a new financial aid allocation formula that increased the number
of students receiving aid, that program was mainly feasible because
the library and the computing center jointly lobbied for additional
students to support information resources across campus. Had the
infrastructure for such collaboration not been in place, such a program would probably not have been doable.

## Partnering with Campus Computing

During the mid-1980s, when people such as Molholt and Battin
were developing visions of the digital library, a number of writers
suggested that the electronic era would necessitate a convergence of
the library and the computing center. What became known as the
"merger debate" faded in the late 1980s but resurfaced in the mid-
1990s with the advent of the networked information environment.[10]

Although the evolving digital library is not the sole driving force
behind the mergers that have taken hold, it has compelled the academic library to look more closely at its relationship with the computing center. Traditionally, college libraries have enjoyed a rich collaboration with computing centers because relatively few such libraries have the know-how, staff size, or financial resources to be autonomous in the area of information technologies (as were many larger
institutions in the 1970s and 1980s). Whereas early relationships at
the college level tended to evolve around the implementation of integrated systems with the library playing the role of client, the develop-

ment of networking and its transformation of the scholarly communication system have revitalized the potentialities for the library–computing center partnership.

Strong synergies can be realized through such partnerships, but how they actually come about is highly dependent upon the traditions and cultures of the academic institution. For the Oberlin Group, there are many different levels and styles of interaction, formal and informal. A 1995 survey of member institutions by Larry Hardesty found that fifty (two-thirds) engage in some sort of a cooperative effort with the computing center.[11] Of the twenty-five Oberlin Group institutions that responded to my survey in 1997, practically all of them reported a deepening or formalizing of those relationships, but the structures used to foster collaboration are as varied as the institutions that adopt them.

Joseph E. McCann and Roderik Gilky sketch a continuum of structural options for organizational partnering: cooperative agreements, limited partnerships with resource pooling, joint ventures with autonomous ventures created, strategic alliances, acquisitions, and mergers.[12] Within the Oberlin Group, every structural option can be found and, within a single institution, relationships can include more than one option. It is not uncommon for a college library and computing center to engage in one or more joint ventures (e.g., developing a campus Web, or supporting both a digital library and a local area network), to have a cooperative agreement (e.g., maintaining the OPAC or the CD-ROM towers), as well as for each unit to work independently in areas with no overlapping responsibilities. Oberlin Group libraries tend to adopt structures that allow them to preserve unique library services and identities while collaborating on new services and products in areas where territorial claims are less well defined.

Alliances are often built via committees, whether at the administrative or the operational level. Bates College has a broad-based administrative structure that might be called *CIO-by-committee* (as opposed to the usual individual campus information officer). At Skidmore, the same approach takes the form of an information resources managers group, which meets weekly and is responsible for strategic planning and capital budgeting of all campus technology.

For the Oberlin Group as a whole, the respective directors of the library and the computing center often sit on collegewide technology advisory committees or are ex officio members of each other's advisory group. At a few institutions (Skidmore, Oberlin College, Connecticut College, Mills College), the library director participates in high-level information technology *policy making*. Operational (or functional-level) initiatives, driven by opportunities or demands, are more common than strategic committees. Campuswide information systems, Web and Internet training, and other computer-related instruction were cited most by survey respondents as areas for which there are either committees or formal joint efforts. At Bates College, computing and library staff are planning joint instructional programs for first-year students and meet weekly to resolve problems related to instruction and service delivery over the campus network.

At some of the colleges, however, relationships are much less institutionalized, being more dependent on the individuals involved. There may be, for example, informal regular meetings between the heads of the two units, or the systems librarian may serve as the liaison between the units. At Skidmore, the systems librarian reports to the associate director for academic computing, though his office is in the library and his day-to-day responsibilities are dictated by the library's needs. This arrangement was selected because the library felt that someone formally associated with academic computing would have more leverage for the library. At Denison University, the electronic publishing coordinator, though reporting to the library director, is advised by a group that includes several nonlibrary units, including the public affairs office. At Lake Forest College, where the library director oversees the computing center, one of the academic-technology specialists has an M.L.S. and works at the library reference desk as her schedule permits. As the director noted, "this helps to tie the library and the computer center together further in a small but visible way."

The key to successful collaboration is to ensure that members of converging or collaborative units are valued for their distinctive competencies and cultural strengths. Over time (perhaps a long time), as staffs from different units share responsibilities and experiences, one can expect a shared culture to evolve. But McCann and Gilky note that, even in a fairly dynamic corporate environment, it may take up to five years to restructure an organizational culture. In the highly decentralized academy, the time it takes to develop a hybrid scholarly–technological culture may be even longer. (Sometimes what appear to be the most auspicious conditions have elements of serendipity: At one college, the coordinator of faculty computing is the wife of the systems librarian, and two technicians in the computing center are married to two support staff in the library.)

## Collaborating with Faculty on Information Literacy

The growth in demand for library instruction at Skidmore closely parallels the rise and diffusion of online resources and services. Faculty have turned in ever-increasing numbers toward librarians to provide themselves and their students with pragmatic, procedurally focused instruction in library databases. As Cerise Oberman has observed, information technology has led librarians to forsake teaching concepts in favor of computer-driven protocols and procedures.[13] Although that is not a surprising trend (given the short time allowed for computer-based instruction sessions), the essential point is that such sessions are not particularly effective. Skidmore's research on undergraduate information seeking shows that, despite a doubling of the number of course-integrated instruction sessions and numerous independent workshops, students simply are not learning how to do effective (comprehensive yet relevant) research in the networked environment.

By cramming specific procedures into the one or few sessions allotted, the library loses the opportunity to teach critical concepts related to search strategies, information structures, and retrieval outcome evaluations. Faced with mounting evidence that the typical instruction session fell short of even modest goals, Skidmore is piloting two new models of instruction. One model seeks to develop an information literacy curriculum embedded in the course sequences of particular majors. The rationale for this approach is based on the Skidmore study's finding that students who had the most accurate model of the overall information environment and the most expert strategies for information seeking were ones who had a strong grounding in the disciplinary information structures of their major area. The other model is focused on a single course for which library instruction has been designated an integral, semester-long component. Librarians and faculty work together to develop a class Web site and explore, through a series of course assignments, the types of information resources available on a particular subject.

There are now a few movements to institutionalize computer literacy programs in college academic programs. At Kalamazoo College, the library has formalized its teaching role by setting up an Information Services Advisory Committee in which the faculty participate in planning research instruction programs. At Oberlin College, a faculty/librarian task force designed a month-long information literacy workshop for faculty to integrate information literacy skills into the curriculum. At Skidmore, the college administration has set up a joint subcommittee (from its Educational Planning and Policy Committee and its Information Resources Policy Planning Committee) to begin to look at information literacy as an institutional issue, rather than one relegated to the library. Such approaches are not altogether new in higher education, of course, but for colleges having very limited staff resources they can be risky ventures. Still, the outcomes can outweigh the time and work involved. Tom Kirk credits the instruction program at Earlham College with a general lessening of demands on the reference desk, noting that through its program which depends upon strong collaboration between teaching faculty and librarians, "students get the routine stuff without having to ask at the reference desk."

Although librarians are co-opting teaching faculty in the area of information literacy instruction, faculty have occasionally co-opted librarians in the development of digital resources, such as course Web pages. At Colgate University, faculty who want assistance have teams from both the library and the computing center help them, with the library coordinating the activity. When faculty use Web pages or other networked resources as lecture materials, they bring the library into the classroom in a way that fundamentally transforms the students' educational experience while furthering their understanding of the information environment.

## Expanding Consortium Relationships

Most member institutions of the Oberlin Group belong to other consortia as well. Whereas consortia generally enable libraries to purchase digital resources at reduced costs and provide opportunities for staff training and continuing education, college library consortia have a special niche in facilitating different institutions to share certain staff positions. Some consortia share a catalog which resides at one institution. Costs for personnel to support the system at the host institution are then shared by other members of the consortia. This model is found at the Five Colleges (a western Massachusetts consortium comprising Amherst College, Smith College, Holyoke College, Hampshire College, and the University of Massachusetts-Amherst). But these institutions are also looking beyond systems support to enhance their personnel resources. The Five Colleges have used grant funds to hire two training consultants—one specializing in multimedia technology and the other in the use of the Web—while another college consortium in Ohio is seeking funding for a shared training specialist. Also, Colby, Bates, and Bowdoin libraries received a Mellon Grant in 1997 to implement a shared catalog and develop other coordinated services. Although there are no new personnel resources associated with this grant, such shared projects allow libraries to undertake significant restructuring by leveraging expertise at individual institutions and eliminating duplication of effort.

This organizational strategy of sharing positions among colleges within commuting distance has the advantage of providing a specialized personnel resource with minimal cost. Few colleges can afford discipline-specific computing specialists, yet applications for different fields are ever increasing in complexity and the potential audience for such applications continues to expand. Colby, Bates, and Bowdoin also received a grant from the Mellon Foundation to establish a Foreign Language Computing Consortium. The grant funds four positions (one of which is for the coordinator of the program and the other positions for a coordinator at each institution). Although early adopters were often self-reliant in support of disciplinary tools, the next tier of users generally has neither the interest nor the time for such self-reliance. If support in their areas does not exist, they probably will not bother with the technology. Consortia hold distinct promise in this area.

## Conclusions

The evolving digital library, which has become a nearly sufficient information environment for undergraduate needs, has outpaced existing organizational models for library public services. Liberal arts colleges, which have very limited personnel and financial resources, must find creative means to use existing staff more effectively. At least one of the seven organizational redesign strategies discussed in this chapter is being tried in all but a few of the institutions of those that responded to my survey. Although a small minority of the libraries are utilizing nearly all of the strategies, most of them have chosen a few that seem to fit their respective campus cultures and traditional institutional arrangements. Oftentimes, beginning with a single strategy creates opportunities and incentives to move on and explore additional ones. Overall, the Oberlin Group has demonstrated a certain risk taking which, however prudent and necessary, is atypical of much of higher education.

### NOTES

1. Pat Molholt, "On Converging Paths: The Computing Center and the Library," *Journal of Academic Librarianship* 11 (Nov. 1985): 284–88; Patricia Battin, "The Electronic Library—A Vision for the Future," *EDUCOM Bulletin* 19 (summer 1984): 12–17, 34; John R. Sack, "Open Systems for Open Minds: Building the Library without Walls," *College and Research Libraries* 47 (Nov. 1986): 535–44.

2. Nancy Evans and Mark Kibbey, "The Network Is the Library," *EDUCOM Review* 24 (fall 1989): 15.

3. Dina Gan, "America's 100 Most Wired Colleges," *Yahoo!: Internet Life* 3 (May 1997), at http://www3.zdnet.com/yil/content/college/intro.html.

4. Steven W. Gilbert, "Making the Most of a Slow Revolution," *Change* 28 (Mar./Apr. 1996): 25.

5. Larry R. Oberg, "Rethinking Reference: Smashing Icons at Berkeley," *College and Research Libraries News* 54 (May 1993): 265–66.

6. Virginia Massey-Burzio, "Rethinking the Reference Desk," in *Rethinking Reference in Academic Libraries: The Proceedings and Process of Library Solutions Institute no. 2* (Berkeley, Calif.: Library Solutions Pr., 1993), 44–45.

7. Chris D. Ferguson and Charles A. Bunge, "The Shape of Services to Come: Values-Based Reference Service for the Largely Digital Library," *College and Research Libraries* 58 (May 1997): 252.

8. Gilbert, "Making the Most of a Slow Revolution," 24–25.

9. Lisa Guernsey, "William Paterson Trains Students to Be Its Technology Consultants," *Chroncile of Higher Education* 44, (Sept. 1997): A36.

10. Pat Molholt, "What Happened to the Merger Debate?" *Journal of Academic Librarianship* 15 (May 1989): 96a–b.

11. Larry Hardesty, "Library and Computer Relations: The Human Side," Star Gate Conference on Information Technology presentation, Oct. 25, 1995, Winston-Salem, N.C.

12. Joseph E. McCann and Roderick Gilkey, *Joining Forces: Creating and Managing Successful Mergers and Acquisitions* (Englewood Cliffs, N.J.: Prentice Hall, 1988), 6.

13. Cerise Oberman, "Library Instruction: Concepts and Pedagogy in the Electronic Environment," *RQ* 35 (spring 1996): 320.

# Caught in the Crossfire: Organizational Change and Career Displacement in the University of California Libraries

*Rita A. Scherrei*

O ne result of the now commonplace organizational downsizing, restructuring, and flattening of academic libraries has been the displacement of many midcareer librarians. Adaptation to new technologies and the resultant changes in work flow and job content, as well as realignment of budgets and new management and organizational theories, are usually the reasons for the reassignments.

On the positive side, such dislocations prevent or reduce layoffs. For librarians in the early stages of their professional lives, adaptation may not be too difficult, for if there is unhappiness, there is also enough personal flexibility to find a more suitable position elsewhere. However, uprooting midcareer academic librarians from their chosen career paths and placing them in different positions more often than not interferes with professional prospects and activities, and with collegial and personal relationships. Typically, it is harder, or at least less desirable, to move to other institutions beyond a certain stage in one's career.

The study is described in this paper focuses on such midcareer disruptions. Having observed the reactions of many librarians who

231

had undergone administrative transfers in the University of California system, I became aware that this side effect of budget reductions and well-intentioned institutional changes can create unanticipated trauma for those affected.

## Hypotheses
Informal observations and conversations led to the following framework for examination and discussion:

• *Hypothesis 1*: Librarians who are transferred from a managerial position to a nonmanagerial position perceive the change as harmful to their professional careers.

• *Hypothesis 2*: Librarians who are transferred from a subject specialty position to either a nonspecialist position or another subject perceive the change as harmful to their professional careers.

• *Hypothesis 3*: Librarians who are transferred from a position in which a particular clientele was served to either a different clientele or a more general service position perceive the change as harmful to their professional careers.

• *Converse hypothesis*: Changes in the opposite directions—toward managerial or nongeneralist positions—would be perceived by librarians as career advancements, or at least as enhancements.

To examine these hypotheses, I looked at ten variables to see how changes in career aspirations, professional activities, professional self-identity, and job satisfaction are associated with career disruptions. In addition to investigating the formal hypotheses, I explored the librarians' attitudes toward the process of change as they had personally experienced it and asked what advice they had for library administrators managing similar staff restructurings in the future.

## Population Studied
The librarians who participated in the study were all from the University of California (UC) system. Their selection was not random. I gathered names of librarians whose careers had been significantly altered by administrative transfers for organizational reasons from colleagues at the nine campuses. Thirty-two librarians of the forty-three identified agreed to be interviewed. Two of them were unavailable at the times of the interviews, so the total number in the study was thirty.

The librarians were all midcareer; a few had entered the profession as a second career and some had gone to library school after working for several years in libraries. Of the thirty, fifteen (half) had obtained their MLS between 1970 and 1974; another ten (a third) between 1975 and 1979; the remaining five (a sixth) between 1980 and 1992. The average number of work years in the UC system was fourteen. Twenty-six (87%) reported they were in their forties; the other four said they were in their fifties. Twenty-three (77%) of the career-impacted librarians were women; seven (23%) were men. Three (10%) were members of ethnic minorities.

## Methodology

Individual interviews with the UC librarians were conducted in spring and fall 1995. Each interview was scheduled for one hour; the actual time of an interview varied from thirty-five minutes to nearly two hours. After initial demographic questions (covered in the previous section), I raised open-ended questions covering the following ten variables: original job at the library; career progression in the library since hiring; most recent reassignment; reason for the recent reassignment; career aspirations prior to reassignment; career aspirations now; professional interests and activities prior to reassignment; professional interests and activities now and in the foreseeable future; overall reaction to the reassignment; and overall reaction to the process of the reassignment. Finally, I asked for open-ended suggestions about managing change should similar restructurings take place in the future, and for any other comments.

## Hypothesis 1 Group

Ten of the librarians' career changes involved being removed from managerial or significant supervisory or coordinating positions to greatly reduced or even nonmanagerial roles. This group formed the hypothesis 1 group.

Of all the librarians, this group had undergone the greatest changes in professional aspirations. Seven of them had seen their career tracks moving them into associate university librarian or large unit-head management jobs. At the time of the interviews, these librarians were almost all unclear as to what they would be doing in the future. They felt derailed; most expressed great disillusionment and reduced loyalty to the library and the university. Some talked about going through a process similar to grieving, not only for their career loss but also for the loss of the relationship with the institution.

On a professional level, they had thought of themselves as managers; now they were finding new identities as reference, instructional, or collection development librarians. For the most part, their professional activities, whether in organizations or in writing and research, had been related to management. Some had decided to drop outside activities for the foreseeable future as they struggled to find new niches—usually in subject areas for which they had very little background and, in some cases, limited interest.

On a positive note, however, nine of the ten were finding a degree of satisfaction in their new positions. They expressed the need to be realistic and to get involved with their new jobs. They viewed themselves as professionals and wanted to obtain the necessary training and skills to do their new assignments well, at a level reflecting their senior librarian status. The same qualities of decisiveness and assertiveness that had contributed to their becoming managers helped them to be quite self-directed in learning new subject matter and skills.

## Hypothesis 2 and 3 Group

This group was composed of ten librarians who had been transferred from one subject and/or client specialty to either a broader, generalist role or another subject and/or clientele area. For the most part, these librarians had expected to remain in their specialization or to continue working for the same client group for the duration of their careers. They had framed their professional activities and campus involvements around that assumption of career stability. They were struggling with learning new subject areas; with serving in larger, less-specialized libraries; and with working on a much more impersonal basis with faculty and students with whom they did not have familiar professional relationships. They expressed the feeling that their long years of experience and service had been devalued.

Like the displaced hypothesis 1 managers, many had withdrawn from outside professional activities and were focused on the new job at hand. They were unsure of what they wanted to do professionally in the future, if anything. In general, this group was also working hard at trying to become accustomed to their new roles. More of these librarians, however, were considering leaving librarianship as soon as they could take an early retirement or find another career. Others planned to move to a different kind of library, such as public, special, or small college, where they could resume their accustomed (more specialized or more personal) service.

## Converse Hypothesis Group

Ten of the thirty librarians in this survey had undergone types of changes that they viewed as quite positive; for example, expansion of administrative or management responsibilities or movement into highly specialized roles from generalist positions. These librarians appreciated the administration's recognition of their skills and abilities. They were actively engaged in their new positions and tended to view their career moves as promotions.

## Additional Findings

Another interesting set of findings was the librarians' reactions to the stated reasons for their displacements and to the process of job restructuring. Nearly all the respondents could identify an administrative rationale for the change. In some cases, it was budgetary; in others, it was for needed building space; in still others, it stemmed from an administrative desire to restructure for technological or other operational reasons. However, particularly for those librarians who had not adjusted to career displacement, there was great cynicism about the validity of the rationale. Many of these librarians believed that there were underlying motives behind their transfers and that the stated reason was merely, or at least partly, a "cover story."

Nearly all the librarians, even the ones who adjusted to their new positions, believed that imposed career changes should be discussed thoroughly in the overall context of a restructured library for the future. They were not satisfied that budget or space constraints were sufficient; they wanted to understand the strategic context for the decisions that had displaced their careers and, in many cases, their lives. They would strongly encourage the university librarian and the appropriate assistant or associate university librarian to have a one-to-one courtesy call—even if brief, at least open and honest. Remarkably, that was done in almost none of the cases; not surprisingly, the librarians believed they deserved it. They also felt that their prior contributions should be publicly recognized. They knew their years of service had been valuable to the library and to faculty and students, and were sorely disappointed by the administration's lack of such acknowledgment.

They suggested that counseling, both individual and group, be made available, and that stress resulting from career displacement be at least acknowledged by library administrators and unit heads. Many alluded to stress over career displacements spilling over to their personal lives. They talked about their feelings of powerlessness, suspicion over motives, and genuine anger at the absence of complete information and an opportunity for dialogue and input with decision makers. Virtually all of them prescribed earlier and better communication in any restructuring process affecting careers.

## Conclusions

Although the population interviewed was limited to the University of California system and was relatively small, the study's findings about harmful changes to careers warrant serious consideration. It is clear that reassigning midcareer academic librarians impacts a whole array of professional prospects, activities, and relationships. Ultimately, the reassignment, if it is perceived as a downward step or a derailment, leaves a strongly negative residue on professional and personal lives. It is possible, however, to mitigate much of this negativity if the job restructuring process is open, consultative, and placed in an overall strategic context.

Thought also should be given to training and preparation for new assignments. The shock of suddenly feeling like a newcomer after having been an expert was a key factor of stress and dissatisfaction. Although these librarians were generally at levels that enabled some of them to retrain themselves with peer assistance, formal recognition of such needs would have eased the stress of transition. In addition to benefiting the librarians, investment in training and preparation for new assignments will obviously result in productivity gains for the library. Having highly paid professionals in essence working at beginning levels represents a significant and irretrievable cost.

Finally, for these quite experienced librarians, most of them at fairly senior ranks, the human dimension often involved trauma and a resulting career crisis of uncertainty. Though they were trying remarkably hard to learn new jobs and become involved in their new responsibilities, many were left with significant residual mistrust and bitterness. They were grateful not to have been laid off, but many of them wished that the process had been kinder, more consultative, and done with a broader, publicized strategic vision.

For administrators managing change—and there will surely be more as technology reshapes collections and services—the lessons are clear: Communicate early; communicate honestly; communicate fully; communicate often. Consult to the extent possible. Invest in training. Take librarians' careers seriously.

# One Purpose: The Research University and Its Library

*Charles B. Osburn*

The future of higher education in the United States appears uncertain these days, and the future of research universities and their libraries seems particularly unclear. A pessimistic assessment would find this an unfortunate and improbable conclusion to an otherwise brilliant chapter in American history. But a more optimistic assessment would find opportunity. This chapter discusses select elements in the intertwined history of American research universities and their libraries that have shaped relationships not only between these institutions but also among them and the rest of contemporary society. It proposes that they seize the opportunity to expand their natural role in scholarly communication and enhance their social service.

## Background
In the late 1970s, observers of science and scholarship in the United States and elsewhere began to note change—and the potential for greater change—in scholarly communication and in the scholarly communication system. Change was then synonymous with the advent of electronic technologies to manage information. Librarians, operating as mediators within this system, were among the first to recognize emergent threats to the system's functioning in the best interests of the scholar. They also detected threats to the stability of

their own profession. Librarians, in general, and academic research librarians, in particular, rallied to find opportunities for enhancing the system and to identify possible dangers of the electronic environment.

Due in no small part to the efforts of academic research librarians, learned societies and scholarly publishers began to shift focus from immediate, local, specific business matters to long-term, more generalizable implications of rapidly developing information technologies. Consequently, the literatures and activities of the societies and publishers now reflect lively involvement in the sea change affecting some of their most fundamental principles and practices.

In the midst of this reenergized, albeit inchoate, system there is a singularly important agent that sponsors a very large proportion of scholarly communication, from the point of creation, through mediation, to consumption: the research university. Throughout the past two decades of rapidly evolving social change, the university stands out as an institution that has analyzed its situation as intensely as any other. Yet, the university's response to the emergent electronic society has been primarily in the form of ad hoc projects and programs, undertaken evidently out of desperation and without thoughtful reconsideration of the concepts and principles that underlie the institution's mission. In view of the crucial role of the university, not just in scholarly communication but also in many other social systems, it is now reasonably clear that scholarly communication will function in the best interests of society if the university comes to the determination that scholarly communication is its very essence, from which all its other services flow. The focus of that determination can lead to a stronger mode of operation incorporating both the efficiencies demanded by contemporary society and the effectiveness that continues American higher education's great tradition of social service.

As employed here, the term *scholarly communication* is generic, subsuming scientific communication. It also embraces teaching and learning at all levels of serious investigation and discourse not limited to the academy. The academic research library's position in scholarly communication has developed from a plainly passive stance for most of twentieth-century history to an active role of restructuring and strengthening that system in recent decades. For these reasons, the mission of the university and that of its library have the potential to become perhaps not identical, but more congruent.

Far ahead of its time, the Alexandrian Library of ancient Egypt offers the clearest example of such congruency. Closely binding mission and function, it prefigured by two hundred centuries the model of the academic research library for the twenty-first century. For the Mouseion, as the facility was called, was at once the library and the classroom, bringing teachers and learners together for a free-flowing interchange of ideas, stimulated and reinforced by the documents close at hand. Learning was the primary goal. Teacher and librarian were one and the same, having not yet been affected much by either bureaucracy or professionalization. In principle, at least, the great library at Alexandria provided convenient access to all the knowledge that had been recorded around the globe. But that was long ago. Between then and now, much has transpired to bifurcate the purposes of universities and their libraries and to separate each institution's mission and function. Why research universities and their libraries responded quite differently to developments in the scholarly communication system, and how scholarly communication in the future could become the forum of a shared purpose and function to serve society, unfolds nearly as a case study of the contemporary academic enterprise.

## The Research University

The Industrial Revolution made it clear that knowledge and education presented an avenue to advancement for those not satisfied with the lot of the assembly line worker. Education became a doorway to options for one's future. The general public in America began to see higher education as useful—thus breaking with European tradition then—and, to varying degrees, this vision has significantly influenced colleges and universities ever since. In a similar fashion, during the mid-nineteenth century, the principle of *egalitarianism*—fundamental to the social fabric of the United States—was linked synergistically to the attitude of *utilitarianism*. Consequently, unprecedented numbers of those who once would not reasonably have aspired to higher learning and to a place among the professions were attracted to, and accommodated by, the universities. All that strengthened the rationale of utilitarianism for higher education.

During the 1950s and 1960s in the United States, the egalitarian spirit was codified into law and enforced, altering society abruptly. Concurrently, societal debate about the U.S. military involvement in Vietnam energized general reform, most dramatically on university campuses. Driven by an aggressive and sometimes militant spirit, these long-overdue legal and social reforms hit the most conservative of institutions—the university. Overwhelmed by the extremes by which the reform wave swept the country and the world, universities came to adopt a laissez-faire posture in administration of higher education. More than any other phenomenon, this withdrawal from institutional authority conduced to the subsequent, serious loss of identity and purpose in American universities.

Meanwhile, other forces also were testing traditional modes of university operation. The student body changed as many sought education for second and third careers; part-time enrollment also increased. By the 1970s, any notion of a typical student had to be revised completely. A tightening of the general economy also affected higher education with the public beginning to demand more accountability than ever before, no longer taking for granted an inherent public good of social and governmental institutions. Eventually, citizens and their political representatives assigned a greater priority to the growing problems of health care, poverty, and crime than to postsecondary education. By 1990, the general economy clearly was being driven far more by market demand than by any other set of goals and principles, generating an environment to which the university has begun to adapt.

## The University and Scholarly Communication

The foregoing enumeration of challenges to higher education may be old hat to anyone who achieved adulthood a decade or more ago, but it serves as a useful backdrop to examination of the university response to developments in scholarly communication. We have now arrived at a crucial moment, perhaps a historical juncture. For the first time, both the emergent medium of scholarly communication and the communication medium in demand by all segments and strata of society at large (not just an elite) are the same, the common feature being the seductive convenience of electronic information technology. This concurrent emergence of the so-called information society and the electronic scholarly communication system opens an era of unprecedented opportunity for the university to serve society through a new kind of relationship. Moreover, the academic research library possesses the potential to be instrumental in realizing that innovative relationship.

Efficient and effective adaptation to new information technology will require even more fundamental change in universities. One could argue that this is unlikely to happen because resistance to change is a venerated tradition in the academy (except, of course, for disciplinary progress). It may be worth bearing in mind, for example, that ancient Greek objections to the introduction of writing into higher learning had to do with that medium's not being interactive, as well as with a fear of its power to dull the memory. Later, the invention of printing was fought by some in higher education because it made scholarly communication a bit too convenient, because the student could learn in the absence of the teacher. Nonetheless, writing and printing have carried the day. Resistance to innovation in scholarly communication is a time-honored tradition but, eventually, higher education adapts itself to forces from without—perhaps because, in due time, they tend to become the forces from within. Likewise, it was not without resistance that academic research became closely entwined with the federal government as an immediate result of extraordinary demands of society during and following the Second World War. For the universities, however, monetary and prestige values of this new relationship far outweighed critical voices from both within and without, so the relationship remains strong even to this day. Growth in federal grants and contracts to universities stimulated a vast output of research which, in turn, stimulated a prodigious production of books and journals. As universities generated more of these products of scholarly communication, their libraries consumed more of them. All that drove up the costs of the scholarly communication system, to be borne principally by the academic institutions.

In this dynamic environment, the notorious and now tiresome debate about teaching versus research began to flourish. Because universities have not addressed this issue in a direct and decisive manner, it lingers and obfuscates fundamental matters of institutional purpose that must be resolved if mission and function are to be reconciled. Over the past half-century, mission and function could be viewed only through dim light, because the very nature of scholarship was undergoing fairly complicated reorientation. The new partnership with the federal government demanded an emphasis on societal problems, global concerns, and disciplinary crossings in the effort to discover new applications of theory and fact; this expansive thrust has tended to grow stronger over the past half-century.

Whether research crossed disciplinary boundaries or stayed within a discipline, since the 1970s the general tendency has remained that of specialization. Apart from the advantages of such focused research, few outside a given specialization can understand (never mind appreciate) a specialist's research—a breach in communication by no means limited to the sciences. The reward system in the academy was rapidly becoming a conglomeration of meritocracies, all functioning within bounded spheres.

As old as scholarly communication itself, what has come to be known as the "invisible college" assumed special importance in this environment. The allegiance of large groups of scholars drifted away from the institutions sponsoring them to the disciplines recognizing their work. That left universities with faculty whose role in institutional governance is largely ambiguous and not necessarily dedicated to concern for, or even understanding of, the status of the institution. With some caution, an allegation of neglect can be extended to charges about indifference toward students and learning in general. For example, regardless of the high levels of theory informing pedagogy, the absence and even denigration of canon (or some mainstream of thought) in the discourse of many disciplines reflects a preoccupation with debate within the discipline rather than with the education and well-being of students.

Into this environment of increasing research output and specialization came a rich array of information technologies offering hitherto unknown power and convenience to the scholar. The scholarly communication system was gearing for even greater productivity and dynamism. The academy was well conditioned for this by the earlier introduction of the computer in some of the sciences and humanities during the postwar era, in the social sciences during the 1960s, and in other areas of the humanities more recently. Influenced markedly, perhaps irrevocably, by even rudimentary capabilities of the computer, the conduct of science and scholarship in all fields evinced a growing attraction to methodology, to the extent that specialists began to value it as much or even more than content. Personal computing, networking at all levels, and multimedia software easily and logically became the mechanism, the structure, and the stuff of scholarly communication in the electronic environment. Overall, the ethos to seize new technologies has evolved within disciplines for decades, and the universities have responded with financial support but not with guidance.

## Mission and Motive

The lack of guidance by universities carries more significance than may at first appear. In its role in society and in the scholarly communication system, the research university does not deliberate as a whole and then take some initiative; instead, it strongly tends to respond by reflex action conditioned by centuries-old adherence to certain principles and goals.

Much of academic tradition can, in part, be credited with the success of American higher education, but it now jeopardizes higher education's resilience to function successfully in the coming decades. More pointedly, there is little evidence that the American research university is seizing the opportunity presented by the confluence of electronic scholarly communication and the information society. In fact, strategies to develop a viable academy for the twenty-first century seem to be limited to strategies from three decades ago (recalled nostalgically as the golden age) now set to electronics. The essential difficulty is that the underlying lag of organizational development behind technological change centers on rather fundamental matters: the future of tenure, the emphasis on research and publication as criteria for academic success, the potential for instructional and information technology in the curriculum, the relative importance of graduate and undergraduate education, the prospect for the university to disseminate scholarly and scientific information, the need to protect and strengthen the global network infrastructure, the overly large expansion of postsecondary education, the emerging role of distance learning, the loss of financial flexibility as salaries consume growing proportions of the university's budget, the need to make downsizing and "more with less" realities instead of hollow slogans, the general loss of public support for higher education, the urgency for the university to become more relevant to society and more competitive in the marketplace.

These issues—with major implications for institutional mission, goals, and principles of operation—tend to be addressed one by one, not in relation to each other in a holistic manner that could harmonize mission and function and prefigure a model for the future. In that respect, the fundamentally conservative nature of the university takes a heavy toll. Especially over the past decade, for example, there have been many articles in *The Chronicle of Higher Education* about fund-raising as a growing dimension of the university (with more dramatic episodes in the pages of the popular press). So stifled by tradition are the research universities that fundraising from extramural or nonconventional sources is considered necessary in order to engage in "innovative enterprises" that do not alter anything traditional. The unstated goal is to preserve everything from the past—to change by growing and adding, rather than by breaking with tradition.

In a similar fashion, the university has tended to deal with various aspects of scholarly communication separately, without consideration of the institution's priority role within that system as a whole. Yet, the rapid growth of the electronic environment and its potential role to join the academy and society are compelling reasons for the scholarly communication system to be considered holistically. Economic conditions eventually will force universities to assign a high priority to scholarly communication. But as things now stand, universities appear (from the outside) to have evolved relatively little since the 1970s—reflecting the view (from the inside) that process, principles, and goals have, indeed, remained essentially the same, except for the drive to cultivate new sources of revenue.

## Divergent Paths

Although the library has been influenced by the same forces as the rest of the academy, its function as a service, rather than as a discipline, has made a difference. Indeed, librarianship has developed almost independently from the rest of the academy as a profession in its own right. Beginning on the local level in the 1960s, and on a national scale in the early 1970s with the creation of computerized cooperative cataloging, the academic library's professionalism has centered on designing electronic scholarly communication services, many of which are now taken for granted. Librarians—not administrators or teaching faculty—planned and built that foundation. Although the universities' financial capacity at that time made it possible (and, indeed, they established a half-century ago what is known today as the Center for Research Libraries), the libraries' collaborative success was generally accomplished in spite of institutional priorities or plans.

In contrast to overall university inertia, academic research libraries have established a recent history of initiating changes of the most fundamental kind. They have restructured their organization to facilitate electronic resources; created entirely new kinds of positions and altered the qualifications of most others; introduced many new services, designed in most cases without tested models to follow; created such services without eliminating needed traditional ones; forged new relationships with other units on campus, most notably the computer center, while staff size declined or at best remained stable; established resource-sharing arrangements with other institutions to optimize services on campus; and generally recast their mission and goals to accommodate the changing environment of scholarly communication. The divergent paths taken by the library and its parent institution, the university, were paved primarily by three influences: the differing professional-development patterns of faculty and librarians; the hold of academic traditions on the faculty; and certain funding patterns that drove the library and the university even farther apart.

As noted earlier, the professionalization of the faculty was encouraged by a combination of meritocracy in the local reward system and disciplinary specialization that resulted in broader faculty allegiances to their respective disciplines. The professionalization of librarians took a distinctly different course, in part because it was only in the third quarter of the twentieth century that librarianship began to assume some of the characteristics of a profession, and in part because of its support mission. As the campus underwent change in the postwar era, faculty had less time to devote to the library and unconsciously delegated much of their former authority to librarians. For its part, the library—under the influence of more professional objectives and standards—began to be institutionalized as an entity unto itself. It was related to the university through its service responsibility, yet divergent by a rather unique mission. This mindset proved to be a subtle, yet constant, influence on matters of policy and procedure throughout the several decades of unprecedented library expansion, removing the library from the mainstream of faculty activity on the campus, as well as from the attention of constructive academic concern.

A once-great strength of the academy in the United States and in other similarly economically advanced nations has been its relative freedom from the requirement to operate with strict efficiency and accountability. Indeed, the professoriat offers perhaps the only vocation that allows selected individuals to be employed for concentrated thought of one's own choosing, fairly unconstrained and even unstructured by time interpreted as expense. A fragile condition at best, this fundamental aspect of the academy has steadily been challenged by growing public scrutiny of higher education. Academics have resisted this challenge, sometimes unreasonably, thus leading the public to question academics' authority over other aspects of higher education. In the effort to preserve the academy, university administration has staunchly guarded faculty prerogatives—reaffirmingly to colleagues on campus, but defensively to others outside higher education. The problem has become one of societal understanding and balance. At the same time, owing to the sheer ambiguity surrounding conditions directly affecting the operations of these large, complex social institutions, there has been a steady dissipation of authority on campus. The early established authority of faculty over the curriculum, for example, has now spread to faculty control of many other areas of academic administration, more often by default than by design. Confluence of such conditions generated a broader resistance to orderly organizational development that has become excessive even within the staunchly conservative institutional arena of higher education.

Much of this evolving conflict over the need for the academic community to plan and operate as a single organization was, until now, subdued by available funding. In spite of the common practice during the 1960s and 1970s for universities to end each year with substantial financial surpluses—to be disposed of at the last minute by the library—no one should conclude that these institutions had sufficient funding. But it is a realistic inference that there was enough funding to obviate the need for serious institutional strategic planning and the establishment of operational academic priorities. It was precisely that set of circumstances that fostered, in a symbiotic way, the divergent paths of the university and the academic research library.

The void in university planning was filled on the library's side by a strengthening of professional principles, as well as by the developing of the library as an institution rather than just a service. In extreme manifestation, this dual professional–institutional vision for the library became an ethos, if not a mystique. Consequently, the library began operating independently of the rest of the university. As the faculty lost understanding of the library's agenda, their support of it waned, except in platitude. Gradually, the image formed of the library by faculty and administration became that of a discrete unit, not integrated into the academic enterprise. The library had lost focus on its scholarly purpose, and the university had lost focus on its library's service mission. The lack of institutional coordination of programs with finances explains the apparent propensity—apart from any budgetary capacity—to adopt new programs and responsibilities on the implicit assumption that the library would follow suit, essentially carrying the burden of research resources and services. The "bottomless pit" metaphor, which came to haunt librarians in less-affluent times, is largely a product of this phenomenon. But that is also the simplistic characterization of a situation that arose, more fundamentally, out of the administrative withdrawal from academic matters. When days of restricted funding came along in the 1980s, they were not met with a concerted effort to plan how to do "more with less," despite of all the talk to that effect, but, rather, with a deeper belief among all parties (faculty, library, and administration) that the academy had entered just a temporary phase of aberration (rather than a return to normalcy). In a similar spirit, university administration wishfully heralded the advent of advanced information technologies in the 1990s as the solution to dramatically escalating library costs.

## A Climate for Change

If two decades of extraordinary financial support for the research universities unduly encouraged research specialization and output to the detriment of the university's mission of service to society, it is now possible that more balanced and reasoned goals for higher education will prevail in contemporary times of normal funding. Although the will to accomplish this is the key factor, a number of financial and technological developments already under way may well establish a new relationship between the university and its library. First, there is the institutional jolt experienced by the stabilization or drop in funding generally for higher education, together with the rise of costs to adopt and maintain the rapid influx of new information technologies. The dual impact of these forces attracts growing attention in the academy, for the faculty can no longer avoid the truth that for so long had been overlooked or ignored: There really are trade-offs to be made and priorities to be applied. Library issues need to be addressed as they have not been for decades. That means that the library will be given closer scrutiny, no longer taken for granted. There will even be occasional debates on campus about the future role of the library in the electronic environment. There will also be opportunities to involve both faculty and administration in library planning in significant ways, thereby creating an overture for the reintegration of the library into the academic enterprise. This series of developments may lead, as well, to an understanding throughout the university of options for varying types and levels of library and information services affecting the scholarly communication system. Precisely in that realm, the university may seize the opportunity to act on a corporate mind.

Academic research librarianship has already recognized that its ultimate business is scholarly communication. It may be highly advantageous for the university to follow suit and focus on scholarly communication in designing its own business plan. The terms *restructuring* and *reorganization* are standard fare in the 1990s to announce major change in large, complex organizations, and surely a good deal of that will be required in the academy. But all the reorganization and restructuring in the world will not carry the day if the university does not recast its vision to the common horizon occupied by the scholarly communication system and the information society in higher education. The establishment of mission, goals, principles, and strategies to cultivate this common interest may well stimulate a level of public understanding of higher education that has not been in evidence for decades. Discourse on the commonalities of scholarly communication and information society would encourage a reinterpretation of traditional academic values, principles of higher education, and library services.

Higher education would then place a new emphasis on both learning and technology in the curriculum—local and networked—to become more efficient and effective in the increasingly competitive environment. In doing so, the academy would reach out to society as never before. It would also have great potential to pervade society with the very medium that society needs to conduct everyday business, creating a logical bond of dependency and service. Higher education, and particularly the research universities, could occupy natural leadership positions in the community. Universities will regain public support of their leadership only when the public reconsiders them more closely relevant to societal aspirations.

In the now increasingly businesslike effort of the academy to join its mission and function with emerging societal goals, two considerations in particular need to be addressed: the kind of service infrastructure that a research university can design to serve the information society, and the efficiency and effectiveness of such service to warrant public financial support. Underlying any such discussion should be an understanding that far more information exists in digital format than is apparent from the way it is presented, let alone distributed, today. And because much more is being created every day, at some point in the not-distant future, a critical mass of societal reliance will be achieved. Truly, the so-called knowledge or information society is on the brink of this sea change.

## Concluding Remarks

Teaching, research, and service—concepts that have long served to lay out the mission of research universities and their libraries—need to be reshaped in the wake of the rapidly evolving scholarly communication system. These concepts can be keys, in turn, to analysis of broader concepts that link the concerns and aspirations of an information society to those of the academy in the 1990s and beyond. Specific functions and service programs follow in the form of library electronic capabilities.

The process to accomplish this kind of institutional self-reassessment may suggest new organizational structures or it may not. What is clear is that little of this can be accomplished without strong leadership to ensure that such issues are addressed and that appropriate decisions and actions follow. A renewal of leadership would have to extend from top university administration down to colleges, departments, and individuals, including librarians; it would reach from the academy up to political bodies and the public at large. Certainly, such leadership must pervade the scholarly communication system as well. The dual usefulness of the research university and its library to society will be demonstrated through the determination of common purpose. Technologically, financially, and socially, the time has come.

## Related Readings

Altbach, Philip G., Robert O. Berdahl, and Patricia J. Gumport, eds. *Higher Education in American Society*. Third Edition. Amherst, N.Y.: Prometheus Books, 1994.

Ashby, Eric. *Adapting Universities to a Technological Society*. San Francisco: Jossey-Bass, 1974.

Dolence, Michael G., and Donald M. Norris. *Transforming Higher Education. A Vision for Learning in the 21st Century*. Ann Arbor: Society for College and University Planning, 1995.

Butler, Nicholas Murray. *Scholarship and Service: The Policies and Ideals of a National University in a Modern Democracy*. New York: Scribner's, 1921.

Geiger, Roger L. *Research and Relevant Knowledge: American Research Universities Since World War II*. New York: Oxford University Press, 1993.

————. *To Advance Knowledge: The Growth of American Research Universities, 1900–1940*. New York: Oxford University Press, 1986.

Immerwahr, John, and James Harvey. "What the Public Thinks of Colleges." *The Chronicle of Higher Education* (May 1995): B1–B3.

Kennedy, Donald. "Another Century's End, Another Revolution for Higher Education." *Change* (May/June 1995): 9–15.

Laing, Jonathon R. "Campus Unrest." *Barron's* (Nov. 1995): 25–29.

Levine, Arthur, ed. *Higher Learning in America, 1980–2000*. Baltimore: Johns Hopkins University Pr., 1993.

Pew Higher Education Roundtable. "A Calling to Account." *Policy Perspectives* 6 (July 1995): 1–11.

————. "To Dance with Change." *Policy Perspectives* 5 (Apr. 1994): 1A–12A.

————. "Twice Imagined." *Policy Perspectives* 6 (Apr. 1995): 1A–12A.

Ruegg, Walter. "The Academic Ethos." *Minerva* 24 (winter 1986): 393–412.

————. "The Traditions of the University in the Face of the Demands of the Twenty-First Century." *Minerva* 30 (Summer 1992): 189–205.

Shapiro, Harold T. "The Functions and Resources of the American University of the Twenty-First Century." *Minerva* 30 (summer 1992): 163–74.

Shils, Edward. "Do We Still Need Academic Freedom?" *American Scholar* 62 (1993): 187–209.

————. "The Service of Society and the Advancement of Learning in the Twenty-First Century." *Minerva* 30 (summer 1992): 242–68.

# Strategic Planning in Academic Libraries: A Political Perspective

*Douglas G. Birdsall*

Although rarely linked, there are a number of similarities between strategic planning and organizational development. Both approaches are used by administrators to manage change in a systematic fashion. *Strategic planning* emphasizes environmental scanning and goal setting, whereas *organizational development* relies on intervention techniques, such as benchmarking and team building. The focus of this chapter is on organizational politics of strategic planning, an interdisciplinary subject that is often overlooked in both management and library literatures. Its thesis is that, by acknowledging the political basis of decision making in organizations, library administrators can build coalitions and alliances in their institutions at large.

## Universities as Complex Organizations

Strategic planning for academic libraries has greater impact when administrators understand the political nature of the decentralized academic system and particularly how decisions are made in their institutions. Universities are "loosely coupled" systems in which actions undertaken in one area need not be integrated with other areas.[1] Consequently, organizational development becomes an "accretion of hundreds of largely autonomous actions taken for different reasons, at different times, under different conditions, by different people."[2] Pervading this political model is a basic "dissension concerning preferences, criteria, and definitions on what the organization should be doing."[3] Library administrators, however, even when engaged in strategic planning, often skirt around anything deemed political in academe, preferring to place their faith in a "rational" order of organizational goals, objectives, and strategies. Such an approach will not have lasting success if it ignores the pluralistic character of modern universities, in which different campus groups use various forms of political power to pursue what each considers best for itself, as well as for the institution.

Strategic planning emerged after the Second World War when program development and budgeting began to be used for long-term planning activities, usually in increments of five-year forecasts. During this period, the Harvard Business School stressed the importance of designing an overall corporate strategy that included all facets of operations, including production, finance, and marketing. It was not until a series of funding crises starting in the late 1970s, however, that analysts applied strategic planning concepts in higher education to determine which programs should survive and the levels at which they would be funded.[4]

For many academic libraries, strategic planning is initiated by senior administrators who require all campus units to submit plans for the overall purpose of developing institutionwide planning cycles. The library director who understands that this system of planning is linked to the strategic allocation of resources is more likely to ensure that the library's mission and goals are closely aligned with those of the university. Such understanding is an acknowledgment that the rational activity of planning coexists with the politics of academe.

Although librarians have become adept at strategic planning methodologies, and may become campus leaders in designing and implementing this process, libraries are typically given scant mention in the strategic plan of the institution. Given the political environment of the university, how can academic libraries best conduct strategic planning? There are three main political strategies for maximizing planning outcomes. These are to build upon the diversity of stakeholder interests, to form alliances and coalitions for the advancement of the library's own interests, and to market a persuasive planning document.

## Building Upon Diversity of Viewpoint

We begin with the ground assumption that there are multiple viewpoints on any campus about the proper goals of the library and the kinds of policies that should be undertaken to achieve them. Because library strategic planning centers on such major issues, it is unrealistic to expect strong or immediate consensus when so many people, both within the library and throughout the academic institution, have an interest in the future of the library. A few examples illustrate the diversity of stakeholders' interests. First, increased access to information resources may appear to be an easily agreed-upon goal; however, there are significant numbers of librarians and faculty who question the wisdom of shifting more dollars each year from acquisitions and staffing budgets to access services, such as document delivery and a seemingly endless number of electronic databases. Second, individuals who staff the reference desk may represent a wide spectrum of opinions about which services are most important and what qualifications those who provide them should have. Next, the viewpoint of catalogers on the importance of database management may be quite different from those held in other library departments. Faculty members, for their part, remain polarized on the importance of high-priced journal subscriptions. Finally, library directors and university development officers may disagree on how fundraising efforts for the library should be coordinated.

Strategic planning works best when the richness of stakeholder diversity is recognized and techniques are used to encourage full participation in the planning process. In this way, differences can be recognized and conflicts mitigated, if not resolved; or, general policies can be formulated to stand, in effect, as treaties among interest groups. Although such policies may not reflect a true consensus, they should approach a reasonable level of agreement among the parties. At Harvard College Library, for example, strategic planning in 1990–1991 involved four task forces, with members chosen from a pool of more than three hundred volunteers at all employee levels. Nearly a hundred faculty members also participated in a series of interest group meetings, and a variety of student committees and associations were consulted. This "bottom-up" approach to strategic planning also featured the creation of fifteen staff focus groups. Susan Lee, in a case study of Harvard's experience with this process, observes that it developed leadership skills among a broad spectrum of staff, raised commitment among task force members, and lowered resisting forces' tensions. She concludes that Harvard College Library "became a more open organization, better prepared for future change, and better able to engage in organizational learning."[5]

A feature of the Harvard model is its focus on long-term organizational development throughout the planning process. A task force was charged with defining a strategy to address organizational norms, management of change, communication channels, problem-solving processes, team building, resistance to change, and human relations.

## Forming Alliances and Coalitions

As we have seen, utilizing a broad base of library staff in the planning process helps to ensure that there will be a high level of internal acceptance of the strategic plan. A more difficult goal is to generate coalitions of support and advocacy among external campus groups. Nevertheless, this must be accomplished if adequate levels of funding are to be directed to library endeavors, and if campus partnerships are to be formed that will serve the long-term needs of all constituencies. Budgetary constraints in higher education generally, and access-versus-ownership issues in particular, are of great concern to faculty and administrators, who naturally want the best possible libraries for their institutions. With Oliver D. Hensley, I proposed a strategic planning model that emphasizes collaboration between the library and its campus constituencies in each of six phases of planning: deciding on the planning leaders, scanning the environment, analyzing strategic options, designing plans, setting the agenda of goals, and adopting the plan.[6]

Although most of the library literature on strategic planning concentrates on planning procedures internal to the library, some accounts describe the importance of involving others in the university community. Notably, when the Massachusetts Institute of Technology Libraries initiated strategic planning in 1987, they set up communication channels with campus stakeholders. The library director kept the provost and the faculty–library committee apprised of developments during the eighteen-month process and, upon completion of the planning document, scheduled meetings with the dean of each school to discuss the plan and its implications for academic programs. Shirley K. Baker's study of this process found that its reception on campus "was very positive and [that] funding for new initiatives was forthcoming."[7]

Meredith Butler and Hiram Davis, in an insightful article on strategic planning at the University at Albany, SUNY, and at Michigan State University, go beyond the level of informing key campus officials about the library's plan to that of establishing a dialogue with important campus groups on the issues. Butler's and Davis's respective experiences show that strategic planning can "set the stage for engaging university officials, faculty, and other major stakeholders in discussions about institutional policies and priorities for library resources and services."[8] At the beginning of the planning process at Albany, a "working dinner" was scheduled with university vice presidents and the director of university planning to discuss environmental trends in higher education and goals for the institution. That single event bred considerable interaction among the participants and was followed in succeeding weeks by a whole series of meetings with university deans, directors, and leading faculty. At Michigan State, "stakeholder luncheons" were held to provide a setting for dialogues about university and library plans. Butler and Davis note that in both institutions, those meetings were the first opportunity many faculty and librarians ever had to engage in substantive conversation about faculty needs and library services.

Coalitions of support for information technology have led, at some institutions, to an administrative merging of libraries with campus units such as computing services. Sheila D. Creth prefers a partnership relationship rather than a formal merging, as the "issue of administrative control pales in comparison to the more fundamental issue of what might be, and should be, accomplished with information technology if library and computing professionals were to combine their expertise in activities such as strategic planning."[9] A reengineered user services operation at Rice University combined several library units with several computing units, and one of the new department's first tasks was to develop a shared mission and goals statement.[10] Whether the result of administrative realignment or the creation of true partnerships, there is great potential for both mutual planning and political clout when coalitions form on an operational level.

The greatest potential for alliances occurs when library goals become a prominent part of the institution's priorities. Patricia Senn Breivik poses three questions that campus planners need to ask about their libraries and computing services:[11]

• "How can information resources and technologies best support institutional priorities?"

• "How can we best organize our information resources and technologies to make the strongest contribution to the identified priorities?"

• "How can we best deploy our limited human and fiscal information technology resources so that all graduates are information literate?"

Strategic planning in academic libraries can reach its full potential when the university community addresses such questions and then integrates solutions into institutionwide planning.

## Marketing the Plan

A third political approach to strategic planning is to orchestrate the presentation of the plan to the academic community. This involves both designing a persuasive document and marketing it to anyone who would be an advocate for library objectives. Butler and Davis note that strategic planning "provides wonderful public relations opportunities and can serve as the vehicle for moving the library more dynamically into the university environment."[12] A poor planning document will not only be counterproductive but even harmful to the long-term credibility of the library.

Decisions involving the format of the planning document are important ones, as the written plan symbolizes the library's future and the character of its leadership. An impressive strategic plan will convey the message that the library is in control of its future and worthy of fiscal support. Conversely, otherwise good goals and strategies may be overlooked in a plan that is ill conceived in parts or written in a pedantic style. In a recent study, I analyzed strategic plans currently in use among seventeen members of the ARL.[13] From a campus political perspective, the most effective plans all have a clear sense of their potential readerships. Strategic directions should be consistently aligned with both institutional goals and particular interests of key stakeholders; otherwise, the plan will appear to be merely an internal statement intended for library managers. The planning documents of two ARL libraries in particular are successful in this regard.

Wayne State University Library System's "Strategic Plan to the Year 2000" is a forty-eight page booklet that provides mission and vision statements, a four-tier arrangement of goal areas and objectives, an evaluation process, and links to the university's strategic plan.[14] What is distinctive about this document is that it is presented as a professionally designed publication. An attractive layout, color photographs, drawings, and sidebars work together with the document's textual content to convey a very positive impression about the Wayne State University Library System—that library initiatives are important and the organization is doing the kind of planning that would best serve its constituencies. The attractive format allows for wide distribution of the publication to campus officials, key legislators, potential donors, and others who would be advocates for the library.

Harvard College Library's plan, "Commitment to Renewal," has a different appearance but one that is also successful in conveying a positive message.[15] This twenty-page publication is simple, but elegant. It has no photographs or graphics. Instead, its authors chose a narrative style that cogently presents major issues facing the library with specific goals and objectives for the 1990s. Its effectiveness lies in the care taken to craft an articulate essay on the library's readiness to face the future.

## Conclusions

Like other organizations, libraries engage in strategic planning in order to learn about environmental challenges and to set goals for overcoming them. This chapter argues that for strategic plans to be more than internal writing exercises, library administrators must understand the politics of influence in their institutions and then develop specific strategies that will garner support for their organizations.

Three general strategies may be useful. First, acknowledge that plans, programs, and policies are politically rational only when they can be accepted by affected constituencies. This requires the kind of library leader who understands that multiple interests exist among various stakeholders and who is committed to developing processes for resolving important issues of conflict. Second, form alliances and coalitions among key library stakeholders. Finally, create persuasive and attractive planning documents that can be widely distributed to external constituencies. Specific strategies used by Harvard, MIT, the University at Albany, Michigan State, and Wayne State are described here. (More examples of such publications would be a useful addition to library science literature.)

Although a knowledge of the political nature of the university does not ensure success in strategic planning endeavors, library leaders who do understand such things, and thus are able to build coalitions with external constituencies, will be in a far better position to achieve their goals. The most effective leaders will be those who forge connections between strategic planning, organizational development, and technological change. This is a salient new area for research and analysis, and our progress will be marked by the improvements made in organizational development and the influence we gain in the university community.

## NOTES

1. Karl E. Weick, "Educational Organizations as Loosely Coupled Systems," *Administrative Science Quarterly* 21 (Mar. 1976): 1–19.

2. Michael D. Cohen and James G. March, *Leadership and Ambiguity: The American College President* (New York: McGraw-Hill, 1974), 104.

3. Jeffrey Pfeffer, "Power and Resource Allocation in Organizations," in *New Directions in Organizational Behavior*, ed. Barry M. Staw and Gerald R. Salancik (Chicago: St. Clair Pr., 1977), 239.

4. George Keller, *Academic Strategy: The Management Revolution in American Higher Education* (Baltimore: Johns Hopkins Univ. Pr., 1983) was the most influential forerunner of this literature.

5. Susan Lee, "Organizational Change in the Harvard College Library: A Continued Struggle for Redefinition and Renewal," *Journal of Academic Librarianship* 19 (Sept. 1993): 228.

6. Douglas G. Birdsall and Oliver D. Hensley, "A New Strategic Planning Model for Academic Libraries," *C&RL* 55 (Mar. 1994): 149–59.

7. Shirley K. Baker, "Strategic Planning for Libraries in the Electronic Age," *Iatul Quarterly* 3 (Dec. 1989): 205–6.

8. Meredith Butler and Hiram Davis, "Strategic Planning as a Catalyst for Change in the 1990s," *College & Research Libraries* 53 (Sept. 1992): 398.

9. Sheila D. Creth, "Creating a Virtual Information Organization: Collaborative Relationships between Libraries and Computing Centers," in *Building Partnerships: Computing and Library Professionals*, ed. Ann G. Lipow and Sheila D. Creth (Berkeley, Calif.: Library Solutions Pr., 1995), 86.

10. Beth J. Shapiro and Kevin Brook Long, "Just Say Yes: Reengineering Library User Services for the 21st Century," *Journal of Academic Librarianship* 20 (Nov. 1994): 288.

11. Patricia Senn Breivik, "Investing Wisely in Information Technology: Asking the Right Questions," *Educational Record* 74 (summer 1993): 47–52.

12. Butler and Davis, "Strategic Planning as a Catalyst for Change in the 1990s," 397.

13. Douglas G. Birdsall, "Strategic Planning Models in Academic Libraries," *Encyclopedia of Library and Information Science*, 59/suppl. 22 (New York: Marcel Dekker, 1997), 292–315.

14. *Wayne State University Library System Strategic Plan to the Year 2000* (Detroit: Wayne State Univ., 1994).

15. "Commitment to Renewal: A Strategic Plan for the Harvard College Library," *Harvard Library Bulletin*, n.s. 3 (spring 1992): 27–46.

# Epilogue: Balancing Restructuring Efforts

*Charles A. Schwartz*

The primary problem of academic libraries—the lag of organizational development behind technological change—raises the prospect that the restructuring process will entail recurring bouts of instability. This book has treated that prospect rather matter-of-factly, as something that is hardly avoidable but largely manageable provided that restructuring is based on incremental, ongoing programs that build toward more significant advances in organizational development. Yet, libraries would face organizational decay if they either put a premium on the avoidance of instability at the expense of any major change; or, conversely, attempted to restructure too aggressively, with ill-prepared radical changes.

This final chapter draws some explicit correlations between organizational development and decay. My interest in this area is not to dramatize organizational decay but, on the contrary, to describe its rather ordinary and varied origins on a practical level. Indeed, instability or decay does not result only from technological lag but can crop up in four general ways. Thus, a restructuring process can be deflected or impaired for reasons that are remarkably independent of what prompts the restructuring.

262

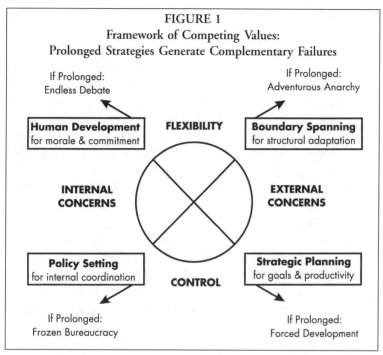

FIGURE 1
Framework of Competing Values:
Prolonged Strategies Generate Complementary Failures

Figure 1 depicts what a balanced and stable organization looks like in terms of four competing orientations.[1] On the right side of the figure are two orientations of *external* concern:

• *boundary spanning* for structural adaptation to new technological (or environmental) challenges;

• *strategic planning* for organizational productivity and effectiveness.

On the left side are two opposing, yet complementary, orientations of *internal* focus:

• *policy setting* for coordination of structural adaptations;

• *human development* for morale and commitment to strategic plans.

Successful restructuring requires that these orientations be brought into balance periodically by making them roughly equivalent in importance and compatible with one another. What makes restructuring such an interesting, sometimes emotional, undertaking is that the orientations are contradictory *moral* positions about the qualities of a "good" manager, as well as a "good" organization. Figure 1 should be considered on those dual—organizational and personal—levels.

On the personal level, the external–internal orientations (boundary spanning versus policy setting, and strategic planning versus human development) represent not only competing values but also natural inclinations and abilities. Some managers are *leaders* who think about shaking up the status quo; other managers are *administrators* who are much more adept at setting down policies and procedures. Few managers both lead and administer equally well. Likewise, some managers are good at devising strategic plans but somewhat lax when it comes to addressing human development concerns, whereas others are better team builders than strategic thinkers. Again, managers who do both well are rare.

For the organization as a whole, prolonged efforts in the direction of any orientation eventually become counterproductive, generating complementary failures on other fronts. An external emphasis on restructuring by boundary spanning must periodically give way to the opposite orientation of policy setting in order for structural changes to be internally consolidated and eventually institutionalized. Restructuring by boundary spanning must also allow for the other two orientations to come into play: an adjustment of strategic plans, and a renewal of human development.

Eventually, a prolonged effort in any direction breeds organizational instability or decay. Thus, there are four general organizational patterns that library administrators should avoid:

- *frozen bureaucracy*—policy setting without external initiatives becoming a blind perpetuation of habits and traditions;
- *rampant confusion*—boundary spanning without internal coordination upsetting policies, procedures, and communication channels;
- *endless debate*—human development without strategic planning for organizational productivity and effectiveness becoming self-centered to an extreme;
- *forced march*—strategic planning without humanistic values and preparatory measures producing an unrealistic agenda.

In a nutshell, successful restructuring requires periodic shifts in the organization's attention to the balancing of external and internal orientations and values.

## NOTE

1. Figure 1 is adapted, in a highly simplified way, from Robert E. Quinn, *Beyond Rational Management: Mastering the Paradoxes and Competing Demands of High Performance* (San Francisco: Jossey-Bass, 1988), 70. This framework of competing values is used in some workshops by ARL's Office of Management Services.

# Contributors

**Barbara McFadden Allen** is Director of the Committee on Institutional Cooperation's Center for Library Initiatives and Assistant Director of the CIC, a consortium of twelve teaching and research universities. She received both her A.B. in Library Science and her M.L.S. from the University of Missouri-Columbia. She has served as resource sharing and automation consultant to three state libraries, and is the author of a number of articles on the subjects of resource sharing and cooperative collection management. E-mail: bmallen@uiuc.edu

**Douglas G. Birdsall** has been Associate Dean of Libraries at Texas Tech University since 1989. He was previously Assistant Director of Libraries for Collection Management and Reference Services at North Dakota State University, and Humanities Librarian at Idaho State University. Dr. Birdsall writes on strategic planning, budgeting, and personnel issues, and currently is editor of the monograph series *Foundations in Library and Information Sciences* (JAI Press). His doctorate in Higher Education is from Texas Tech University, and his M.L.S. from the University of Michigan. E-mail: lidgb@ttacs.ttu.edu

**Meredith A. Butler** is Dean of Library Faculty and Director of University Libraries at the University at Albany, SUNY. Prior to her appointment as Dean, she served as Assistant Vice President for Academic Planning and Development in Academic Affairs. She received a B.A. and an M.A. from Ohio State University, an M.L.S. from Syracuse University, and began her career at Syracuse University Libraries. She holds a joint faculty appointment in Albany's

School of Information Science and Policy. She writes and speaks on numerous topics, including copyright, electronic publishing, women and academic success, entrepreneurial librarianship, and the economics of information; and is presently engaged in a project on university libraries and financial development. E-mail: mb801@cnsvax.albany.edu

**Nina Davis-Millis** received a B.A. with honors in Music from Wesleyan University, and an M.L.S. from Columbia University. She worked in the libraries of The Juilliard School, the State University of New York at Purchase, and the Manhattan School of Music before joining MIT's library system in 1985. Since 1993, she has been Associate Head for Information Services for humanities, business, and social sciences; and also serves on the Network User Interface Team, a joint committee of the MIT Libraries and Information Systems to develop network applications. Davis-Millis served on the executive board of the Music Library and has presented papers on library technology for such organizations as the International Association of Music Libraries, the Association of College and Research Libraries, and SUNY/OCLC. E-mail: ninadm@mit.edu

**Stephen E. DeLong** received an A.B. from Oberlin College, a Ph.D. in Geology from the University of Texas at Austin, and in 1973 joined the University at Albany, SUNY, where he is currently Associate Vice President for Academic Affairs and Information Systems. Dr. DeLong's non-scientific interests include the effects of technology on culture and in higher education (see "The Shroud of Lecturing" and "May You Live in Interneting Times!", both at http://hawk.fab2.albany.edu as /delong/shroud.htm and /delong/netimes.htm, respectively). E-mail: delong@poppa.fab.albany.edu

**Richard M. Dougherty** is a Professor in the School of Information at the University of Michigan. He formerly served as Director of Libraries at Michigan from 1978–1988, and at the University of California, Berkeley from 1972–1978. He earned his advanced degrees in librarianship from Rutgers University. Professor Dougherty is a former editor of both *College and Research Libraries* and the *Journal of Aca-*

*demic Librarianship.* He is currently editor of *Library Issues.* He has published numerous articles, editorials and monographs. Dougherty is also president of Dougherty and Associates, a consulting firm that specializes in helping organizations develop and implement change management strategies. E-mail: rmdoughe@umich.edu

**Joan R. Giesecke** received a B.A. from SUNY Buffalo, an M.L.S. from the University of Maryland, an M.A. from Central Michigan University, and a D.P.A. from George Mason University. Dr. Giesecke is Dean of Libraries and Professor at the University of Nebraska-Lincoln Libraries. Previously, she was Associate Librarian and Head of Technical Services at George Mason University. She has taught graduate courses in library science for Emporia State University, and does research in the area of organizational design and decision making. She was co-Principle Investigator on an NSF grant for planning the electronic library for the state of Nebraska. She is a former editor of *Library Administration and Management,* the author of numerous articles on management, and the editor of *Practical Help for New Supervisors* (ALA, 1997). E-mail: joang@unllib.unl.edu

**William A. Gosling** received a B.A. in History from Bates College, and an M.L.S. from the University of Pittsburgh. Following an Internship at the Library of Congress and two years in the US Army, he returned to LC where he was Administrative Officer, MARC Development Office, and CIP Program Manager. Currently Assistant Director for Technical Services and Library Systems, and Interim Director (1997), of the University of Michigan Library, Gosling compiled *Canadiana in United States Repositories* (Dalhousie University, 1994), has published several articles on technical services, and serves on four journal editorial boards. E-mail: wgosling@umich.edu

**William C. Highfill** received an M.S. from Kansas State Teachers College, Emporia, and a Ph.D. from the University of Illinois, Champaign-Urbana. From 1973 until 1995, he was Dean of Libraries at Auburn University. Since then, he has served as a social sciences reference librarian there. He has written about the status of librarians; library cooperation, particularly in the areas of planning and resource sharing; and the role, functions, and governance of academic library consortia. E-mail: highfill@lib.auburn.edu

**Caroline M. Kent** is Head of Research Services in the Widener Library, and Assistant to the Associate Librarian for Public Services in the Harvard College Library, positions she has held since 1989. She received her undergraduate degree from Connecticut College, her library degree from Simmons College, and is currently working on an M.A. in History at Harvard University. She has worked in the Harvard, MIT, and Brandeis University libraries; has published several articles and book chapters; and is a co-author of *Teaching the New Library* (Neal-Schuman, 1996). E-mail: cmkent@fas.harvard.edu

**David F. Kohl** is Dean and University Librarian at the University of Cincinnati, where he has served for seven years. His previous professional experience includes positions at the University of Colorado-Boulder, the University of Illinois-Urbana at Champaign, and Washington State University in Pullman. Dr. Kohl received a master's degree and a doctorate from the Divinity School at the University of Chicago, and an M.L.S. from the University of Colorado. He recently concluded a term as President of RASD (now RUSA), serves as reviews editor for *RQ*, represents OhioLINK on the U.S. Department of Commerce's Conference on Copyright and Fair Use, and represents the Association of Research Libraries as a delegate to IFLA's Document Interlending Section. He publishes and speaks widely on library issues, particularly in the areas of library management, change and consortium development; and is the author of the series *Handbooks of Library Management*, six volumes (ABC-Clio, 1985, 1986). E-mail: David.Kohl@uc.edu

**David W. Lewis** received a B.A. from Carleton College, and an M.L.S. from Columbia University. He holds certificates of advanced study from both the Graduate Library School at the University of Chicago and the School of Library Service at Columbia University. He is currently Associate Executive Director of University Libraries at Indiana University Purdue University Indianapolis. He previously held positions at the University of Connecticut, Columbia University, Franklin and Marshall College, and Hamilton College. Lewis writes on library management, technology in libraries, and the economics of scholarly information. E-mail: dlewis@iupui.edu

**Rebecca R. Martin** holds a doctorate in Public Administration from the University of Southern California, and an M.L.S. from San Jose State University. Dr. Martin is Dean of Libraries at the University of Vermont, a position she has held since 1990; her previous administrative positions were in the libraries of San Jose State University and the University of California, Berkeley. She holds a faculty position in the Public Administration program at UVM, where she teaches seminars in organizational behavior and human resources management. She is the author of *Libraries and the Changing Face of Academia* (Scarecrow, 1994) and numerous articles on a range of library management and service issues. E-mail: rmartin@moose.uvm.edu

**Lisa McClure** earned a B.A. in English from the University of Michigan. She was graduated from that university's School of Information in June 1996. Her contribution to this book (with Richard Dougherty) was part of an advanced management seminar.

**Sue O. Medina** received her Ph.D. and M.S. from Florida State University. Since 1984, Dr. Medina has directed the Network of Alabama Academic Libraries, a consortium of academic institutions supporting graduate education and research programs. She is a past editor of *Interface* (newsletter of the Association of Specialized and Cooperative Library Agencies) and the author of numerous articles on library services and resources in collaborative environments. E-mail: smedina@asc.edu

**Charles B. Osburn** is Dean of Libraries at the University of Alabama and Professor in the School of Library and Information Studies. He earned masters degrees at the University of North Carolina and the Pennsylvania State University, and a Ph.D. at the University of Michigan. Dr. Osburn has served on the boards of the Association of Research Libraries, the Center for Research Libraries, and Solinet; and on the OCLC Research Libraries Advisory Council. He has published a large number of articles and book chapters, as well as *Collection Management: A New Treatise* (JAI, 1991), *Academic Research and Library Resources* (Greenwood, 1979), and *Research and Reference Guide to French Studies* (Scarecrow, 1968, 1981).E-mail: cosburn@ualvm.ua.edu

**Thomas Owens** studied English at the Ohio State University and the University of Arizona. He began his professional career with automated library systems at Ohio State University in 1970. Since then, he has led computer operations at a number of university libraries, worked as an automation consultant for large academic and public library consortia, and managed a customer support desk for Geac Computers. At the time his chapter (with Nina Davis-Millis) was written, Owens was Head of the Library Systems Office at MIT. Currently, he is a project manager at Endeavor Information Systems. E-mail: owens@endinfosys.com.

**Derrie B. Roark** is Associate Vice-President for Learning Resources Services at Hillsborough Community College in Tampa, Florida. She holds an Ed.D. from Florida State University, and a B.A. and an M.L.S. from Louisiana State University. Dr. Roark serves as president of the boards of the Tampa Bay Library Consortium and the Tampa Educational Cable Consortium; was the inaugural Advisory Board chair of the College Center for Library Automation; and has served on the LAMA Editorial Board. She has written several articles and chapters on community college learning resources, and is co-editor (with Wanda K. Johnston) of *A Copyright Sampler* (ACRL, 1997). E-mail: roarkd@mail.firn.edu

**Rita Scherrei** is Associate University Librarian for Administrative Services at UCLA, a position she has held (with some variations in title) since 1982. In addition, Dr. Scherrei teaches in the UCLA Department of Library and Information Science. Her Ph.D. in Higher Education is from UCLA, as is her M.L.S. She received an M.S. in Chemistry from Seattle University, and a B.A. from Mount St. Mary's College (California). She is an active author and speaker on personnel, diversity, and organizational issues, and was the 1995 recipient of the Gale Research/EMIE Roundtable Multicultural Award. E-mail: scherrei@library.ucla.edu

**Charles A. Schwartz** received a Ph.D. in Foreign Affairs from the University of Virginia, and an M.L.S. from Indiana University. He is the author of numerous articles in a broad range of fields and the recipient of both the K.G. Saur Award (ACRL, 1995) and the Jesse H. Shera Award (ALA, 1992). Dr. Schwartz taught comparative politics at the University of Alabama; worked as a librarian at the University of Northern Iowa and at Rice University; and is currently Assistant Director for Collection Management and Technical Services at the University of Massachusetts-Boston. E-mail: Tony@delphinus. lib.umb.edu

**Peggy Seiden** is College Librarian at Skidmore College, Saratoga Springs, N.Y. She previously held positions as Head Librarian at Penn State New Kensington and as Software Manager and Librarian for Educational Computing at Carnegie Mellon University. She received her B.A. from Colby College, an M.A. from the University of Toronto and her M.L.S. from Rutgers University. She writes and speaks on issues of technology and libraries, particularly the impact of technology on library user behavior. E-mail: pseiden@skidmore.edu

**Gloriana St. Clair** is Interim Dean and Associate Dean, Planning and Administrative Services of the University Libraries of Penn State University. Previously, she was a library administrator at Oregon State University and at Texas A&M University. She received a B.A. in English and a Ph.D. in Literature from the University of Oklahoma, an M.L.S. from the University of California at Berkeley, and a M.B.A. from the University of Texas at San Antonio. Dr. St. Clair is the author of numerous scholarly articles and was the editor of *College & Research Libraries*. Currently, she is the editor of *Journal of Academic Librarianship*. She has been the recipient of several academic and professional honors, including The Pennsylvania Quality Leadership Foundation, Inc; appointment to the Board of Examiners for the Pennsylvania Quality Leadership Awards; and 1991 Senior Fellow at the University of California, Los Angeles. E-mail: gss@psulias.psu.edu

**Katherine L. Walter** received both a B.A. and an M.A. from the University of Iowa. She has been Chair of the Serials Department of the University of Nebraska-Lincoln Libraries since 1985 and was promoted to Professor in 1994. She has written and received funding for many grants in the areas of preservation and access. Walter is the author of *Saving the Past to Enrich the Future* (Kansas Library Network Board, 1993) and Project Director for the Nebraska Newspaper Project (NEH-funded). She is active in ALA's Association for Library Collections and Technical Services, chairs the Nebraska Documents Preservation Advisory Council, and serves on the AMIGOS Preservation Service Advisory Council. E-mail: kayw@unllib.unl.edu

**Herbert S. White** retired as Distinguished Professor and Dean Emeritus from the Indiana University School of Library and Information Science in 1995. He now resides in Arizona, but continues to write, lecture, and speak. His twenty years on the faculty at Indiana University followed twenty-five years in government and industrial information management, including executive posts at IBM, Documentation Incorporated, and the Institute for Scientific Information. He served as president of both the Special Libraries Association and the American Society for Information Science, and as treasurer of the International Federation for Documentation. A graduate from the library education program at Syracuse University, he was honored with the first distinguished alumni award from that school. A prolific speaker and writer, Herbert White has authored more than 200 articles and a number of books, including *At the Crossroads: Librarians on the Information Superhighway* (Libraries Unlimited, 1995), *Ethical Dilemmas in Libraries* (G.K. Hall, 1992), *Education for Professional Librarians* (Knowledge Industry, 1986), *Library Personnel Management* (Knowledge Industry, 1985), and *Managing the Special Library* (G.K. Hall, 1984).

# Index